Praise for *A Death in Brazil*:

'An astonishing feat of storytelling' Peter Carey, Booker Prize winner

'Glorious ... fascinating and revealing' *New York Times*

'Robb paints a picture of Brazil quite unlike any other' *Publishing News*

'Electrifying ... enthralling' *Literary Review*

'Fabulous ... Robb writes beautifully' *Irish Examiner*

'Reads like a thriller' *Daily Express*

'Eclectic and inventive ... a wonderful book' *Guardian*

'A brilliant portrait of Brazil' *Sunday Tribune*

'Fabulous ... an utter marvel' *Waterstone's Books Quarterly*

'An intoxicating cocktail of a book' *Time Out*

'Masterful' *Sunday Business Post*

'A brilliantly atmospheric study of twenty-first-century Brazil' *Sunday Times*

'Excellent ... mesmeric ... I eagerly anticipate Robb's next work' *Irish Times*

A DEATH IN BRAZIL

BY THE SAME AUTHOR

Midnight in Sicily

M

Pig's Blood

A DEATH IN BRAZIL

A Book of Omissions

PETER ROBB

BLOOMSBURY

First published in Great Britain in 2004
This paperback edition published in 2005

Copyright © 2003 by Peter Robb

The moral right of the author has been asserted

Maps copyright © by Alex Snellgrove

A CIP catalogue record for this book
is available from the British Library

Bloomsbury Publishing Plc, 36 Soho Square, London W1D 3QY

ISBN 0 7475 7316 6
9780747573166

10 9 8 7 6 5 4

All papers used by Bloomsbury Publishing are natural,
recyclable products made from wood grown in well-managed forests.
The manufacturing processes conform to the
environmental regulations of the country of origin.

Printed by Clays Ltd, St Ives plc

www.bloomsbury.com

IM

Florisvaldo Azevedo de Carvalho

You can put anything into a book of omissions.
Reading one of these never worries me at all.
What I do when I get to the end is close my eyes
and think of all the things I didn't find in it. So
many great ideas come to me then, really deep
thoughts.

—MACHADO DE ASSIS

The tram goes by full of legs:
White legs, black legs, yellow legs.
My God, what are all the legs for, asks my heart.
But my eyes
ask nothing at all.

—CARLOS DRUMMOND DE ANDRADE

Brazil made me intelligent.

—FERNAND BRAUDEL

Contents

I	Mixed Blood	3
II	A Cordial Man	31
III	On the Beach	55
IV	Parrot Perch	81
V	Below the Equator	107
VI	Stuffed Goat	133
VII	A World Elsewhere	159
VIII	A Place to Die For	187
IX	Witnesses	215
X	A Used Revolver	241
XI	In Maceió	265
XII	A Win	289
	Sources and Readings	309
	Notes	316
	A Chronology	317

The maps of Brazil (pp. xii and xiii), which have been drawn by Alex Snellgrove, show only places mentioned in the following pages. Likewise, the notes on reading and the chronology at the end refer only to matters discussed in the book.

The tilde over a Portuguese vowel, as in *São Paulo* or *sertões,* stands for a missing *n* at the end and means the sound comes out through the nose. The sound of an *nh* pairing in a Portuguese word is that of an *ñ* in Spanish or *gn* in Italian—so the surname of *Euclides da Cunha* rhymes with *vicuña* in Spanish and *prugna* in Italian.

The currency values that appear here, many of which are necessarily approximate, are expressed in United States dollars valued at the time of the transactions they refer to. So after ten or more years, PC's billion would be a lot more today.

12°

Fortaleza

4°

C E A R Á

P E R N A M B U C O

Olinda
Recife
Porto de
Galinhas

Garanhuns

Palmares

Rio São Francisco

A L A G O A S

Guaxuma
Maceió

Canudos

Penedo

SERGIPE

Aracajú

N

B A H I A

Salvador
de Bahia

Bahia de Todos
os Santos

14°

S O U T H

A T L A N T I C

O C E A N

Santa Cruz
Cabrália

Monte
Pascoal

Like everyone, I went to Brazil to get away. At the start it was easy. At the beginning of the eighties Brazil still had a consulate in Naples. It occupied a vast and gloomy suite with high ceilings and the finest veil of dust in a distinguished Umbertine palazzo two blocks in from the Bay of Naples. On a clear day you saw Capri from its window. The consulate was marked by an oval plaque in burnished brass and you reached the office in a clanking iron cage lift with glowing mahogany seats.

Reception was manned by a tall lady with parchment skin and horn-rimmed glasses on looping chains. Another nearly identical lady lurked within. They wore silk blouses in the heat and cashmere twinsets in the cool. Their dark straight hair was pulled severely back, their feet shod in costly lace-up shoes and they moved softly in long skirts of handwoven tweed. Behind frosted glass yet farther in I once saw a fuzzy silhouette of the consul himself. There was a huge old Underwood typewriter with a cast-iron frame on the reception desk, several wilting aspidistras in pots in the corners and a fly spotted schoolroom map of the Americas on the wall.

I wondered what the old ladies had to do in Naples, and they seemed to be wondering too. There was a Brazilian I knew studying navigation at the Naval Institute, but that was all. A hundred years earlier, hundreds of thousands of southern Italian peasants had sailed steerage for Brazil from Naples. Now a third of Brazilians were of Italian descent, and some of the richest among them. The rich came to Italy to spend and poor Brazilians, if they could, would come to Italy to make their fortune. Most of these were transsexuals who plied their trade at the richer freeway junctions farther north. The Naples consulate was dying of inanition. The fan flicked around noiselessly. Though they made it clear that the consul couldn't be hurried, the two ladies were always very good about my visa. Of course I went to Rio first, via Casablanca with Royal Air Maroc, which had a special offer at the time.

I

Mixed Blood

Murders happen anywhere and mine most nearly happened in Rio. Twenty years later only the scar of a small knife wound on my arm reminds me that this is a memory and not a dream. The night went on and on like a dream, with a dream's ungraspable logic, or a Brazilian soap's. Details become wonderfully vivid, like the old carving knife with a long curved and darkened blade carelessly left earlier on the kitchen bench of the Copacabana flat, in the moment it was being held at my throat. My Portuguese lost its rudimentary awkwardness and became unreally fluent very fast. Words I'd never known I knew came pouring from my throat. Things flowed with a dream's weightless speed. The danger lay in the speed. A flailing knife blade moves faster than thought. Movement had to be slowed, the heat lowered. It was the one thing I understood. Let nothing happen. Respond to violence, speed and noise not with violence, speed and noise but with ponderous torpidity, envelop each new threat in slowness. The beautiful Portuguese periods began to roll, slowly, slowly, but with what baroque grace, from my amazing tongue. Obtuse fearlessness stayed the hand with the knife, impassive calm put a little wobble in the spin of violence.

Chance put the knife in Adelmo's way. Chance, or Brazilian entropy, had saved me a moment before we worked our way to the kitchen. The hideously old-fashioned Brazilian furniture, in the sitting room where it started, was a wasteful mass of dark stained solid tropical woods and dark brown cowhide upholstery and rows and rows of little brass studs. Adelmo grabbed a lamp and then a chair to smash my head. The lamp's base was cast iron and the chair too heavy to wield. When we got to the kitchen and he grabbed the knife, a tiny part of the first fatal impetus had been lost.

There—elaborately, ponderously, holding his eye hypnotically—I laid out the options. I told him that since he held the knife, if he wanted to kill me he probably could. Yet there was nothing of value in the flat. This looked likely. There were a couple of pairs of jeans and a few faded polo shirts flung around and that was all. The American dollars under the mattress would have been to Adelmo a huge amount, but I didn't mention them. If Adelmo started looking he would find the money in seconds and kill to leave with it. It was important that Adelmo's mind be kept off looking for cash. The baroque periods surged and crashed, like the thunder of surf in the night, as Adelmo learned that the noise of any assault would be heard by the neighbors in the next apartment. The neighbors, Adelmo heard in an elaborately inserted parenthesis, were close friends of mine. There were several of them next door, young, physically vigorous, and holders of a spare front door key to the apartment we were in. The apartment was vacant, but what was baroque prose for, if not to put a spin on simple realities? Finally, the doorman downstairs—armed of course, and a family friend—was the only person able, from within his reinforced glass booth, to activate the mechanism that unlocked the heavy glass doors that opened onto Our Lady of Copacabana Avenue, and the doorman had strict instructions never to let visitors out of the building unless they were accompanied by myself. A strange order, improbable even, but a slight cause for concern to anyone who might be planning to kill and leave. By name I mentioned the particularly hideous Rio jail where Adelmo would spend the rest of his life.

This little touch kicked in to great effect. Nobody likes to feel trapped, and Adelmo knew all too well the experience of being locked in. He hated it. Later, when the emotional cycle had turned again, he showed me the scars on his legs that had been made by the bullets fired at him by the reform school guards as he ran off. Adelmo had been fending for himself since he was very young. And for the next couple of hours he held the carving knife to me in the kitchen. And talked. He laid out his life in words. The flashing-eyed knife-waving anger dissolved in tears of unhappiness at his lot. The only reason he hadn't killed me, he said with an unexpected sob, was that I'd been so good to him. The restaurant, the respect. He would have killed anyone else. Then the knife was at my throat again. Still holding the knife, he threw his arms around me. *Kiss me,* he said, and I did. It was a very charged and prolonged kiss. The illusion of hieratic distance conjured by ornate prose suddenly vanished. *I already saved you tonight,* Adelmo said. *The guy on the bus was going to knife you.*

Very likely. As the juddering, madly speeding late night bus had swung and hurled us to our destination, a giant of a black man, an amazingly tall and muscular figure in running shorts and running shoes and a tank top, had been toward the end of the journey the only other passenger. He seemed to know Adelmo. They had talked apart for a while, and the stranger glanced across at me from time to time. *You didn't understand what we were saying,* Adelmo said now. *We were talking carioca slang. He wanted to roll you. He wanted to knife you and I said no.* What I remembered was that in one of his huge hands the black man was kneading, while he and Adelmo talked inaudibly, a rather finely made gold spectacle frame, an elderly person's spectacle frame. The lenses were gone, and his hand was reducing the frame to a tiny compact ball of twisted gold wire. I wondered what had happened to the owner of the glasses.

Adelmo didn't often get the chance to talk about himself and in those days I was a good listener, even without a knife at my throat. Adelmo was happy that, maybe for the first time in his life, he had an audience. Through all the moods and phases of the night, however, the kitchen knife was always there. Once, as if to remind me of my place, Adelmo slashed my arm with the knife. The cut wasn't deep but the flowing blood raised feelings of danger, violence and panic. *You'll tell them I attacked you.* Adelmo slashed his own arm and started bleeding too. He calmed down. *I'll tell them you knifed me first.* He was pleased at the logic of his self-wounding. The danger passed and he went back to telling me about himself, between declarations of love and spasms of murderous rage. We went on for hours, standing in the little kitchen. In the end we were clinging to each other and too exhausted to go on. We wiped off some of the sticky blood and went downstairs. The doorman hardly woke as he buzzed us out. The sky was getting lighter over the Atlantic.

I caught sight of Adelmo again the following night, crossing a square in the centre of Rio. He was hard to miss. He was wearing, at a very rakish tilt, a beret in shocking pink angora. It set off his virile features in a striking manner. He waved cheerfully and seemed on top of things again. It was the last time I saw him. I left a couple of days later and it was years before I went back to Rio. The night in the kitchen at Copacabana with the carving knife felt like the logical and personal conclusion of various other things I'd seen and experienced on that and earlier visits in the early eighties. It was hard not to feel that visiting Rio was asking for trouble. Things were starting to break apart in Rio. The signs were everywhere.

In that very building, the day I had rented the apartment a few months earlier, I came home to a foyer full of military police. One grabbed me and threw me against a wall and a couple of others began, not gently, to search me. Someone said, *That's not him,* and I was flung aside. Police were swarming all over the building. When I got upstairs, I glanced out of the window, which gave onto a kind of small enclosed garden. One or two stories below was a sloping roof that stopped at a wall on the garden. The wall was built up a little beyond the bottom of the roof to hide the slope, and in this gutter between roof and wall, partly hidden by some opulent green foliage, I was looking down on a poorly dressed black youth who was lying very low and very still. Later the police left and when I looked out again the boy was gone too.

Another time a boy raced barefoot across the promenade, the cycling track, the palm lined central island and the multiple traffic lanes of the Avenida Atlântica, away from the beach and heading for one of the transverse streets that led through Copacabana and, eventually, to the mountainside that rose behind the strip of apartment blocks, sheer out of the flat coastal strip, walls of rock, clefts of green. A watch bracelet was glinting in the boy's hand and the military police were shooting at him, and into the crowd on the footpath. They missed the boy, and the schoolchildren and housewives and street vendors and the people heading home from the beach and the taxi drivers talking and smoking while they waited for fares. The police didn't always miss, when they shot into a crowd of Brazilians.

The boy was making for the precarious jumble of shacks that clung to the rocky peaks. This was the *favela* and his home. In a reversal of the world's more usual urban growth, which had the hovels of the poor clustered at the base of green hills where the rich lived in their big houses, Rio's peculiarity had the twentieth-century apartments of the wealthy spread along the beachfronts—first of Guanabara Bay and then of the long ocean beaches to the south—while the unaccommodated poor, flooding to Rio from all over Brazil, made their flimsy homes on the breathtaking and dangerous heights of the monoliths looming over the concrete real estate. Shacks crashed into green crevasses with every downpour, but the view from Rio's favelas was stupendous. I climbed up once to look around, and found a pastoral settlement whose most dangerous inhabitant was a huge brown sow wandering its paths. Twenty years later, no outsider would dream of entering a favela without protection. The name of the favela came from a long way away. In the remote hinterland of Bahia in the Northeast of Brazil there was a rocky peak rising by a flat riverbed called Monte Favella. At the end of the previous century thousands of Brazilian troops had been sent from Rio and other places south on a terrible punitive expedition and they had camped on Monte Favella, which gave its name, after they came back, to the encampments of the poor on the spectacular hills of Rio. But it would be years before I learned what happened at Canudos, the place overlooked by Monte Favella.

One day, changing some of the Yankee dollars I had smuggled out of Italy, I was given twice as many greasy wads of big red *cruzeiro* notes as even the day's exchange rate warranted. The sheer distractedness about the value of money that Brazil's rate of monetary inflation promoted was another symptom of social breakdown that was almost as vivid as the children on the streets and the police shooting into crowds. The supermarkets of Rio were being looted in those days by people who left the money and took the sacks of beans and rice. Money in Brazil was something you dealt in fistfuls. You didn't bother to count it.

Brazilians were living through the long dragged out death of a military dictatorship that had lasted for nearly twenty years, though there was no sign then of an end to the agony of military rule. Brazil under the military had lacked the kind of drama that caught the world's interest. There had been none of Chile's bombing of the presidential palace, no murder of an elected leader, no massacres in the football stadium, no *caravan of death*. Neither had there been the disappearances of Argentina, the unmarked gray Ford Falcons, the unspeakable tortures, the still living bodies dropped into the sea from helicopters, the ignominy of a lost war in the South Atlantic. There was in Brazil no brilliantly sustained urban guerrilla resistance to match the exploits of Uruguay's Tupamaros, no permanent guerrilla army in the jungle like Colombia's or Peru's. For the world there was something dispersive in Brazil's hugeness, something that made it hard to focus on. When the Brazilian military had taken power a decade before the others, it happened so blandly that the world hardly noticed. The United States, poised between Kennedy's murder and the Vietnam War, prized stability and acquiescence in its hemispheric neighbors and thought military rule in Brazil would be a good thing, and so in 1964 did a lot of people in Brazil. The governor of Rio tried to rally the troops against their leaders, but he failed and followed the president into exile.

For years the military had it easy, riding Brazil's late and remarkable industrial boom, and the euphoria and pride that went on for years after Brasilia was built. The stunning modernist capital that went up almost overnight in the empty highlands of Brazil's very center projected a land of great resources and endless confidence. This and a little money and a lot of soap operas kept people's minds off who exactly was running the country and how they were doing it. There was resistance, however. Students were imprisoned. Foreign diplomats were kidnapped and exchanged for the prisoners, who were flown to safety in Cuba and Mexico while the Brazilian military looked foolish. More prisoners were taken. The screw turned in 1968. The military closed down the Congress altogether and began *a counterrevolution within a counterrevolution* in which murder and torture became routine instruments of the government's control. The resistance responded by kidnapping the American ambassador. Advised by great and powerful friends, Brazil's dictators developed the model of government that the military of Chile and Argentina would soon make their own. Subversives—who might be anyone who did not loudly acquiesce to the military— were hunted down. Most of Brazil's democratic leaders had already left the country.

Lacking an entire political class and the smartest and bravest of its younger generation, who were overseas or dead or vanished within the regime's prison system, Brazil was not well placed, after ten years of military rule, to deal with the drastic downward turn the world economy took in the 1970s. A few years of floundering and the less cruel and obtuse of the military wanted to tiptoe backward out of government, only not too precipitately, in case people noticed. Control without responsibility was what they wanted and never achieved. By the eighties the bankers and industrialists were despairing. There was no way Brazilian generals could manage one of the world's larger industrial economies, let alone avert at the same time a social disaster that only the boom had held off. Power was draining from the military, but still they were afraid to let go.

People were quietly coming back. There were amnesties. Unreported and unnoticed, particularly by holidaying foreigners with no desire at all to involve themselves in the travails of underdevelopment, things began to stir. In 1979 the movement produced a minuscule grouping of recently exiled and tortured intellectuals and some industrial workers who were raising their heads. Grandly, the little group called itself the Partido dos Trabalhadores, the Workers' Party. Late one afternoon I was on the Avenida Rio Branco, in the center of Rio, just as darkness fell. Down the splendid street, choked with buses and their black exhausts, and all the yellow VW Beetle taxis running on sugar-cane alcohol, marched a little procession of demonstrators. There were twenty of them at the most, and I think they were march-ing about education. They were carrying a red flag with a black star, as well as the banners. They seemed a tiny and frail looking group, determined but a bit intimidated, a lot less assertive in their persons than the messages on their banners, in danger of being crushed by the traffic and a general indifference. It was a surprise to see them in the brutal and hedonistic Rio de Janeiro of the last years of military rule. Their banners identified them as members of the Workers' Party. I wondered how long they would last. I wondered how they were able to exist at all in that Brazil, in Brazil as it was at the start of the eighties.

The desperation of some of the younger Brazilians—people like Adelmo, whose concentration on personal survival left little space for the big picture—was reflected in a film made around this time, a gritty and technically economical film that recalled De Sica's and Buñuel's images of another generation's lost chil-dren in Naples and Mexico. The new movie was called *Pixote* and was seen by a lot of people. I saw it in Rio, and watched the rather obvious back projections of Arpoador beach—which showed that the group of reform school fugitives from São Paulo have arrived in Rio—in a cinema that was a few hundred meters from the beach itself, the little kink between Copacabana and Ipanema, in full vibrant color with real bodies. *Pixote*'s young actors, in the true vein of neorealist art, were what they played, or near enough. The child who played Pixote, the pale and watchful youngest of the group, and the feeling center of the film, was an eleven-year-old from São Paulo. Fernando Ramos da Silva was the only one of the group who didn't quite live on the streets. He was one of a family of ten children from the industrial outskirts of São Paulo. His father was dead. Father and mother were country people from the Northeast who had come south to pick coffee and like so many others from the Northeast were sucked into the megalopolis of São Paulo, the biggest, richest, dirtiest and most dangerous city in South America. Mother and children survived by hawking lottery tickets on the streets.

A lot of people saw *Pixote* in Brazil and around the world, but not many doors opened for Fernando. He had a few small acting jobs, but he never really left the world of his origins. When he was seventeen he married a girl a year younger and they had a child. He had a few run-ins with the local military police, and he felt they picked on him because of the film. He felt typecast for life as a derelict and killer by his childhood role as *Pixote*. In 1987, when he was nineteen, he was playing cards at home when the military police raided the neighborhood. He hid at a neighbor's place, and when the police found him hiding under a bed they fired seven shots into him point-blank. They reported that Fernando had died while resisting arrest. There had been no charges against him. Because *Pixote* had been seen by millions of people, the death was picked up by the international wire services, and the Italian papers, who felt the news embodied either a confirmation of everything the film had foreshown or a bitter irony about the way art could take over a life. Which it did. Both readings were true, though in Brazil it was a very ordinary death, a death like thousands of others that were happening every year.

The deaths still happen. In 2003 another Brazilian film came out called *City of God,* which was the name of a Rio favela and the title of a novel by a young Brazilian writer called Paulo Lins, who had grown up in the City of God. From childhood he had lived through the City of God's fall from a quickie housing estate knocked up in the days of the military into the blood soaked stamping ground of the drug gangs who worked out of it. The drug gangs, winners and losers, living and dead, millionaires and foot soldiers, had been Paulo's childhood friends. His novel and the film enacted the spiral of violence and terror that all Rio's favelas have known in the last twenty years. Even more than in other countries, drugs are a growth industry in Brazil, which shares long and uncontrolled borders with all the biggest producers of cocaine. For several of these countries Brazil is both a vast market and their outlet to Europe and the world. Drugs are the only economic activity possible in the favelas but are not confined to the favelas. The drug runners of Rio now blow up cars, stop traffic and stop business in the smartest seafront suburbs. You would have to be a Brazilian to know what it means for Paulo Lins to have made it out of the favela and become a student, a poet, a researcher, an admired novelist, but the favela is pursuing him. The favela is overtaking Brazil.

The film of *City of God* has great visual flair, but it convinces, like *Pixote* twenty years before—if not as much as the novel— because its actors are real. And like the boy who played Pixote, the young actor who plays the boy who rises to control the favela's drug business has remained trapped in the world he came from. A few months after the film went around the world, he was arrested after a police chase along the beachfront in the smartest part of Rio. The teenager had made nothing out of his film and had a cocaine habit to feed. Like most of the other hundred or so who played in the film, he still lived in the favela. One of the actors became a model, a few got parts in a soap called *Women in Love,* a lot of them did a film workshop. Most of them were still living on hope rather than money. The film's director said that *to give these boys money . . . would only lead them back to cocaine addiction.* The violence of the drug business is a new mutation of the old, old violence of Brazil, which is a country of immense natural wealth, at peace with its neighbors and facing no unusual turbulence or social unrest within its borders. Yet the killing rate in Brazil, tens of thousands of violent deaths a year, falls within the parameters of the United Nations' definition of a low intensity civil war.

It was natural that a film about the lost children of Brazil's cities be played out along the narrow axis of Rio and São Paulo, which are only a few hundred kilometers apart. Everything in Brazil revolves around Rio and São Paulo and it has been like this for more than a hundred years. The building of Brasilia merely triangulated the airline traffic patterns. There is more money in the cities of the Southeast than anywhere else in Brazil, and more killing. Rio on Guanabara Bay sprawls over the habitable parts of the most beautiful site in the world. It was the slave and sugar city of the south, snatched from the French in its infancy and francophile to its marrow, the old capital of imperial Brazil, dazzling in its disease riddled belle époque, reimagined as the *marvelous city* of flying down to Rio and twentieth-century dreams of beaches, music, football, drugs and sex, ringed and overlooked and now increasingly invaded by its favelas. For the world, Rio goes on being Brazil.

São Paulo lacks Rio's splendor of place but it has the sex and drugs and the violence, a lot of money and even more people than money. A Jesuit mission station in the sixteenth century, inland from Portuguese coastal power and near the *índio* souls God wanted, for centuries it stayed a little inland cattle town. Its tough and cruel settler *bandeirantes* were the first Europeans to penetrate Brazil's interior on their long slaving forays against the índios. The hills around São Paulo were perfect for coffee shrubs and in the latter days of slavery São Paulo was transformed by money from the worldwide coffee boom. The European immigrants flooded in to replace the slaves. A million Italians, hundreds of thousands from Portugal, from Japan, from

Syria, from Germany, these were the first. São Paulo created and supplied its own demands, and when industry came to Brazil it came first to São Paulo. Now twenty million people make São Paulo maybe the fourth biggest human agglomeration on the planet. Rio is huge and lovely and terrifying. São Paulo is huger and more terrifying and not lovely at all. The immensely rich hover over the city's canyons in their own helicopters, fluttering at sunset between the corporate tower and the gated residence. São Paulo has more private helicopters than any other city in the world, more armored limousines, more armored ordinary cars, more armed security personnel and more desperate people than any other urban center on the face of the earth.

———

Seven years later, I got an early morning train to Rome and caught the afternoon flight to Lisbon. The Portuguese airline flew out of Lisbon at one in the morning and touched down in Recife at daybreak. Recife is nearly two and a half thousand kilometers north of Rio and the flight to Recife from Lisbon took a lot less time than any flight to Rio or São Paulo. It took me to another country. It took me to the Northeast—more exactly to the Northeast's oldest settled states, narrow Pernambuco and Bahia, which is bigger than France—and to a sense of the Brazilian past.

The Northeast is seen in Brazil as a problem. From its larger coastal cities, it can look very like the Southeast. The model is always Rio. There are the rows of high and shoddy new apartment blocks—each with the name of an Italian old master painter or a culturally prestigious place in France in wrought iron script on the fortress street-level wall—built along the Atlantic beaches at the edge of the city. They are the same in every coastal city in Brazil, and it is easy to forget for a moment which particular city they belong to. Which city you are in. Geography and architecture and climate are all equally unhelpful. The same vast resort hotels stand at every strategic point, always doing so much less business than they were built for and showing the same underpaid figures in uniform idling out front. But these appearances deceive. The Northeast is different.

The past is present in the Northeast. Rio and São Paulo destroy as they grow, but walk down certain streets in a northeastern city and you might be in the 1940s. There is the cream painted curved art deco cinema, with its turnstile and its popcorn vendors, there is the milk bar with stools and tropical milkshakes, there are the lean men with hats over their faces, asleep on the tray of a beat up old truck. Walk around a corner and slavery seems not to have ended. You see black women with huge bundles on their heads and shirtless men straining to move a two wheeled cart and not a car in sight. A bell clangs in the tower of a baroque church, the homeless clustered in its porch. A thin choir drones in the flimsy chapel of an evangelical sect.

Go through some tiny town of the northeastern outback. Pass the silent people on the stone front steps of their pastel washed and windowless one-room houses. The houses are built in rows along the beaten unpaved street, and along the beaten track a skinny mule pulls some sacks on a decrepit dray, and then a darker long eared mule ambles past under a barefoot boy in a big straw hat with a fraying brim. He's riding bareback with a slack rope halter resting in one hand, while the young girls with chairs and mirrors do each other's hair on the dusty verge. The narrow road that brought you there goes on forever, the hills undulate mildly until lost in the haze and if you lose yourself in the present you lose your bearings entirely. The interior of the Brazilian Northeast is a world apart—high, bare, hot and terribly dry. The coast of the Northeast is moist and lush and follows that eastward jutting shoulder of the South American continent that seeks the matching indentation in the west coast of tropical Africa. Recife is on the shoulder's easternmost bulge.

Recife was built on the islands of a river delta, where the Capibaribe River and the Beberibe and the Pina and the Tijipio and the Jordão all flowed into the Atlantic, under the protection of that slim but effective line of rocks that runs along the coastline a little way offshore. This was the crucial reef, the *arrecife* that gave the city its name and protected its shipping by breaking the force of the Atlantic swell. Recife had no splendid bay like those of Salvador and Rio, no dramatic cliffs or monolithic outcrops, just this stubborn little line of barely visible rocks. Recife didn't even have the amenity of a splendid green hill looking out over the Atlantic and cooled by ocean breeze. Olinda, the old capital, was built on such a hill. Olinda was adjacent to Recife, but still separate and special. The Portuguese had built Olinda in 1537 and it was one of the oldest settlements in Brazil, but in the early seventeenth century it had been knocked out by the Dutch. The Netherlands were scrabbling for a foothold in the continent, and clung for twenty years to a strip of coast in the Northeast. They were the people who had founded Recife a hundred years after Olinda. Caught in time, the old city of the landowners and the church stayed on its hill, run down and incomparably more beautiful, snatching at the crumbs of a hand to mouth tourism. From the middle of the seventeenth century Recife, with its merchant houses and its docks, was where the action was.

Where the bus tipped me out at first light, groggy from the Lisbon flight, was somewhere on the island of Santo Antônio. Guided by helpful hands, I stumbled into a small hotel whose modest entrance was hidden by a rank of yellow-canopied vendors' booths. It was called the Nassau, after Prince Maurits of Nassau, the man who founded Recife. The hotel was not large, but taller than the buildings around it, and taking coffee on the top floor you got an exhilarating oblique glimpse of hazy seafront and cobalt ocean in the morning sun, and a lungful of warm salt air. Nearer by was a confusion of baroque bell towers, domes, terracotta tiled roofs, and raw low-cost office blocks, their untreated concrete sides blighted by huge blotches of black tropical mold. The big avenue below was packed with rows of buses that were hardly moving, some little cars, and crowds of tiny people on foot, their foreshortened legs striding out very fast in every direction.

The footpaths teemed with people, and the streets were almost impassable from the number of hawkers' stands. The hotel was in a cobbled space called the Largo do Rosario, and the handsome church was at one end. A few yards away, in the wedge shaped space in front of Nossa Senhora do Carmo, lots of sellers had no stalls. They came from the country and spread their fruits on a cloth, little mounds of mangoes, little hands of delicate bananas, pyramids of limes, assortments of bell shaped *caju* fruit, pink and pale yellow, with the poisonous green *castanha* still attached, which when roasted would become a cashew nut. There were *cajá*, a kind of yellow plum, as well as *caju*. There were guavas and pawpaws and custard apples in small heaps. Most of the fruits had only their índio names. Sharp red *pitangas* and twigs of *pitombas* like clusters of suntanned Ping Pong balls. Women squatted with a pan of palm oil over a charcoal fire, frying *acarajé*, their African bean meal patties with a dried shrimp embedded in the top like a red jewel.

The mouse gray blanket of the rat poison man, positioned discreetly just around the corner, with its carefully arranged display of the mummified corpses of dozens of rodents dispatched by his product, always drew an absorbed knot of onlookers. Even more stopped to look at the anaconda writhing around the shoulders of the man selling barks and herbs and little bottles of his own special remedies. The herb vendor was an orator and a performance artist as much as a healer, and he and his snake held large crowds transfixed, until he paused to give them an opportunity to buy. Some of the pedestrian alleys were so jammed with the plywood stalls of watch repairers, vendors of coconut and banana and chocolate cake, or roast corn, or hot dogs, or combs and necklaces and wrist bands or used vinyl records, that you could hardly move. The jewelers—watch repairs and trinkets—had their own alley. Sellers of used comics and agricultural magazines, old physical culture reviews and odd encyclopedia volumes and other reading material concentrated in the literary area under the arcade of Avenida Guararapes by the Bar Savoy, where on Friday evenings a lady in her forties sang on the footpath with an electronic keyboard and snare drum player. The side alleys off the arcade were entirely given over to hot dogs and sticky cakes. The green coconut-juice stands stuck with the browsers along the arcades and the crowds jostling at the bus stops. The sellers of pencils, string, brown paper, envelopes, ballpoint pens and postcards had their own specialized stands over on the other side of the avenue around the post office steps. But anywhere at all in the city someone might be standing on the footpath by a tiny trestle table with a few choice digital watches, a heap of garlic, some coconut sweet, a luminous toy on a string or some objects of religious devotion.

A lot of the dense mass of people moving on foot through the city carried wares with them. Most of the crowd moved really fast, flinging out their legs and arms in a way only Recife people did when they had somewhere to go. People with something to sell were sometimes only semi-ambulatory, like the popcorn vendors and the hot dog men, who worked from big glass boxes mounted on bike wheels or pram wheels. The others traveled lighter and faster and were often underage. The newspaper sellers were emblazoned with the masthead colors of the

Diario de Pernambuco, the oldest paper in South America, and edited out of a stately nineteenth-century edifice near the Largo do Rosario, or its rival from a newer building around the corner, the modernizing *Jornal do Comercio.* The shoeshine boys lugged their heavy wooden boxes on a leather strap or a cruel rope over their shoulder and kept their eyes to the ground for those leather shoes striding along among the plastic flip-flops and the cheap runners. The shoeshines concentrated on the bars and restaurants, since sitting shoe leather was half the battle and after a few beers even better. Shoeshine was the most thankless job of all. The kids who stood around in the Praça do Carmo all day, leaning on a sign announcing *I buy gold,* had it easy.

The food sellers also hung around the bars. There were an awful lot of bars in Recife, a bar consisting largely of a few rickety folding tin tables and like chairs set up on an uneven footpath, and an awful lot of kids to service the hunger pangs that follow a few drinks. Toward the end of the afternoon the streets filled with boys carrying broomsticks over their shoulders. Around a nail at each end of the broomstick were suspended little plastic bags of *amendoim,* which were peanuts. They came raw or roasted or steamed, ready to shell or preshelled, in large bags or small. You could also buy cashew nuts and quails' eggs. Other children spent their evenings lugging little braziers around, made out of old paint tins and filled with glowing charcoal, like a church censer. In the other hand was a tray of long blocks of white cheese impaled on wooden skewers. Your skewer of cheese was grilled over the little brazier while you drank your beer and waited. The cheese was the Northeast's white *quiejo coalho,* made from curd. When darkness fell—and the sun dropped out of the sky in the space of a few minutes—the older youths arrived who had spent the day trudging along the sand at Boa Viagem with dishes of shrimps or buckets of oysters and now came to town to move what was still unsold.

Between the Largo do Rosario and the *Diario de Pernambuco* was a small garden at the confluence of several streets around which there were a lot of people gathered on account of the many bus stops for the different lines. The small garden itself was busy with the meeting and greeting of unattached ladies and unattached gentlemen, who I noticed often left in pairs after striking up an acquaintance. At one end a crowd had gathered around a wiry middle-aged man with skin like finely polished wood. He was wearing a black cowboy hat and dark glasses and a very clean, slightly frayed, short-sleeved blue-and-white-check cotton shirt and playing an old acoustic guitar that he had wired up to a primitive and even older amplifier and a battered black speaker box. He was thrumming the guitar and not so much singing as chanting or intoning a long ballad that had the bystanders gripped. Each strophe finished with a flourish and the listeners laughed. I couldn't make out what he was singing about in his hypnotic way. It seemed to go on forever, but the singer knew how to hold an audience.

On the corner, a few yards away, another man was squatting by a display of leaflets. There were dozens of them and they were the words of songs like the one being sung. At once crude and beautiful, the long rhymed ballads were hand-set in ancient irregular letterpress, printed on folded sheets of the cheapest pulp paper. Some of the libretti were laid out on the ground and others were held up for sale on a frame strung with clotheslines, to which they were pegged and fluttering like drying underwear or trapped birds, with a crude and vivid woodcut on the cover. I bought half a dozen at a few cents each for their gorgeous letterpress. Others might have wanted them for their woodcuts. Music, story, image were here combined. I bought a ballad about a girl who turned into a snake and another on the arrival in hell of Lampião—the outback bandit who wore steel rimmed glasses and an outback leather hat studded with silver medallions, and was the greatest of the Northeast's primitive rebels. I unpegged the story of a boy who didn't know how to make love to girls and the account of a football match in purgatory. The black man and the rubber tapper. The boozer and the believer. Not quite Homer, or even Ovid, they had their moments. Newer songs fed into a repertory of workings and reworkings of favorite local themes, which was why a new take on the one-eyed Lampião was still a good bet fifty years after Lampião and his girlfriend and his men had been cut down in an ambush by the military police. The armies of type, poor and a bit ragged but impeccably in step, were marching now through pagelet after pagelet of newsprint already dry and yellowed under the piercing sun.

The bafflements of Recife derived from more than the clutter of its streets and the busyness of its traffickings. The flatness of the interlocking delta islands, and the network of mysterious waterways that cut across the reclaimed land, the number of similar but different bridges, made walking around town like covering the pieces of a big jigsaw puzzle. The lay of the land gave you no help and neither did the direction of the water flow, for the rivers were all tidal, and their waters ran both ways. I walked for hours on some early forays, convinced I was heading inland, only to end up on the waterfront on the island of São José, Recife's oldest part, where the old warehouses and the customs station and shipping offices clustered. This was a largely deserted and somewhat sinister place after nightfall but in the daytime you could get a man to row you out to the reef and pick you up later, and lovers used to do this. Beyond the reef, finally, there was nothing but the ocean and Africa.

———

Recife's streets had a strangely familiar feel. Their random intensities reminded me of Naples. They also recalled a book. Many

years before, on a wet day in Edinburgh, I had found a copy of
the first edition in English of Gilberto Freyre's *study in the development of Brazilian civilization . . . translated from the Portuguese of
the fourth and definitive Brazilian edition by Samuel Putnam,* as the
title page had it, bound in a black cloth like oilskin and published in New York by Alfred A. Knopf in 1946, thirteen years
after its original had first appeared in Brazil. In English it had
become *The Masters and the Slaves.* Freyre was a descendant of
sugar plantation owners and Recife was his city. In this first
book, which he wrote out of homesickness and published in
Brazil in the early 1930s, he described in sweeping generaliza-
tions and intricate, gripping detail the culture of the sugar plantations in colonial Brazil. The two poles of that culture, as the
title of his book made clear in Portuguese, were the *Casa-grande
& Senzala,* the big house of the white masters and the slave
quarters of the captive African workers. The piercing light, the
lush green of the fields of tall waving sugarcane, the cobalt ocean
off the coast, the humid heat and farther inland the bone dry
cruel clarity linked the Mediterranean culture of the masters and
the African cultures of the slaves and the tropical American culture of the displaced índios in the enclosed and isolated world
of the big sugar estates.

What linked the masters and the slaves was sex. In Freyre's
intricately documented study, every matter of life on the sugar
plantations led subtly back to sex. The sex was so deeply present
in his material that Freyre hardly needed to be explicit about it.
It was sex enhanced by the gorgeousness of the climate and the
sweetness of the sugar, and also sex made perverse by the cruel
relationship of masters to slaves, of the Roman Catholic Church
to African practices and indigenous forest life. Every new theme
he turned to became an aspect of sexual life. It was a very seductive picture of a slave society, a lot more complex in its reciprocities than I had ever imagined. The Brazil of the sugar

plantations was, in Freyre's account of it, profoundly influenced by the values and practices the captives had brought with them from West Africa, so that in time the culture of the Portuguese masters had been subtly but radically transformed by the ways of the people they used as chattels. Brazil had turned into a society vastly different from that of the slave owning southern states of North America through the intimacy that existed on all levels between masters—and mistresses, and the children of the Portuguese masters and mistresses—and their slaves and their slaves' children. If in Protestant North America sex with slaves had been nasty, brutish, short and a matter of profound shame, particularly when the children were born, in the lax Catholic Brazil of the tropics, sex across the divide of race and ownership seemed to be at the very center of plantation life. Sometimes, reading Freyre, you wondered how they ever got the cane harvested and crushed and the juice boiled down.

In Freyre's view all this produced, over the four centuries and more of Portuguese settlement in Brazil, a much more fluid relationship between black and white than the English or North American or Spanish colonies ever knew. The Portuguese had been enthusiastic about sex with the índios too, until they had killed most of them off with their European diseases and their attempts to enslave and Christianize them. Brazil was peopled with black, whites, índios, and descendants of black and white, black and índio, índio and white, and endless further variants of the three as the generations passed. Sexual mixing laid the social ground for a benign equality in diversity of all Brazil's races and cultures, once the institution of slavery itself had dropped away, as it did at the end of the nineteenth century. By then the diversity was being enriched with a flood of Brazilians from other parts of Europe and from the Middle East and Asia. It was immensely seductive, Freyre's tropical pastoral of the vanished world of the sugar estates, conjured in sensuous and loving detail. Most seductive of all was the idea that out of Brazil's sensual and promiscuous past a new society had grown where the races flourished and racism was extinguished. The *new world in the tropics* that Gilberto Freyre wrote about so exuberantly and so prolifically in book after book was a marvelous dream.

To Brazilians in the 1930s the image Freyre held up of their own society had been quite startling. The Brazilians who shaped Brazilian institutions—the white Brazilians—had always lacked confidence in their racially bastard society. The blacks and the bastards were so many and the honorable white *fidalgos* so few. Even ordinary white people were not all that thick on the ground. There was nothing they could do about it. The solution, it seemed, might be to give up the idea of a ruling caste altogether—the idea Spanish America clung to—and go for modernization. In 1889, a year after she had formally abolished slavery in Brazil, Princess Isabel and her thoughtful and once astute but now elderly and infirm father, the emperor Dom Pedro II, who was now known around Rio as Pedro Bananas, were startled to find themselves escorted to the docks by the military, put on a boat and shoved off to Europe, where Pedro would die a couple of years later in a modest hotel in Paris. The army was in power. The Brazilian republic was proclaimed.

The republic's motto, *Order and Progress,* girdling the globe with the stars of the Southern Cross on Brazil's beautiful new green, blue and yellow flag, proclaimed its positivist values; and betrayed, in its very peremptory formulation, the new rulers' deep anxiety about their new body politic. It gave away their eminently military sense that keeping a tight grip on things was an even higher priority than moving things forward. The republicans were about control. Their aspirations were entirely European and in sweaty, chaotic, sensual Brazil, whose wildly oscillating economy was entirely based on export agriculture and controlled by the commodity markets of Europe, there was a lot to embarrass people who wanted Brazil to become a nation-state of a European or North American kind. The past was even more embarrassing than the present. Centuries of indiscriminate couplings had produced a people of bastard voluptuaries. If the positivists and the social Darwinists were right, and the founders of the republic of Brazil were convinced they were, Brazil was doomed to underdevelopment because so many Brazilians were inferior material. There was a terrible tension between the expansiveness and optimism that were generated in even the tightest mind by Brazil's gorgeous climate, its vastness and beauty and abundance, and the nagging fear of being doomed to backwardness.

When the nineteenth century ended Brazil was a little less entirely a society of the great landed estates, ruled by the sugar growers, the cattle growers, the rubber growers, the coffee growers. The cities were growing, especially the capital, Rio, and the new Brazilian republic was the creation of the city middle classes, the businesspeople and professionals who mediated between the landed barons and the rest of the world. The economy was booming and the city people of Brazil's belle époque were resolutely staring across the Atlantic for a glimpse of Europe, whence all the fine things came that they were now importing. Especially they were trying to make out France, which was entertaining its own unrealities at the time, like the rest of a Europe already drifting toward the Great War. Imported into the latterly slave society of tropical Brazil, the unrealities of the nineties boom blossomed with a heady luxuriance in Rio.

Then there was the world war and the world bust. For Brazil it was the crisis that ended the old republic and introduced— another new European fashion, in its way—the dictatorship of Getúlio Vargas in 1930 and its enhanced version, the New State, in 1937. It was into the newly uncertain Brazil of the early thirties, where the bust of world capitalism was no less amplified than the boom had been, that Gilberto Freyre's amazing book was born. It amazed everyone. It celebrated everything that the intellectuals of the new Brazil had been in deep denial about for fifty years: the bad old world of the slave plantations and their brutal, lustful patriarchal tyranny. It announced that out of this world, and specifically out of the sexual life of slave owning society, in the backward and embarrassing culture of the rural Northeast, the uniquely splendid civilization of Brazil had been born.

The paradoxes of Freyre's case were greatly perplexing for Brazilian intellectuals trying to make sense of their country's place in the modern world. Young Gilberto was barely thirty when he wrote *The Masters and the Slaves.* He had spent time in Europe and studied in the United States and maybe for this reason had no sense of inferiority about Brazil. His book was also disconcertingly well written, slangy and extravagant, exuberantly, vividly particular and filled with the sights and smells and tastes of the Northeast. Gilberto's familiarity with the jokes and locutions of Brazil's illiterate masses, his knowingness about their social and culinary and sexual habits as well as their language, shattered decorum. Food and sex had never been held to be a part of culture at all, let alone considered with Gilberto's playful unadornment. It was especially startling to the guardians of ruling values that the entirely white and irreproachably fidalgo grandson of plantation masters should have been so familiar with the daily life of his social inferiors—it seemed like a betrayal of his class and race. Other Brazilians, and especially northeasterners like the young Jorge Amado, who was in his teens and already starting to write the popular life of northeastern Brazil into novels that would be read around the world, were simply dazzled. Never mind that most of its Brazilian readers knew nothing of the Northeast, let alone the long gone life of the old sugar estates. Brazilians recognized themselves in Gilberto's book. The verdict in the end, though it was a long time coming and never entirely unqualified—Gilberto Freyre has been in and out of favor over the years, and has a singular way of disconcerting both right and left—was Amado's, that *Gilberto's work leaves us all more Brazilian.* The unfamiliar pleasures of his style lowered resistance to his thesis and seduced his readers into embracing all the pleasures of a racially mixed Brazil.

Gilberto was a prolific writer, but none of his later work ever quite matched this first young man's book in its impact. He went on writing the same book over and over. There were two sequels—completing a massive trilogy on the uniqueness of Brazilian civilization—and a flurry of smaller books. Each new book was a variant reworking of the first, elaborating and embellishing its argument, and taking the story into his own time. All shared its marvelous sensitivity to the significance of the physical details, the concrete particulars that give the theory its seductive life. Fat footnotes thrust their way up every page, stories nested within the stories of the principal narrative like the *Arabian Nights,* under the guise of additional facts. The current Brazilian edition—the forty-second—unwisely confines these to the end of each chapter, whereas the splendid design of Knopf's put them in legible double columns at the foot of the pages they often occupy almost entirely. Freyre's translator, Samuel Putnam, was even more irrepressibly devoted to the footnote than the master himself, and his own further notes were interspersed with and sometimes added to and qualified Freyre's own. The reader had to make his own way through their typographical luxuriance.

Gilberto Freyre was not an ideas man. He snatched at whatever looked useful—or even merely interesting—and worked it into his tale. A later Brazilian anthropologist complained that

Gilberto always compromised his findings by intruding a novelist's touch. He didn't mention the readiness to draw support from some of the cracker-barrel racists, mad phrenologists and weird theorists of the psychosexual who were pullulating in the twenties and thirties, the mental sludge of the very positivism Gilberto's book dispatches so finally. The vice is marginal, and the bibliography has its own fascination. *The Masters and the Slaves,* and the other two books of Gilberto's trilogy on the making of Brazil, *The Mansions and the Shanties* and *Order and Progress,* and all the satellite works like the book on sugar and confectionery, are in the end a single great Brazilian buildungsroman about the making of Gilberto, a Proustian attempt to recover his own past disguised as the description of a civilization.

II

A Cordial Man

Brazilians are Mediterranean and African in most of their ways and as Mediterraneans they are lunch people. Big lunch people. It is a problem in northeastern Brazil not to be a lunch person and sometime after sundown that difficulty starts making itself felt for a dinner person. People in Recife did their eating in the day and their drinking in the evening. You could get a cheap and abundant worker's lunch almost anywhere. And in a place with white tablecloths and good china and uniformed waiters bearing elaborate menus, you could get the kind of vast and traditional midday meal described by Gilberto Freyre, consisting of many dishes and side dishes served with spoon and fork, expertly wielded by a single hand in the best French manner against a background of *azulejos*—the beautiful blue-painted white Portuguese tiles—dark wood, white linen and with whatever drink you fancied. At night all the enticing restaurants were boarded up. Places where people drank did food of a kind, but since food was an odd thing to look for in the evening they weren't geared up to supply anything decent. This was where the boys with broomsticks and braziers came in.

One evening I headed down a short narrow alley off one of

the busiest streets—the sun long down by now—and entered a calm cobbled space that was closed to traffic. A tall baroque church in eggshell blue with sandstone quoining rose behind a spiked railing at one end of the square. Narrow roads went off each corner, and the other three sides were lined by little colonial houses of one or two stories. The houses were painted in pastel colors, their ornaments picked out in white. Some of the houses had tables and chairs outside. People were drinking and the broomsticks and braziers were busy. People were even having their shoes shined.

None of the places had visible names, and the outside tables of one were continuous with the outside tables of the next. It was a beady eyed waiter who swept me in as I peered through the door. Even in the tropics I like to sit inside to eat or drink, to have a roof over my head and a solid wall behind me, a table that sits foursquare and a noncollapsible chair. Outside is edgy. So while the people outside, who were mostly young, were jostling over their drinks and prey to birds, mendicants, sudden rain, violent assault, unsteady tables and the importunities of tiny children and the entrepreneurial youth, I was waved into a room that was pleasingly half full. It had walls of white-painted brick, a dark wooden floor and a long communal table of heavy dark wood down the middle of the room, with long wooden benches to sit on. At the front, by the windows, and along the sides were smaller tables and stools.

At the back of the room, framed by a massive, irregularly shaped contraption of huge dark wood, was a low bar. Bent over a glass and grinding with a wooden pestle was a slightly built man of middle age with a beaky nose, sharp black eyes and spiky, ruffled iron gray hair. He wore a neat short-sleeved shirt and a severe pair of half-moon glasses sat low on his nose, loops of granny chain swinging on either side as he mashed a lime with sugar and ice to make a *caipirinha*. Behind him a massive old dresser's endless compartments held spirit bottles, postcards, openers, spike files of bills and receipts, photographs, a calendar, glasses of various sizes, several bunches of keys, pencils and a ballpoint pen, some paper flowers in a little vase, a bottle of some strange and murky homemade liqueur, a paperweight and a couple of little human figures in unglazed terracotta. On the dresser's main ledge was an ancient manual adding machine by Burroughs with a crank handle and a ribbon of white paper spilling out the back. To the left of the bar a stockade of varnished saplings led out to reeking pissoirs, and against the wall on the right was a further empty space, a little frame within the frame of the bar that from time to time was abruptly filled by a primitive dumbwaiter, hauled up on pulleys with a load of dirty glasses or lowered with a bump announcing plates of food. Behind the dresser a kind of stepladder led up through a square hole cut in the ceiling to a kitchen hidden under the eaves. From time to time a pair of well shaped and tanned bare female legs descended through the hole and rested on a rung, while their owner spoke with the beaky man behind the bar. The legs then rose again out of sight.

The waiters raced in and out with trays of sweating beer bottles and glasses wrapped in napkins. Sometimes they carried food, of which I tried to snatch a glimpse. The beer, which in Rio had always been draft, in Recife was always in bottles, and the bottles here were tended and nurtured in the freezer so that they emerged at zero degrees centigrade without having actually frozen, and arrived before you with a bluish frost on the glass like the bloom on a plum. From time to time there was a miscalculation, and the beer solidified when the crown cap was removed, spilling endless frozen amber foam like ice cream. Sometimes a customer would wander off without having paid and a waiter sprinted after him.

The man with the beaky nose worked away behind the fronds

of green coconuts, which were spilling out of a trough in the wooden contraption in front of the bar, grinding limes and ice into tumblers and adding the sugar and the slug of *cachaça* and presenting the drink with a white paper napkin folded around the base of the glass to absorb the condensation. Even when the trade winds moved the air after sunset, there was always condensation on the drinks glasses. Cachaça and beer were the universal drinks in Brazil. The beer was pale, cold, low in alcohol and superfluous sugars and malts and gases, and practically indistinguishable from one brand to another. At this time, however, in Recife the Antártica was being brewed with water from a mineral spring that made it ambrosial. Cachaça gave you a hit of something altogether more interesting. The white distillation of the sugarcane was not a fancy booze. Neat cachaça put fire in your belly and stilled the pangs of hunger. Caipirinhas gave you a simultaneous hit of ice's cold, alcohol's fire, lime's ascorbic acid and cane sugar's energy rush. In Recife the cachaça was Pitù, poured from the bottle with the picture of the red freshwater crustacean on the label. The same picture was on walls all over the city. The coconuts were there to have their ends hacked off with a murderous cleaver when someone wanted a glass of their juice. There were people drinking whiskey with coconut juice too. Juice extraction was deft and rapid. One hand wielded the cleaver, the other held the fruit for slicing and upended it over a waiting jug in a single movement while the other hand was replacing the cleaver on the bar. The cleaver was a worry, lying there on the bar, as things got lively.

Bangüê was the place's name. It was carved in big letters on a panel of varnished wood above the bar. I had stepped into the plantation world of Gilberto Freyre. A *bangüê* was several different things in slave life on the sugar plantations of early Brazil. Gilberto, describing *the morose, melancholy, indolent life* of the plantation wives in that man's world where the wives bore heirs and the men had slave women as their lovers, said they went out *only in the hammock . . . or in the bangüê, or litter,* with its leather top and curtains, carried by African slaves. A bangüê was also the stretcher that carried away the bodies of slaves when they died, and the hand barrow made out of liana thongs that was used to remove the used husks of the sugarcane. Bangüê became the name of the trough in which raw hides were washed and tanned. Bangüê—*one of the most characteristic of Brazilian regional terms, with a number of meanings and shades of meaning,* chipped in the translator in one of his footnotes—was also the furnace and the boiling pans in which the sugarcane juice was rendered down, or the tiled runnel in which it was drained off to crystallize and solidify, and so it got to be in the end the name given for the whole sugar producing estate in its collective sense, the plantation, the mill, the refinery, and now the drinking place that evoked this world.

The bar itself was a dark and massive wooden trough, with a great wooden beam horizontal above it and at one end a vertical wooden screw with its thread carved into a smoothed and polished tree trunk. The huge piece of wooden machinery must have come from one of Pernambuco's old sugar mills, like the old leg irons, balls and chains, and weapons of assault that hung on the walls. There was an ancient baby's crib made of reeds hanging from one wall of white-painted brick. There were a few knives and guns and some clay pipes for smoking. And there were a couple of big portrait photographs on the walls of sun-baked musicians from the drylands of the interior playing instruments they had made. There was also some rather fine wood carving on panels. On your way to the amenities you had to squeeze past a wooden sedan chair with round portholes for looking out the side, massive as the other plantation things, an unbelievable weight to stagger around with in the sun, even without one of the plantation wives—the women of the big house, who never lifted a finger on their own account, were seen with some malice in the sketches of European travelers—lapping over the sides in all her indolent melancholy. The sedan chair, minus the leather roof and curtains, was now being used to store beer crates in and was probably the eponymous bangüê itself. There were tottering stacks of beer crates, full and empty, by the door, and more between the shafts of the sedan chair. A thickset man in shorts, with twisted, powerful shoulders, came and went in a rapid oblique shuffle with crates on his back, changing empty bottles for full, staggering slightly under his load. A golden patina of old smoke covered the walls and nobody seemed to be there for the decor.

The hard-pressed waiter flung a menu down and it skidded across the polished wood. The list of the day was typed on a sheet of paper stapled to a woven reed fan, like a paddle with a handle, such as slave girls used to keep the air moving around their mistresses' necks and breasts as they swung in the hammock or the rocking chair. It was hard to choose. *Sarapatel. Arrumadinho. Chambaril. Xarque.* The waiter pursed his lips with concentration as I ordered a drink and then he shuffled off, a small sturdy workhorse in short-sleeved shirt and carpet slippers. The Bangüê had an excellent menu of a daily special for every day of the week except Sunday, but only for lunch. I was in trouble again. But only partly, and only for a while. The menu's longest section was its list of *petiscos,* and the place called itself a *petisqueira.* The petisco was a superior version of the snack. A simple snack in Brazil was a *lanche* and you found it in a *lanchonete,* or a glass box on wheels. A petisco, like a *quitute,* was altogether superior food, inventive, complex, refined, delicious— serious food for the serious drinker, to be shared around, had in any order or combination, wolfed down or picked at over time, and the Bangüê promised well. After flinging a couple of preliminary inquiries at the waiter, and getting rapid-fire answers that were too complex for a first go, I settled on *carne do sol com macaxeira.*

Sun dried steak might seem tough and overcooked, but it was always dense with flavor, enhanced by a few sautéed onion rings and complemented by the waxy translucency of boiled *macaxeira.* Macaxeira was a long pale root with a pinkish skin that might grow to a meter long, one of the kinds of manioc that were a Brazilian staple. Sellers wheeled stacks of them around the city in barrows, announcing themselves with a drawn out macaxeira street cry. The carne do sol arrived with a bottle of homemade *pimenta,* a suspension of pounded red chilies, and another bottle containing clarified butter. This was another product of the process that produced the white curd cheese, no less prized than the cheese itself and de rigueur with carne do sol. The next evening I had *agulhas fritas,* half a dozen fried needlefish neatly aligned along an oval plate. If you took the head and the tail in your fingers, the dry white flesh lifted neatly in a single piece on either side of the skeleton.

At what point, during what lull, did the bird of prey behind the bar acknowledge my presence? I no longer recall. The waiter, whose name was José Antônio, kept the cold beer arriving at the right moment, as each night I worked down the list of petiscos. One quiet moment early in the week the person behind the bar with the hooded eyes came over and we had a conversation about food. He talked as he looked, in such a rapid staccato way that a lot of his recommendations were lost, apart from breadfruit. Then he asked if I was a researcher.

Gilberto Freyre had brought me to Recife—or rather Gilberto's books, the man himself having died at eighty-nine three years before—and since Gilberto had had an insatiable curiosity about everything that was really human in Brazilian history and life, human in the sense of appetites, desires, pleasures, vices and consolations and the ways these were realized, as against the country's myths, illusions, lies and rationalizations, a curiosity about the details that made up the real rather than about sustaining big pictures, I said yes, I was a researcher. The bird of prey, whose name was Vavá, accent on the second *va,* short for Florisvaldo, didn't press me for details. He had known a number of researchers from the exterior—the exterior being anywhere not inside Brazil—and I seemed to fit the pattern. Most of the Europeans who did research in Pernambuco were looking into poverty, homelessness, malnutrition, illiteracy, corruption, violence, human rights violations, child labor, life expectancy, health problems and things like that. Problems of underdevelopment, and this was not material for conversation over an evening drink and a petisco. Other researchers came to Pernambuco to look into popular culture, oral traditions, the rituals of Carnival, dance and music, and if I was one of these, well, there was plenty of time.

Vavá jumped up and went back to work, to meet and greet, being best friend of every paying customer who crossed his threshold, to mix drinks and keep things moving. Almost hidden behind the dresser, there was another head behind the bar, staring out from among the green coconuts through giant designer lenses. The head belonged to a seated woman who was cranking away intermittently at the Burroughs calculator. She had a headful of golden ringlets, each one defined as if carved in stone, and large eyes behind the enormous glasses. She was Dona Lia, Vavá's wife, and Dona Lia was the business part of the Bangüê.

Vavá and Lia—it would take me ten years to find this out—were in crisis. They had taken over the bar as an offshoot of their main activity, which was a small art gallery of work produced by painters and sculptors and wood-carvers and potters in the interior of Pernambuco. The art gallery was in another little house not quite next door to the bar, and the back of this house, or its front, opened as a shop front onto the busy avenue running behind one side of the Pátio de São Pedro. That shop was a bookshop, the Livraria de Cordel, and as its name announced it sold the little booklets with the words of the ballads sung by the wandering singers at the bus stop. Vavá had started with the bookshop, selling the cordel libretti and other books about Pernambuco and the Northeast, and then set up as a dealer in local art. He and Lia had taken over the Bangüê when it came up for sale several years later. Taking on the bar turned out to be a smart move.

———

One night I stood by a parked truck not far from the Bangüê and listened to a man called Lula speak. It was a turbid evening after a hot wet winter's day. Night had fallen suddenly and hid the inky clouds that were trailing low over the city roofs. The truck was parked in a shallow triangular plaza, alongside the high iron railing that defended a seventeenth-century convent. The convent chapel's white baroque façade, edged in dark unpainted stone, glowed in the dark at the end of an avenue of palms. Behind the truck and next to the convent were the plain but blotchy dark green front and the dim fluorescent lights of the Parrot Restaurant, which at that hour was nearly empty of drinkers. Lula was a stocky, vigorous man with matted and kinky black hair growing low on his brow and a thick black beard on his face. He stood on the back of the truck in a worn short-sleeved shirt, leaning forward on one strong hairy forearm, looking down at the crowd of us standing around, and holding a microphone on the end of a cord. You could see he was missing a finger of the hand holding the microphone. Lula was a man like many in Recife. He might have come in from up-country Pernambuco to sell farm produce or buy stuff at the city's São José markets. Lula was a Brazilian battler, recognizably one of those northeastern battlers who hurled their stocky bodies into the daily struggle to put food on the table, and sometimes, like Lula, were taken a long way from home by the requirements of that struggle. There seemed to be a great intimacy in his words to the crowd. He wasn't raising his voice, and he wasn't making promises. He certainly wasn't spinning through any rhetorical hoops. He was just talking in a low-key, concrete, practical but utterly compelling way about the troubles in their lives and what, practically, could be done about these troubles.

Lula was more widely acquainted with the hardnesses of life than most of his listeners in Recife. He knew the underside of the industrial megalopolis down in the south of Brazil. Lula had been taken to São Paulo as a child, one of the millions of north-easterners who had made Brazil's great internal migration from drought and starvation to feed the industrial growth of the south. He had known, shining shoes and selling peanuts on the streets as a child, what it was to be despised as a northeasterner by big city people. After a remarkable few years as a union leader of São Paulo's metalworkers he had seen out the dictators and he was now a leader of the Workers' Party, that heterogeneous cluster of revolutionary Marxists, liberation theologians, ordinary parliamentary social democrats and trade unionists which had been formed ten years earlier, as the power of the military waned, to act for people whose voices had not been heard in Brazil for a long time. Lula himself was not an ideologue, or even much of a book reader. He had become the voice of the Workers' Party around Brazil for the same reason he had been so effective as the metalworkers' leader, for the same reason that I and dozens of others were now standing rapt in the dark as he spoke from a truck.

Listening to him speak, you forgot that a few months earlier, at the end of 1989, Lula had come remarkably close to being the president of Brazil and that he bore the mark of a loser.

Lula's recent nearness to power seemed an illusion, because the man who defeated Lula, when the two of them had pulled away from the other pretenders and gone to a final vote six months before, was now so compellingly Brazil's new leader that it was hard to imagine the vote could have gone otherwise. Fernando Collor de Mello was a northeasterner too, though he seemed to come from another world. You also forgot, looking at the dynamic new president, that a year earlier Fernando Collor and not Lula had seemed the unlikely candidate. Nobody knew much about Fernando. There didn't seem much to know. But he was tall, much taller than Lula, stylish in a way Lula could never be, apparently much younger, though the difference was four years, and very personable. He promised to modernize Brazil, after the decades lost by the military dictators, sell off the sclerotic state corporations, end protection, stop inflation, open up the economy and make Brazil globally competitive. This was advanced talk at the end of the 1980s, and it sounded fresher and more exciting in Brazil than anywhere. Fernando had a terrific TV presence—people were entranced by the jogging, the motorbikes, the glamour. They knew the lifestyle from TV. Fernando was the future.

Before the long night of the military, only a tiny group of Brazilians had ever been allowed to vote and the chosen one was always the choice of the landed wealthy, of the sugar people, of the cattle people, the rubber people, the coffee people. Even so, in sixty years the country had elected only four presidents, and only two had seen out their terms. In 1954 Getúlio Vargas—*I am standing in a sea of mud*—retired to the presidential bedroom and put a bullet through his heart. Juscelino Kubitschek, who got Brasilia built in 1960, finished his term and handed over to an elected successor, but Juscelino himself was a creature of the military. In 1960 only one adult Brazilian in four was allowed to vote, and Jânio Quadros, who won, gave up after seven months as president, claiming *hidden forces* were forcing him out. His vice president, João Goulart, took over and was removed by the tanks and troops in 1964.

In 1985 the retreating military had let only the Congress vote for the president; the winner died and the first president of a newly democratic Brazil was little José Sarney, a northeastern landowner rooted in the past whom nobody had ever imagined as its leader. Brazil had changed out of sight since the military coup. It was now a complex industrial and metropolitan society and the vote of 1989 was momentous because it was the first really democratic election ever held in a country of 150 million people. It was momentous too because one of the candidates came from Brazil's industrial workforce, who made the country go and had no say in its running, and received the thinnest trickle of the immense wealth Brazil generated. Lula's presence was deeply disturbing to the players of the old game. After years of repression and then the bitter disappointment of 1985, a lot of Brazilians were feeling ready in 1989 to choose the man who wanted to change the rules entirely. The old players had no credit at all. Panic grew on the upper floors of São Paulo and in the mansions of Rio. Who could be found to represent big money and make big money's interests attractive to all those Brazilians who were struggling in the middle, eager to move up, afraid of being dragged down?

This was Fernando's chance. Up he popped, from a little state people had barely heard of, confident, articulate, visually strong, seemingly untied to the past and savage in his attacks on the outgoing president. The contest of 1989 was big enough and polarized enough to seize the imaginations of people outside Brazil, and the world watched from afar the relentless rise of the former metalworker and the drama of the charismatic unknown who looked like a playboy. In Italy I remembered the violence and decay of years before and suddenly I wished I could see what was happening in Brazil. People were turning out in hundreds of thousands to hear Lula in Rio and Saõ Paulo in the days before the vote. Others were scared of Lula's radical words and soothed by Fernando's talk of modernizing Brazil, and saw Fernando as a hope for change without pain. How could you tell, unless you were there? By the time I got to Brazil it was all over, and Fernando had been sworn in a couple of months earlier and here was Lula on the stump for some local man. But I hadn't lost my curiosity. This was my research. I had no idea then how much these lives might show about the oddest and most thrilling country in the Western Hemisphere.

It started raining again while Lula spoke, lightly at first, then heavier and heavier. The sound of the water falling on the stones almost drowned the noise of Lula's amplified words coming from the clusters of loudspeakers. Umbrellas were useless under the weight of the water. Office workers who had stopped to listen held plastic satchels over their heads. It was all useless. Shirts were plastered to shoulders and hair was flattened on scalps. Shoes filled with water. Beads of rain were caught by the spotlights as they gathered in heavy pearls along the ropes of electric cable that looped from overhead lines to the truck and the speakers and the lights and snaked along the ground and through pools of water. What if the cables came down? Lula went on talking calmly, his four fingers gripping the mike, standing upright and beating the rain with his other arm now for emphasis. Nobody moved until he finished.

The rain was still falling heavily when the loudspeakers played a hymnlike little tune sung by quavering maudlin voices. It was called "Our Star Is Going to Shine." This was the new anthem of the Workers' Party. The star was the red star of revolutionary class struggle, but some in the party had decided that the color and the imagery and the talk that went with them were putting people off, people who might otherwise be won over, like house-wives and others unlikely to clench a fist. A few less people frightened and Lula might be changing the world in Brasilia, instead of standing on the back of a truck in the rain. The jingle was one of the direst inventions of the newer and nonthreatening Workers' Party that was quietly being elected to the government of more and more cities and states around Brazil. The jingle sounded like something heard in one of the evangelical sect halls that dotted Brazil ever more thickly. The new and militantly evangelical churches, some of them huge and vastly rich already, were deeply hostile to the Workers' Party. The hostility was reciprocated. Evangelists were the other contenders for the hearts and minds of the Brazilian masses. It was no mistake that the Workers' Party's sickening new song sounded like an evangelical hymn. From the music or the rain, the crowd scattered fast and headed for shelter as soon as Lula finished speaking.

The odd darting figure, satchel still gripped over head, was still running for cover. Otherwise the streets themselves were empty now. Along their edges in the shadows were the night people, black on black, gripping their flattened cardboard boxes and their small children, huddled under available overhangs, waiting for the storm clouds to exhaust themselves so they could go to bed. A few older children stalked apart like wingless insects, emaciated and detached from the human clusters, gray rags flapping off their limbs. Their heads were mostly shaved and they clutched glue bottles to their breastbones, under their filthy knotted T-shirts and running singlets. They looked serenely beyond all human care. The next day was blue on blue, gold on white, hot and dazzling.

Harried José the waiter was clearly one of the ground down northeastern working people Lula spoke for. José used to set off on his interminable journey home toward midnight, after hours and hours on his half-crippled feet. He worked only some days and received no salary. Like all the bar waiters he made only the ten percent service charge on the drinks he served and he lost the price of the drinks when a client absconded. This was why he looked harried, throwing anxious glances out the window every time he came inside to pick up a new order. He looked, as Vavá pointed out once with a seraphic detachment that contained a feeling he couldn't afford to indulge, many years older than his real age. One night I mentioned Lula. José's face grew twisted with dislike, and with a kind of embarrassment. Lula was ignorant, incompetent, illiterate. He hadn't been fit to lead Brazil. What would people think if he went overseas? Lula had done pretty well in the Northeast, and splendidly here in his own state of Pernambuco, but it suddenly became clear why he hadn't won Brazil. José hadn't wanted Lula as his president because Lula was too like himself. Slumming foreigners might look on Lula as a working class hero, but when José saw him he felt pained and humiliated and he hated himself and Brazil. He wanted to be represented not by a stumpy bearded metalworker who had lost a finger in a lathe and got lost in Portuguese syntax, but by a tall, elegantly suited and mellifluous graduate in law, a person who knew the world and could meet with foreign leaders as an equal and an ornament to Brazilian civilization. Someone like Fernando.

Fernando and Lula seemed to come from different countries, and in a sense they did. Brazil was a country where the richest one percent of the people had fifteen percent of the wealth. The poorest forty percent had less than a tenth. If you looked at the gap between the wealth of the richest twenty percent of Brazilians and what the poorest twenty percent had, Brazil came in at the bottom of a list of eighty-five countries. The gap between rich and poor was more than six times the difference in countries like India, Egypt, Pakistan, Indonesia. It was more than double the wealth gap in Russia, Mexico, Nigeria. Double the gap in Chile, Venezuela, Colombia too—the only Latin American country that came anywhere close to Brazil's inequalities was Guatemala. Brazil's wealth gap was more than six times Japan's or Germany's, four times Canada's, more than three times the differences in Britain, the United States or Australia. If you compared wealth inequalities in the countries of the world, Brazil came third to last in a list of the ninety-three countries for which data existed. Fernando was a winner in a country where Lula and all the people like him were born to lose. The Brazilian people themselves had just confirmed it.

Fernando's first act of modernization was a shock for almost everyone. The day after he took office in 1990, Brazilians woke to find the government had confiscated, for eighteen months, all their money in the bank, above a ceiling of just over a thousand dollars. People were not reassured when the new minister of the economy was unable to explain on TV just how the Collor Plan was going to stabilize the currency. One morning after breakfast, and a couple of months after the freeze, I met the hotel's owner in the lift. The lift took some time to come down from the terrace with its view and its breakfast spread, and as it descended the owner filled the space with praise of Fernando. He thought the shock to the system a great thing and told me Fernando was going to save Brazil. A few days later the Bangüê hiked its prices and so did everywhere else. Fernando's plan was already falling apart.

People who had saved now had no money to buy houses or cars, pay schools and hospitals, even to buy food. They certainly had no money to buy works of art. For years Vavá and Lia had been buying the work of artists in outback Pernambuco, mostly carved wood and ceramic figures, and selling it to galleries and collectors in Brasilia, São Paulo and Rio, selling it from their own gallery in the Pátio. Vavá loved being an art entrepreneur and suddenly it was over. He was left with a houseful of carvings and pottery, paintings and fabrics that would get dustier and dustier over the months and years. The Bangüê had become his only hope of making a living. It was why Lia so often paused as she cranked the calculator and stared into space. Things were quiet even in the bar, though business picked up as inflation ballooned again. Two months after bank accounts were frozen, inflation was running at eight percent a month. By November it would be seventeen percent a month. The faster prices rose, the busier the street dealing got and the fuller the bars. I never understood why.

There was one client of the Bangüê's who even in the slow times turned up every evening around six and stayed for an hour or so. He was the only person in the bar who ever wore a jacket and tie, usually a bone colored tropical linen jacket in patrician style. Among the dark wood and the country appurtenances he looked like the plantation owner. He was in his forties, had an amiable face and smiled often under a large dark mustache, and he had a bon vivant's girth. He never sat down, and drank whiskey standing up by the serving bar, wedged between the green coconuts and the stacks of plates and glasses, in front of the dumbwaiter. He stood by the bar so he could speak to Vavá, and the two of them carried on a lively conversation the whole time he was there, inches from the whirling cleaver splitting coconuts. From time to time Vavá would pass him a little plate of cheese with *pimenta* or something special that didn't seem to be on the menu. He never seemed to pay for anything, and I wondered about that.

His name was Cândido and we started talking one evening, over the noise and clatter of the food and drinks. Somehow, we got on to abandoned children. Cândido asked me how serious the street children problem was in Italy. *Street children?* I said. *We don't have any.* A wave of child thieves from the Balkans was just then sweeping through the city streets of Italy—hardly abandoned though. They were slaves run by gangs of adults who tortured them at night if their takings fell short. Their number was relatively tiny. In Italy proper even the street children of Naples were gone. And even in the hardest times, these had always had, if not a family, a locality, a context, a sustaining social fabric they were part of. In Brazil, the street children seemed to number in the millions, and they had no real ties to the adult world at all. Recife teemed with skeletal child glue sniffers. They were the bottom layer of a whole heap of Brazilian children abandoned by the society they were born into, a society whose violence in home and neighborhood made them take their chance on the streets as the lesser evil. The glue didn't always get the children through the day. You needed more than an intoxicating sniff to defend yourself. There were no less desperate adults also on the streets, and other adults who wanted to use you, and other adults again who simply saw you as detritus, something to be removed by whatever means were at hand. Four street children were murdered every day in Brazil—probably more, every day, every year. How were Cândido and I to talk about this? His affability was subdued for a moment.

Brazil's new economics minister, who thought up the bank seizure and found it so hard to explain, was a young woman called Zelia. She was a protégée of Fernando's from his tiny home state of Alagoas in the Northeast. Zelia had no experience of politics and little of economics, or of life. The day after bank accounts were frozen, Zelia turned up unannounced at the president's home in Brasilia. Two days in office, Fernando was not so intimidated by his new job that he didn't feel able to relax. Zelia found him relaxing over a prelunch whiskey and deep in conversation with a middle-aged man—bald, thickset, his face lightly masked by big designer glasses and a mustache. The thickset man was drinking gin. *An admirer of British habits, at lunchtime he recommended a Tanqueray, his favorite, with a slice of lemon fixed on the edge of the glass.* As Fernando glared at Zelia over his tumbler of Black Label, angry at being disturbed, the bald man affably *raised his glass a little, combining the offer of a drink with friendly greeting.* Fernando said, *What are you doing here?*

Zelia knew the middle-aged man. He too was from the little state of Alagoas, whose capital, Maceió, was on the coast not far south of Recife. He had been Fernando's campaign treasurer, the man who paid for everything. He had paid her, when she was an unknown economist on Fernando's election team, thirty thousand dollars cash plus expenses for each of the last six months before the final vote. His name was Paulo César Cavalcanti de Farias and when the election was finally won Fernando had told him, *Without you I wouldn't even have made it to the second round,* but hardly anyone else knew of his role in Fernando's victory. For PC Farias, whose friends called him PC, this private praise from the president was enough. The people who did know PC were nearly all from Alagoas.

When Zelia interrupted them halfway through the president's second day in office, PC and Fernando were talking about a matter that had grown from the way PC had run Fernando's campaign finances the year before. PC had done too well. He had raked in $160 million and had only spent $100 million on getting Fernando elected. *What am I going to do with these sixty million dollars, Fernando?* PC had asked. PC had never seen so much money in his life, and was still a bit dazed by the liberality with which people had given. The election had been close, and people had responded generously, even extravagantly, to PC's solicitations. Several of Brazil's banks had given $3 or $4 million each, and all the big industrial groups had given at least as much. Andrade Gutierrez, the construction, telecommunications and real estate group, gave more than $7 million. Almost none of the people with money to lose had let PC down. The more they had to lose and the higher Lula rose in the opinion polls the more freely they had given. Only the Globo media group failed to give to PC.

Manage it, Fernando told PC of the $60 million. It was an unusually large amount of spare money to manage, but electing a president was an unusual experience for Brazil. Fernando was happy to have the money and didn't want to be bothered with details. PC saw it as a challenge. He had to manage letters of credit, stocks and shares, cash checks, bank checks, checks from account holders who didn't exist, bills of exchange, dollar notes, dollars held in offshore accounts. The gifts had come in all these forms and all the gifts were a long way outside the law's idea of the acceptable present. PC managed to manage the money and in the months after the election he paid out $2 million of it for Fernando's personal and family expenses. PC learned a lot from the big industrialists who had given the money—new ways of money laundering, new ways to keep money hidden inside Brazil and offshore, refinements in the methodology of keeping parallel accounts. He set up new offshore companies and opened bank accounts in the Caribbean, the United States, France and Switzerland. For the first few months of Fernando's presidency, he paid out in cash or in checks drawn on his own accounts. Later that year he worked out a system of payment by checks from nonexistent account holders and he stuck to this.

PC had been Fernando's treasurer for four years, ever since the campaign that saw Fernando elected governor of their home state of Alagoas. PC had smoothed away an impasse between Fernando and the sugar growers. He had always been more than a money man. He was Fernando's mediator with the business world and the administrator of Fernando's own affairs. Fernando, who was an impatient person, came to rely on PC almost entirely in money matters, to the point where it was unclear quite what money was whose. For his part, Fernando had the social and political connections that PC's business activities required. Quite early in the campaign, when all was still in doubt, PC had gambled $2 million of his own money—a lot for him in those days—held in a Panama bank, on Fernando's election. *I'm staking everything I've got on this,* he told his incredulous brother. Fernando's fortunes and PC's now rose together. The symbiosis was total. When Zelia asked the president what to do about PC's intrusions into her running of Brazil's economy, Fernando told her, *Play along.* And Zelia, who was minister of the Brazilian economy, did what she was told by PC, who was no one at all.

The commonality of goods meant there was something for PC in the surplus. He paid himself back the two million from his Panama account. He finished off the house he was building, a $5 million concrete fortress on a hilltop whose interior was done out with priceless baroque religious carvings, contemporary designer kitsch and things PC had picked up on his travels, and whose master bedroom suite took up fifty square meters. PC also spent $10.5 million on a couple of jet planes for himself. He loved flying and he loved planes and nursed a secret plan to own a major airline. In one of his planes he flew his biggest giver, Sergio Andrade, from Rio to Havana. The Andrade Gutierrez group was interested in building floating oil platforms for Cuba and PC himself wanted to do business with Havana. Fidel Castro took them to dinner and gave PC a box of cigars personalized with the name *Don Pablo* on the band of each. From then on PC received regular supplies of these from the Cuban embassy in Brasilia, and he liked to talk about these gifts from Fidel, who seemed to have understood from the start exactly what the game was.

———

One Friday afternoon I moved to a cheaper hotel. A run-down place in a dilapidated nineteenth-century mansion by the river looked dense with character, and so it was. On the verandah a very tall, very old and very thin black man rocked all day in his rocking chair with a flat checked cap tipped down over his eyes. The building stank of rancid fat and the hot shower device in the bathroom gave out nasty electric shocks when you turned on the water. Shortly before daybreak someone in the street below took out my windowpane with a rifle, filling the bed with glass shards. It seemed time to move on. From a classified advertisement in the *Diario de Pernambuco* I found a flat on one of the upper floors of a huge and scary block of low-rent housing. The building was so vast and its cardboard thin walls of crumbling cement so flimsy that it felt ready to fold up and collapse at any moment. The walls vibrated with the life they were so imperfectly built to contain and big pieces of the honeycomb brickwork enclosing the staircase that spiraled up the side of the building had already fallen off into space. The holes in the staircase wall, the torn patches of blinding light, induced vertigo. When the lifts didn't work you climbed thirteen floors past these sudden holes. The lifts when they did work were so few and so slow and their users so many that you could make that climb in the time you waited for a packed and sweaty ride.

At dawn on Saturday I woke to a tremendous banging on the door. I jumped out of bed into ankle deep water. The next door neighbor was banging to warn me. He was a black schoolteacher who said people on the floor above had gone away for the weekend leaving a tap on and a sink plugged. *They're always doing this,* he yelled over the sound of cascading water at the end of the passage. He told me that the entire building went without water during the daylight hours—unpaid bills, the teacher said.

People had to collect their daily needs during the night. Our neighbors had left town with the tap turned on while the water was cut off. Their apartment was locked and nobody had a key. I noticed now that all the front doors on this floor except mine were protected by a flood barrier across the floor. I spent the rest of the morning trying to sweep water out of the flat, along the corridor and down the stairs, encouraged by a neighbor, whose light dress was tucked well up around her thighs on account of the ankle deep water. Then the building's water was cut off again.

Dried out, the apartment was basic and practically unfurnished. I learned to shower after dark and before dawn. The window had a splendid outlook on the city and the sea. And if you looked straight down there was a wide ledge below, not much above street level, and beyond the ledge a narrow pedestrian alley which ran the length of the block and was filled with the tiny stalls of locksmiths, cobblers, knife sharpeners and the folding tin tables and chairs of a string of tiny bars which interspersed the shops, each of which had its own improvised awning of translucent corrugated plastic. The people in the building used to throw their rubbish, quite big bags of it at times, out of their windows. Most of it landed on the ledge and slowly disintegrated there in the sun and the rain. Pleasure in the view was always punctuated by a falling plastic bottle or a floating ice cream carton, and it was unwise to put your head outside. Sometimes a bag of kitchen scraps tossed distractedly from an upper floor would miss both the ledge and the awnings and land from a great height on a group of citizens relaxing over a cold beer. From above it looked as though an ants' nest had been poked with a stick. Inside the building, my neighbor the teacher had an endlessly active social life and his rambunctious visitors—his students? surely not—were soon mistaking my door for his and banging at two in the morning. There was a great deal of coming and going at all hours of day and night in the Edifício Ipiranga. And just over the road was the bus stop for the beach.

The beach at Boa Viagem was a long, long narrow strip of sand that ran north-south behind an exiguous rib of rock a few meters out from the shore. Boa Viagem was the new part of town, the usual strip development, blocks of apartments built along the beachfront and a promenading pavement of mosaic stones in the Rio manner, with coconut juice stalls at intervals. Farther back were the hypermarkets, the shopping malls and barbecue joints as big as football grounds. At high tide the reef was covered, and at low tide in many places there was no water at all between sand and rock. In other places, and when the tide was halfway, shallow warm protected pools formed where the slothful wallowed for hours and small children played and peed. I always struck out well beyond the reef, looking for clearer water away from the crowds and wanting to get some distance covered. I never did find really clear water. *The abattoir outlet,* Vavá explained.

III

On the Beach

Black winter squalls would roll up over Recife, blowing sheets of rain off the Atlantic. Winter on the northeast seaboard was never cool though often wet and stormy. Fine days were for swimming and on the beach you needed a drink supplier and deck chair provider, who kept an eye on your things while you were in the water. I settled with Neuza because she was the only woman, a single mother competing with a congeries of inter-related family groups strung along the sand. Neuza was a lean and rangy black woman who might have been an athlete. She had three teeth left in her head and three small sons by three absconding fathers, the eldest eleven and the youngest barely able to walk.

Neuza did all the work. Her elder sons, who had long thin limbs like her though they were much lighter skinned, were too dreamy and distrait and far too weak to help their mother move the heavy blue wooden cart across the soft sand. The cart held the tub with ice and bottles, and the folded chairs and umbrellas when it was time to go.

Sometimes a squall swept in out of a brilliant morning. Black clouds and driving rain came up from nowhere over the sea, and the rain was so cold on the skin that people ran for the shelter of coconut palms or huddled under the umbrellas. One mean day, bad enough to keep almost everyone off the beach, Neuza saw from some way off a gang of marauding youths moving down the beach. We tucked such valuables as we had under the struts of the umbrella and gathered the chairs in a defensive circle around the cart. The wind howled off the ocean as the menacing long limbed figures got nearer, strung out along the beach, looking for trouble, and raised flying sand around their feet. The kids watched them silently. There was nothing we could do if they attacked us. Neuza's eyes were narrowed and wary. She had recognized these boys from a long way off and knew the signals. We can't have looked worth the trouble and so they passed us by, heading south, shorts and T-shirts flapping in the wind, wild and scary in that moment as the sky.

Whatever the weather a long train of food vendors trudged along the sand in an interminable caravan. The ones of most inter-est bore boiled prawns and fresh oysters—they were the ones you saw at the Pátio in the evening if a downpour had interrupted beach sales. One lady who always sold out early wore a kerchief and aluminum framed glasses and left the island of Itamaracá—an island of the delta with a big Dutch fort from the seventeenth century—before dawn to get to the beach with a fat lidded alu-minum cooking pot on her head. In the pot were big red and white shelled mud crabs from the island, caught by her husband and boiled in the pot with coconut milk, palm oil and unidenti-fiable African spices. The oysters were also from Itamaracá and when they arrived I forgot the cholera lately come from Peru and sweeping northern Brazil. A boy knelt in the sand by his galva-nized bucket, levering open shell after shell with a broken bladed knife. On each a single drop of fresh lime juice was enough, and gulps of Neuza's cold Antártica.

If you kept on going south along this beach, and followed the coast for twelve or thirteen hundred kilometers—until you were halfway to Rio or just past that point—you got to the place where the Portuguese first landed on this continent. Pedro Álvares Cabral was supposed to be heading around Africa to India in 1500 when he happened on the coast of Brazil. It seemed an odd mistake to make. The Portuguese navigators were consummate realists, empirical and incremental and quite unlike brilliant, mad Columbus, who had landed in the Caribbean eight years earlier, trying to sail westward to Asia and believing he had got there. The Portuguese were not people to sail off into the unknown. They had turned down Columbus's proposal of a westward sailing exploration because they already had a lot invested in getting to Asia by sailing east around Africa. Since 1433 Portuguese ships had been sailing farther and farther down the African coast, ready to strike east. One of their ships had already reached the mouth of the Congo by 1484, and four years later Bartolomeu Dias rounded the cape at the bottom of the continent. Only a mutiny made him turn back.

Then Vasco da Gama made the full sea journey around Africa to Asia. He reached Calicut, the great pepper emporium on the Malabar coast of India and was back in Lisbon in the summer of 1499. Portugal, one of the smallest and poorest countries in Europe, with a population of little more than a million, was now preparing to set up a string of fortified trading stations along East Africa and the coast of India, as it had already done along the Atlantic coast of Africa. The follow-up expedition left Lisbon the next spring. Pedro Álvares Cabral commanded thirteen ships carrying twelve hundred men, the most formidable Atlantic fleet ever assembled, and ready for the longest sea voyage ever made. They sailed out of the Tagus in March 1500. The ships took supplies for an eighteen-month voyage and cargo for the Portuguese trade offensive in Asia. The northeast trade winds carried Cabral's fleet past the Canary Islands in five days and down the coast of Africa. A week later they passed the Cape Verde Islands. Then one of the ships disappeared in the night, apparently in calm weather, and was never seen again. The other twelve ships spent two days searching for it, and perhaps lost their bearings. In any case, the fleet sailed far to the west of any expected course down Africa. After six weeks at sea and four weeks after passing the Cape Verde Islands, the sailors saw great quantities of drifting seaweed, and the next morning they saw shearwaters flying above their ships. That evening they caught sight of land, a high round mountain dominating a strip of coast. It was the unknown and still unnamed Brazil. They called it the Land of the True Cross, a name which would fail to stick, and they called the mountain Monte Pascoal because it was Easter.

The fleet anchored offshore and next morning they made out seven or eight people on the beach by a river mouth. By the time the Portuguese landed a boat there were eighteen or twenty Tupi waiting to greet them. The first meeting of Europe and South America was very friendly. The sleek and naked locals seemed quite unfazed by the sudden arrival of smelly bearded white people wearing clothes.

They were dark and quite naked, with nothing to cover their shame. They carried bows in their hands with their arrows. They all came boldly toward the boat, and Nicolo Coelho made a sign to them to lay down their bows, and they laid them down. He couldn't converse with them, or reach any useful understanding, because of the surf breaking on the shore.

In return for a couple of sailors' caps, the leader of the landing party got *a hat of long bird feathers with a little tuft of red and grey feathers like a parrot's . . . a large string of very small white beads like seed pearls.* The next day *two well built natives* were removed from their canoe and as evening fell were brought on board Cabral's flagship, *where they were received with much pleasure and festivity.* It was a chance to get a good look at these unknown men from the unknown land. The Portuguese were struck by the *well shaped* people with *good faces and good noses,* and most of all that *they go naked, without any covering; neither do they pay any more attention to concealing or exposing their shame than they do to showing their faces, and in this respect they are very innocent.*

The locals were also unnervingly unimpressed by the display of European wealth and rank that Cabral put on. Only one of them caught sight of Cabral's gold neck chain *and began to point with his hand toward the land, as though he were telling us that there were gold in the land.* There was doubtless a general narrowing of eyes on the Portuguese side at this point in the meeting of the cultures. When the visitors lay down to sleep on board, attention returned to their nudity.

. . . they stretched out on their backs on the carpet to sleep without taking any care to cover their privy parts, which were not circumcized, and the hair on them was well shaved and arranged.

The men he saw on the beach later were the same. *None of them was circumcized, and all were as we were.* No trace of Islamic contamination in the land of the true cross. If the members of the Portuguese fleet felt a little abashed at the *innocent* and inso-lent physical well-being of the smooth skinned and glossy haired Tupi warriors they encountered, the sensation sharpened into something more when they met the Tupi girls. When Pero Vaz de Caminha was deputed to write an account of this landfall for the Portuguese king, the detached tone faltered when he described the young women. This wasn't like telling your king about an unusual headpiece of yellow tropical feathers, or a bone-pierced lower lip.

> There were three or four young girls among them, very young and very pretty, with very dark hair, long over their shoulders, and their privy parts so high, so closed and so free from hair that we felt no shame in looking at them very well . . . One of the girls was all painted from head to foot . . . and she was so well built and so rounded and her lack of shame was so charming that many women of our land, seeing such attractions, would be ashamed that theirs were not like hers.

The words were perhaps interpolated precisely to arouse the interest of Dom João II in the new land. Cabral sent his men ashore to check out the river and on its bank, Pero Vaz de Caminha told his king, they found

> four or five young women just as naked, who were not displeasing to the eye, among whom was one with her thigh from the knee to the hip and buttock all painted with that black paint and all the rest in her own colour; another had both knees and calves and ankles so painted, and her privy parts so nude and exposed with such innocence that there was no shame. There was another young woman carrying an infant boy or girl tied to her breasts by a cloth of some sort so that only its little legs showed. But the legs of the mother and the rest of her were not concealed by any cloth.

The beauty of the surroundings and the climate, the abundance of food and fresh water, and the untroubled relations with the extremely beautiful local people seemed, as much as the sheer glorious unexpectedness of this landfall, to create a little pocket of pleasure and refreshment out of time for Cabral's thousand or so men. Ahead lay the South Atlantic crossing, Africa, the Cape of Storms, the Indian Ocean, African tribesmen, Arab traders and Asian potentates, riot, massacre and death by water far from home. Many of those who came ashore on this Brazilian beach would never live to complete the journey home to Lisbon. One of their ships had vanished already, in calm weather and known latitudes. The landing turned into a picnic. Diogo Dias, one of the Portuguese captains—and brother of the Bartolomeu Dias who had rounded the African cape twelve years earlier—

an agreeable and pleasure loving man . . . began to dance among them, taking them by the hands, and they were all delighted and laughed and accompanied him very well to the sound of the pipe . . . making many light turns and a remarkable leap which astonished them, and they laughed and enjoyed themselves greatly.

This palled eventually, and the Tupi got bored with the capering of Diogo Dias. Caminha reported more critically of their lack of appreciation that *they soon became sullen like wild men and went away upstream.* The sourness passed after a few days of familiarity and growing trust. Delight kept breaking down the walls of Caminha's own reserve, his sense of belonging to a superior culture, as he wrote to his king. The Portuguese were entirely dependent on the Tupi for fresh water and peace of mind, and the Tupi *skipped and danced with us to the sound of one of our tambours, in such a manner that they are much more our friends than we theirs.* While the Portuguese celebrated mass on an island in the bay the locals pleased them by following attentively, until interest sagged during the sermon. Many of the Tupi, knowing a celebration when they saw one, *got up and blew a horn or trumpet and began to leap and dance for a while.* When the ships' carpenters made a large wooden cross the Tupi were far more gripped by their encounter with the new technology than with the symbol of the true religion. In this enthralling moment they discovered the cutting power of metal tools, and pressed in *more to see the iron tools with which they were making it than to see the cross, because they have nothing of iron . . . they cut their wood and boards with stones.*

At the next mass the visitors were so pleased by the way the locals imitated their acts of worship that it seemed *these people to be wholly Christian lack nothing except to understand us.* One young woman who stayed throughout the mass was intent on following the ritual, but her total nudity distracted the Portuguese men from their prayers. They gave her a blanket, but *she did not think to spread it much to cover herself . . . The innocence of this people is such that that of Adam could not have been greater.* The new arrivals couldn't take their eyes off the bodies of the people they found. At first Caminha presented them as wild creatures, easily frightened, *rather like birds or wild animals . . . and their bodies are so clean, and so sleek and beautiful.* Invidious comparisons and a little abashed self-awareness inevitably followed. The Portuguese couldn't help linking the locals' physical beauty and their good natures. *Our Lord gave them fine bodies and good faces as to good men.* Like the lilies of the field,

> they do not till the soil or breed stock, nor is there ox or cow or goat or sheep or hen, or any other domestic animal which is used to living with men. Nor do they eat anything except these manioc . . . and the seeds and the fruits which the earth and trees produce. Yet they are stronger and better fed than we are with all the wheat and vegetables we eat.

Maybe the Portuguese weren't so superior after all. Could they really consider themselves healthier or happier? In Caminha's letter to the king his honesty went beyond the sharpness and accuracy and abundance of his reporting—and all his detail was ethnographically exact—and admitted a deep personal uncertainty into the larger and increasing wonder of the meeting with these people. As his letter went on, the rhetoric of the sales pitch gave way to an unfeigned sense of wonder.

The message was significant enough and urgent enough for a ship to be detached from the fleet to take it home to Lisbon. It touched carefully on the matters of interest to an empire building Christian king, on the theological—the unsullied souls ripe for conversion—and the commercial—the benign climate, abundant flora and fauna, signs of mineral resources. Yet in the very meticulousness of his recording of what the Portuguese found in the new land, and even more as he described the realities of their encounter with its people, Caminha kept sounding like a delighted boy writing home about the holiday of a lifetime. There was the beauty and animation of the people. There were also the birds, the *very large and beautiful red parrots,* macaws the sailors got for trinkets, *and two little green ones.* The Portuguese also got some green feather caps by barter, *and a cloth of feathers of many colours, woven in a very beautiful fashion.* And fish, signs of cockles and mussels, shrimps, *a very large and fat shrimp such as I had never seen before.*

There is no record of what the Tupi thought as their weird looking visitors sailed out onto the ocean, leaving behind two weeping convicts to be consoled. The convicts were guinea pigs, saved from death sentences back home, brought to be abandoned, to *learn their language well and understand them* and maybe even impart a little Christianity. Mainly the convicts were breeding stock. With a population a fifteenth the size of France's, a seventh Spain's, a third even of little England's, the only way tiny Portugal was going to people its new overseas territories was by engendering colonists in situ with the help of the locals. Nobody knows what thoughts of relief, regret or puzzlement passed through the minds of the Tupi and entered their conversation. Did they have any notion the Portuguese would be back? These particular Portuguese would not return. Within a few months Pero Vaz de Caminha, the author of one of the most tough minded and enchanting letters in the history of Europe, the sole document of a moment of perfect poise in the history of the Old World and the New, would be dead. He was killed in a fight with the people of Calicut on the Indian coast. Cabral himself, who was only thirty when he was given command of the intercontinental expedition, made it back to Lisbon the following year. But once home he behaved badly, fell out of favor with the king and died in obscurity.

The visitors' interest in the unmodified state of the Tupi penis expressed more than mere curiosity. The Portuguese knew a lot about Islamic culture. Portugal itself had been ruled by Islamic powers for five hundred years. Business and religion were inextricably interwined and the Portuguese were increasingly in competition with Arab traders. In 1415 the Portuguese had taken Ceuta, the outpost at the entrance to the Mediterranean on the tip of Morocco. Having gained a foothold in Africa they were setting out to break the Arab monopoly on the spice trade east of Africa and at the same time take the place Venice had long held as Europe's trade link with Asia. The Portuguese knew how rich Venice had become in the eastern Mediterranean by exploiting Asia's overland routes. The trade route through the Persian Gulf was closed to the Venetians after the Turks took Constantinople in 1453, and the Red Sea route was monopolized by Egyptian and Arabian traders. By pioneering a sea route from Europe around Africa to Asia, the Portuguese were about to displace both Arabs and Venetians and change the pattern of world trade forever. By landing in South America on the way, the Portuguese would project Europe irrevocably toward the west. A year and a half later the Florentine banker and cosmographer Amerigo Vespucci sailed into a vast and splendid bay a little farther north of Cabral's landing place, and called it the Bay of All Saints after the day of his arrival, which in Portuguese was the *Bahia de Todos os Santos*. Vespucci, who now went on as far south as Patagonia, had sailed along the northern coast of South America in 1499, and unlike Columbus he understood that this continent had no precedent in European thinking. He wrote home to Lorenzo de' Medici that a *new world* had been found.

Two months later the Portuguese Gonçalo Coelho sailed into another huge and no less splendid bay to the south, gorgeously jungled and marked out by monolithic rocks as big as mountains. The Tupi who lived there called it Guanabara. It looked to Coelho like the mouth of a great river, though it wasn't, and since it was New Year's Day of 1502 he called the place of his landfall the *Rio de Janeiro*. There were more expeditions over the next few years, and then in 1530 Portugal sent out four hundred men to set up a colony on the continent. It was the beginning of Brazil. In the early sixteenth century Cabral's meeting with the Tupi, and the other encounters that soon followed, revived the dream of a lost human innocence and the nostalgic longing for a golden age, just as the mental skies of Europe darkened and the continent's societies were riven by religious reformation and counterreformation. For all the hunter-gatherer tribes of Tupi and Guarani and the others who lived strung along the entire eastern littoral of the South American continent, their gifts of beautiful feathers, fresh water and sexual relief, and their discovery of metal technology and the taste of alcohol, were the beginning of the end.

Cabral's version of events, the magical accident set out in Pero Vaz de Caminha's letter, is in some ways hard to swallow. The founding document of Brazil's history may be more disingenuous than it seems, and Cabral's landfall less fortuitous. There is something odd, for a start, in the way the convoy should somehow have lost its bearings so badly that it drifted right across the Atlantic without the commanders' even realizing where they were until the ships made landfall in South America. This was a formidably equipped fleet, manned by the best seamen and navigators there were, using the best existing maps and the new Portuguese technology of the astrolabe to find its bearings astronomically, advancing in good weather down the well-known part of the African coast on its way to India, along the sea route pioneered by the Portuguese themselves. The letter doesn't ask whether the Land of the True Cross is just another island or part of something larger, as if Cabral and his king already had a very good idea what it was. There is a certain lack of *surprise* in the letter at the fact of the portentous landfall itself, and once the visit was over, the ships' commanders seemed again to know exactly where they were. Things resumed with their usual efficiency, one ship peeling off and heading directly home to Lisbon with the letter for Dom João while the rest of the convoy resumed its journey to India, having claimed the territory for Portugal and lost barely a week making the reconnoiter of the coast.

Given the expertise and daring of Portuguese seamen, and the state-of-the-art design of their oceangoing caravels, and the Portuguese government's determination to develop a maritime trading network ahead of its European rivals—Spain above all—there may have been earlier and unpublicized, not to say highly secret, Portuguese explorations across the Atlantic, following or even preceding Columbus's Caribbean discoveries. The race for the west in the 1490s was seen as a question of survival, and the competition between Spain and Portugal was so tense that the pope intervened in the potentially ruinous conflict. His mediation had established in 1493, a year after Columbus had landed in the Caribbean, a demarcation into zones east and west of an imaginary line running north-south a hundred leagues west of the Cape Verde Islands. The idea was to give Portugal Africa and the eastern trade and Spain what was found in the Americas. That the Portuguese knew more than they revealed about what lay over the Atlantic was suggested by Dom João's immediate dispatch of a delegation to the court of Ferdinand and Isabella at Madrid to renegotiate the deal. Portuguese persistence won out, and the following year Portugal and Spain signed a treaty at Tordesilhas that shifted the line much farther west, to 370 leagues west of the Cape Verde Islands. The new line now passed through the still theoretically unknown South American continent, so that when he was so surprisingly washed up on its coast six years later, Cabral naturally claimed the eastern part of the continent for Portugal. The legal questions had already been looked after.

———

Brazil's splendors are on such a scale that many are only visible from a distance. Once I spent several weeks flying into the continent, hopping from city to city as far as Manaus on the Amazon. The tangle of great silver rivers catching the light among the deep green absorbency of the forest canopy, then the water taking fire in the moments before sunset as the jungle turned into black velvet—this was something you could only know from the air. Flying is the only way to conceive the dimensions of Brazil and the only way to reach its many roadless settlements. The distances make planes an ordinary part of Brazilian life. Those who can afford them catch pancontinental flights like the local bus, as they do in North America and Australia, or grab an air taxi for shorter hops. Others have their own planes, light craft for getting around the farm, executive jets for getting from one meeting to another, helicopters for getting home to the gated community from the office. The little group of Brazil's rich are sylphs inhabiting a little airborne milieu out of sight of everyone else. Their world is far from check-in queues or lumbering mass transport planes, and its faintest earthly traces are the rooftop helipads and private landing strips, and even these lie far from profane eyes.

Air travel's glamour and convenience—and at higher levels its discretion—made planes a special object of desire for PC Farias. President Fernando Collor's first big privatization was of the airline VASP. The buyer was a friend and PC gave him $11 million for a share in it. They still didn't have quite enough to buy the airline outright, and then PC had the idea of getting a ten-year interest-free loan of $40 million from Brazil's state oil corporation, Petrobras; $30 million of it could be handed over as jet fuel. A ten-year interest-free loan, with rates running as they were, amounted to a gift of $40 million, and Petrobras said no. Then the telephone calls began.

The calls from PC came so insistently that the president of Petrobras had them recorded. PC called him a dozen times and visited his office twice. *You're creating a lot of difficulties,* PC said. Then Fernando's chief of cabinet, who was his brother-in-law, rang to express the president's *great interest in the VASP privatization's going ahead.* On a visit to New York, the head of Petrobras started getting calls from PC at his Park Avenue hotel. He refused to take the calls and his wife told PC he was jogging in Central Park. PC got annoyed. The Petrobras chief found himself under attack in the Brazilian press and accused of undermining the Collor Plan and the Brazilian currency. Seven months into Fernando's presidency, the head of Petrobras called a press conference, denounced PC's interference and resigned. Fernando expressed his satisfaction and said he had never *fitted in.* The fight had led to an item in the *Jornal do Brasil* revealing that *the man behind the campaign against the current president of Petrobras . . . is the mysterious PC Farias.* A reporter went to Alagoas to find out who PC was, and a weekly magazine published an article on him. The cover showed a terrible little black and white snapshot of a bald man with mustache and glasses, which was the only picture of PC anyone could find at that time. The magazine was offered money to suppress the article but refused, and other papers started to notice *the government's intrigues, lies and shady deals* and question *PC's rapid rise.*

Fernando's government disliked critics and soon showed its displeasure. The *Folha de São Paulo* was the most influential daily newspaper in Brazil. It was a rather dull broadsheet that took its own views very seriously and had been quite sharply critical of Fernando during the election campaign—even harder on Lula—though it had later supported Fernando's bank freeze. A platoon of armed police raided the paper during Fernando's second week in office, storming through its offices, seizing documents and looking for the owner. They said the raid was a search for fiscal irregularities but the paper felt it as intimidation. Five months later the *Folha* noted the government was handing out advertising contracts without calling tenders. The Brazilian government spent $500 million a year on advertising for the state owned banks and corporations and the contracts were in the gift of Fernando's private secretary, who was an old school friend of PC's from Alagoas. The secretary was feeding the contracts to small businesses who had worked for Fernando's election campaign, and when the *Folha* drew attention to this, Fernando sued. It was the first time a Brazilian president in office had sued for libel. Fernando was still very popular and the *Folha*'s editor was insulted in the streets of São Paulo and feared arrest. Curiosity about PC continued to spread.

Paulo Cesar Cavalcanti de Farias was an honest tax man's son from the interior of the Northeast. There were six boys and two girls and PC was the eldest of the eight. He was born in 1945 in the outback of Alagoas. Their father, whom the children respectfully addressed as *Collector,* worked all day in the local tax office and their mother made the children's clothes, kept house and did the cooking. She was deeply religious and helped their even poorer neighbors and kept her children's noses to their school books. At meal times they only spoke with their parents' permission.

Toward the end of the 1940s the family moved to the state capital, Maceió. The Farias boys all slept together in the attic of a little house and in the daytime they studied at the Marist Brothers college, half an hour's walk up the road, and played football in the street. Their mother wanted one of her boys to be a priest, another a lawyer and a third a doctor. When he was nine PC was enrolled in the seminary at Maceió to learn French and Latin and prepare to serve God. It was the only way a bright poor boy could get a decent education. By the time he was fourteen PC was giving private lessons to help the family. A social photo showed the teenage PC dressed in a black soutane with a wide sash, with a cigarette between his fingers. Soon after the photo was taken, PC's lack of a vocation was obvious to everyone and he switched to study law. He could not afford to go off to university in Rio or São Paulo or Recife, and enrolled in the little state university of Alagoas. There is no record of just when PC decided his father was a loser, but from the moment PC got out of the seminary the constant factor in all his wildly various undertakings was the promise they held out of upward movement. Most of PC's efforts were at making money, but the moneymaking was preceded by activities of another kind that suggested PC's first real interest was power, and that it was only later that he came to understand that power and wealth were more or less the same thing. One entailed the other, and knowing this made him comfortable in the shadows. PC needed recognition from people who mattered. He never sought the attention of the crowd.

He arrived at university in time for the military coup of 1964. While other students around Brazil organized resistance to the dictators, PC began his career as a militant of the right. As president of the students' organization, PC was one of the few allowed to vote in the *indirect* election for state governor of Alagoas, the only kind of election the military allowed, and in 1966 he voted for the winning candidate, who was a cousin of his father's. By the time he graduated at twenty-two, PC had a clerical job in the governor's office and told people he was the governor's private secretary, which opened a few doors. He did some outback legal work in the criminal area, and was paid for his services in crates of fruit and poultry from his subsistence farmer clients. He started selling telephone lines to drylands settlements on commission for the telephone company and discovered his talent as a salesman. He sold a lot of telephones and started making money. Being known, as PC made sure he always was, as a personal friend of the state governor was a big help in signing up new telephone subscribers as PC worked his way through the towns of the interior.

PC used the same talking skills as an announcer on a local radio station owned by the church. The studio was just by the cathedral in Maceió, on a square where people bought and sold used cars. PC and used cars were made for each other, and PC snuck away from the microphone to hang around the car mart. He left an old radio program tape playing on an eternal loop in the studio while he went off wheeling and dealing, trading cars for wristwatches. This was when they started calling him Little

Paulie Gasoline. The bishop of Maceió turned on Radio Palmares for background music during his snoozes after lunch, and realized after a while that he was hearing the same announcements and the same music over and over again. PC talked his way out of dismissal, obtained the bishop's pardon and went on dealing in used cars and working on the radio. Then he went into a serious used car dealership. A sugar planter put up the money and PC moved the cars. He moved on to a gas station and the Chevrolet dealership in Maceió. By 1970 PC had set up a Chrysler dealership that he parlayed into one of the biggest truck sellers in the Northeast of Brazil, his first really serious business. Two years later he added a tractor dealership. When Brazilian cars started running on sugarcane alcohol, PC sold the equipment for cane farming and distillation. But he always spent more than he made and life went on being a struggle, at least on paper. He bought a big black used Ford Galaxie and hired a driver. The driver wore a black chauffeur's uniform with a tie and cap and PC rode around Maceió in the back seat, holding up the financial pages of the papers, driver and passenger sweating like pigs in the tropical heat. PC kept the windows rolled up to simulate the air-conditioning he couldn't yet afford.

The metamorphosis of Little Paulie Gasoline into PC Farias did not happen overnight, and the new personal style evolved slowly. He started holding Friday night soirées, with girls flown up from Rio and the janitor acting as butler in a rented jacket. PC's own look was still based on black silk shirts, alternating with several others in brilliant colors, and the heavy gold crucifix nestling in the chest hairs. There was a lot more gold on the hairy wrists and the thick and unusually clumsy fingers. PC never learned to open a bottle unassisted. His hair started thinning early and he grew enormous sideburns in the early seventies manner. He had always been short and now his whole body was thickening fast as he made his way into the good life. In the words of someone from the Southeast who knew him later in life and knew his history and was nevertheless seduced by PC's silver tongue and not unsympathetic to PC's ferocious efforts to drag himself up from the dirt,

> PC was a special person in Maceió. Unlike others he could talk, he could persuade people, initiate projects. And he was reliable: he never failed to keep his word . . . He was a born capitalist, an ambitious entrepreneur, a man on the make in a wretchedly poor region, a shaky bookkeeper who knew his way around the bureaucracy and the law and knew how not to get caught . . . His goal was to be head of a rich family that owned diverse and powerful business interests, that was respected and politically influential.

As the lifestyle expenses rose, business did not always go well. The plantation of eighty thousand coconut palms seemed in deep trouble even with all the tax breaks from the state government. By 1983 PC was $7 million in debt and receivers were called in. But PC's creative accounting ensured that though he was insolvent in Brazil he had a lot of money in Panama. In 1985, after a ministerial inspection of PC's tractor dealership, the Brazilian attorney general's office laid twelve fraud charges against PC. The tax collector's son was charged with forging receipts and practicing tax evasion. In 1986 the earthmoving business folded and the next year PC's access to rural development funds was cut off. Yet he seemed to have more and more money to spend, despite the travails of his businesses. Which was why the authorities had been curious about his business activities in the first place.

PC's mother made sure he gave jobs to all his siblings, even when he wanted to sack them. *Shut your big mouth, Paulo, and do what I'm telling you,* his mother said, and PC did. He put one of his brothers through medical school in Rio and a specialization course in California. And through his partner in the motor show-room he got to know the Lyra brothers. The Lyras were two of the biggest sugar producers in Alagoas. They also ran several big air taxi companies and controlled a large part of the state's economy and its politics. PC made himself useful to the Lyras and under their auspices his business activities flourished, if not always seeming to. In 1984, just when his businesses were facing bankruptcy, he ran campaign finances for candidates favored by the Lyras, and as their bagman he got to know more people on the political and business scene of Alagoas. At this time he refreshed his acquaintance with a young deputy who represented Alagoas in the federal Congress, Fernando Collor de Mello.

———

Four years later, Fernando Collor and PC had developed a for-midable reciprocity when it came to furthering each other's interests, but the audience for their brilliant double act was still contained within a small circle in the tiny and obscure sugar and cattle state of Alagoas. When Fernando turned up at the headquarters of TV Globo in Rio at the end of 1988 to say he wanted to be president of Brazil and to ask for Globo's support, the founder and patriarch of the Globo media empire—and Globo ran the biggest TV network in the world outside the United States—was one of the few people in the rest of Brazil who knew who this young man was.

Roberto Marinho was immensely rich and powerful and—as practically a self-made man—a prodigy in Brazil. In 1988 he was eighty-three and had been an American-dollar billionaire for at least a decade. His father had begun his working life as a proofreader on the newspapers and founded *O Globo* as an eve-ning daily in Rio in 1926. There were at least a dozen daily papers in Rio in those days and it was no big deal. Three weeks

later, twenty-year-old Roberto found his father dead on the bathroom floor from a heart attack. The son threw himself into
reporting and then into running O Globo with maniacal energy.
Roberto Marinho was a horserider, a spearfisher and a ladies'
man, a smart journalist and a smarter entrepreneur. He made
O Globo grow through the thirties, went into radio in the forties
and television in the fifties, and used TV Globo and Radio Globo
to promote his paper all around Brazil. In 1988 the weekday
sales of O Globo were the second highest in the country and its
Sunday sales topped all, and by then the paper was only a small
part of the Globo empire. Roberto Marinho had a way of getting
on with those in power. He got on especially well with the
military and conspired in their coup of 1964. Interests coincided
and Globo power grew mightily in the sixties and seventies,
along with Marinho's personal clout. These were the years when
TV Globo grew into the world's fourth biggest television network. Before the military there had been fewer than half a million television sets in Brazil, and when the regime faded in 1985
there were nearly twenty-seven million.

What Brazilians mostly watched on their sets were the soaps.
Globo telenovelas brought together a vast and scattered audience
of mainly illiterate people, gave a whole population stories to
share and something to keep them quiet. Endless and anodyne
dramas unwound on the Globo screens. Most of them were about
conflicts over sex and money in immensely wealthy white families living in huge apartments overlooking Rio, which was the
Globo city. Actors flounced into and stormed out of vast car-
peted living rooms, collapsed or clinched on huge ivory Nau-
gahyde sofas, quivered with emotion in close-up as they clutched
a telephone receiver to their cleavage. The unfolding of the plots
matched the weekly market research into audience response,
which was partly why they felt so unstructured. They could be
axed in days if popular interest fell, dragged out for years if

Peter Robb

people liked them. Individuals whose ratings fell were written out of the story overnight and new faces brought in. Fulminant brain tumors and car crashes and departures for the exterior were matched by returns from the dead—memory loss, the wrong body, whatever. The better a soap did, the longer it survived and the more completely it lost any form or meaning beyond the tiny peaks before each commercial break. These soaps were as far as you could get from the tightly wound clockwork mechanisms of American film or British TV. They went on and on forever, as nourishing as chewing gum, and their actors seemed to be chewing gum rather than feeling and speaking.

That a Brazilian soap became a river of flotsam carrying everything on its endless downward flow—that it lacked drama's elements of tension, conflict, resolution—seemed to reflect something you saw in all of the real Brazil's social relations, from the personal to the political. This was the avoidance of confrontation of any kind, an endless elasticity of evasion and spurious amiability. Did it reflect real life inside the Brazilian family, and that unusually complex mesh of promiscuity and repression that had lasted from the days of masters and slaves? Or the contemporary reality that the briefest confrontation with a stranger in the street might lead to a knife in the guts or a bullet in the head? Or did it derive from atavistic fears of a bloody rising by the underclasses? The ancestors of the penthouse families you saw in the soaps, the masters and their wives and children in the remote big houses on the sugar plantations, had often had their throats cut in the night by their insurgent slaves. Dramatic tension had only a relative interest in the television art of a society so many of whose immediate needs could be briefly resolved by a well-aimed bullet or a good fuck and none of whose other needs could ever be resolved at all.

That the tensions being avoided might have had some basis in race was obscured in the soaps by the absence onscreen of any

76

black or colored person whatsoever. On one level, this was mere realism, there being about as many blacks living in penthouses as there were whites in the favelas, but it went beyond this. In the soaps, even the servants were usually white, which was not how things were in real life, and from the preponderance of blue-eyed blondes you might think, if it weren't for the suntans and the skimpy clothes, that the soaps were made in Scandinavia. And when in the nineties, after decades of penthouse drama, Brazilian TV started reaching outside the great cities and outside the immediate present for its material—when it started making drama series out of some of the lastingly popular regional novels of an earlier and rural Brazil—whole northeastern populations of farming settlements in Pernambuco and fishing communities in Bahia changed their color from black to white, or rather golden tan, in their translation to the screen. Art and social realism were fine if they pulled in advertising, but some of the unrealities of Brazilian television lay too deep to change.

The Globo soaps ran end to end from six till ten every evening and the only thing that interrupted them was the Globo evening news at eight. Globo news items were short, simple, carefully selected, heavily weighted to human interest and always presented by white people. As the military faded in the eighties, nothing changed on Globo screens or in the Globo command suites. Leaders of the tender new democracy wanted Roberto Marinho's approval and support more than anything. *I might be fighting with my army minister, but I won't be fighting with Roberto Marinho,* said the *indirectly* elected president of Brazil in 1985, who before he died chose as his minister of communications the owner of TV Globo transmission rights in Bahia. When little José Sarney took his place, the new ministry was vetted by Marinho before it was announced. Anyone looking to follow Sarney in 1989 would also want Roberto Marinho on his side and that was why Fernando came knocking.

Roberto Marinho knew Fernando because he had done business with Fernando's father, who had made most of his money from the TV Globo concession in Alagoas. Marinho suspected that Fernando's father had swindled him in property deals in Rio, and had lately sacked Fernando's elder brother Leopoldo from his management job in Globo, for misconduct. Now he balefully noted Fernando's fancy clothes and for a long time afterward referred to him as *the boy with the French cuffs*. All Fernando got from his first visit to Roberto Marinho was a certain amount of space thereafter on the Globo media, which mattered, however, since most of what most Brazilians knew about Brazil they learned from TV Globo.

Roberto Marinho's coolness toward Fernando didn't mean he was promoting anyone else for the presidency of Brazil. On the contrary, he was worried about the lack of a convincing candidate to stand against the resurgent left. Presidential elections were not really a Brazilian thing, and since there had been no popularly elected president of Brazil for forty-five years, the problem Brazil faced in 1989 of democratically electing its president was one nobody had ever dealt with. And by late 1988 inflation was running at a thousand percent a year and getting worse. The value of workers' wages had dropped by a quarter. The army had been breaking strikes, workers had been killed. In 1989 there was a two-day general strike in March that shut down most of the republic. There were more strikes in April, of dockworkers, metalworkers, schoolteachers. Stones were thrown at troops. Troops fired on strikers. Two million stopped work. The generals were getting restive again but it was too late to go back. Democracy was the future, Marinho realized, as long as the right president could be found, and the right president might be anyone but Lula.

In 1988 Roberto Marinho was newly in the grip of a sexual passion that had outlived fifty intervening years of marriage to two other women. Lily de Carvalho had arrived in Rio from France in the 1930s as a dazzling teenager and Lily and Roberto had danced together in the Golden Room of the Copacabana Palace, but Lily had married Roberto's friend instead. Now she was a widow with $150 million of her own and enchanting as ever, and Roberto Marinho was tired of his second wife's preoccupation with the communist menace and her dozens of cats. However virile and active, Marinho was now an old man. His mind was on the past in politics and love. He still thought the main danger facing his Brazil was the former governor of his own state of Rio de Janeiro. Leonel Brizola was a golden tongued populist who had tried to rally the armed forces against their generals in 1964 and was still a powerfully unsettling presence among many opposing nullities. Brizola would *tread on his grandmother's neck to be president,* as Lula rather spitefully said. But Brizola's influence on the left was quietly draining away. All year he had led in the opinion polls for next president, but now Lula equaled him at twelve percent and by the end of 1988 nobody else came anywhere near. From Brizola or Lula, Roberto Marinho felt that everything he had built up over the decades was increasingly under threat. Where was the leader who was going to defend the Brazil that mattered? Fernando Collor, an unknown politician from the second smallest, second poorest and most benighted state in the republic, unknown to the rest of the country, a spoiled playboy with no history to speak of, did not convince him at all.

When PC called the following year, Marinho agreed to see him readily enough, and listened intently as PC held forth on the candidate, the program, the campaign and the heavy costs of the campaign, and indeed Marinho had a great deal to say himself on these matters and offered his opinions generously. But whenever PC wanted to talk about money the conversation seemed to slither away into another channel. From his meeting with one of Brazil's richest men PC came away empty-handed, without actually having been refused and indeed without having been able to get around to making his request. It was PC's only failure in the year of the election. But what Roberto Marinho had to give as the owner of TV Globo was greater than money, and this in due course he gave to Fernando.

IV

Parrot Perch

A tribal leader's daughter living on the lower Amazon River became pregnant a long time ago. The angry chief used fire and duress to make her tell him the name of the father, but the girl insisted she had slept with no man. The chief was going to put his daughter to death, but a white man came to him in a dream and told him to stay his hand, because the girl was telling the truth and had never slept with a man. Nine months later she gave birth to a beautiful girl child who was white. Her tribe was amazed and so were the people of all the surrounding tribes, having never seen a white person, and they all came to look at Mani, which was the white child's name. Mani was walking and talking in almost no time and then, at the end of a year, without sickness or pain, she died. The tribe buried her according to custom in the ground below her own house. From the ground where they buried her a large-leafed plant sprouted of a kind the tribe had never seen before. It grew, flowered and bore fruit, and the birds who ate the fruit got drunk. The earth split open under pressure from its roots and when they dug they found that the white root the plant was growing from was the body of Mani. They tried the root and so began eating manioc, which in Tupi means *Mani's house.*

The white body of Mani had been providing the main food of the indigenous peoples in the newfound territory since the first millennium before Christ. Now manioc became the plant that fed the Portuguese and enabled the colony of Brazil to get through its first hard times. Pero Vaz de Caminha told the king of Portugal about it when he described the landing on Bahia in 1500 and Brazil's first governor issued an order for its cultivation forty-seven years later. Five hundred years later manioc is still— with rice and beans—the fundamental component of every Brazilian's diet. The *macaxeira* offered to Cabral's men, along with the feathered headdress, timber and fresh water, was the indigenes' first and greatest gift to the usurpers. The ever so slightly sweet macaxeira, or *aipim,* is like a slightly waxy potato with a few soft fibers running through it, and can be served boiled in big strips or used to make fries that make you wonder why you ever bothered with potato chips. The other main type of manioc is full of prussic acid and highly toxic, but the índios had developed a way of removing the cyanide, by grating the roots and soaking them in water and then forcing them into a big woven straw tube called a *tipiti* which drained off the poisonous juice. The secret of their food technology was the índios' second great gift to the invaders, and several millennia after they were first developed, tipitis are still used in Brazilian homes to make the poisonous manioc edible. The detoxified pulp could then be rolled out very thin and baked on a big flat stone to make *beiju,* a very thin and fine kind of unleavened bread still much eaten in Brazil, sometimes made with added coconut or cashew nut, and used to wrap a sweet or savory filling. But the Indios' most common treatment of the pulp was to roast it, grind it, roast it again until it became the coarsely powdered, sand colored and nutty tasting *farofa* that today is an invariable presence at every kind of meal on the tables of every social condition throughout Brazil, the unique and universal indicator of a Brazilian meal, *primary, irreducible, instinctive.*

Manioc flour became the first instance of that complex reciprocity of cultures that grew up between Brazil and Africa in the centuries of slavery. The slave ships stocked it for barter along with Bahian tobacco and cachaça when they sailed back to Africa, and soon in Africa manioc was planted around the slaving ports to supply food for the ships taking new prisoners to Brazil. Manioc grew as well in Africa as in Brazil, and its cultivation spread. Its high nutritional value soon made it one of Africa's staple foods. In Brazil the manioc was also processed as tapioca—another indigenous technique—and tapioca combined with northeastern sugar and the arts of Portuguese confectionery to produce the desserts and sweets that Gilberto Freyre wrote about with such profound emotion.

Farofa will be a part of any memorable Brazilian lunch, and it was of one in particular. One fine day in Recife, the hot skies immense blue and gold, one of those days when high pressure, low humidity and the mild breath of a coastal breeze make you feel coastal Brazil's is the most benign climate on earth, I had a Bangüê lunch. The Pátio was blinding at midday, the pastel houses bleached and flinging the light back into the empty space they surrounded. Crossing diagonally to the Bangüê, I raised the crowd of resident pigeons and intersected with Dona Lia arriving from the unfashionable baroque church of Santo Antônio dos Pretos, the black people's church around the corner where she spent hours on her knees every morning. Vavá was not in sight, but cheerful round-faced Jorge, who worked the lunchtime shift, waved me in. The Bangüê at midday was a restaurant and not a bar. The side tables were let down from the wall and all were laid with white cloths and cutlery. The sunlight outside and the expanse of white linen within made everything airier and lighter

---

than it felt at night. Jorge brought a bottle of Antártica, freezing but not frozen, to the table by the sedan chair. It was *feijoada* day and to try the Bangüê's feijoada had been a deeply pondered intent.

The overhead fans were still, the window shutters flung wide open, and from the mild penumbra of the room the tiny houses across the square were fixed in brilliant detail. Framed in the tall open rectangles, the houses' bright pastel colors and slight irregularity of finish, the animation of people hurrying across the square with outflung arms, like jerky figures in a silent comedy, and the periodically upswirling pigeons were like details in the street scenes of a naïf painter. Brazilian naïfs—there were a lot of them—were maybe less naïf and more realistic than they seemed. I stretched my arm along a shaft of the sedan chair, worn smooth by slaves' labor, and waited for the meal which had its distant origins in the poorest circumstances of the slave quarters' fireplace.

In the mountainous parts of Portugal they still eat a dish of white beans and pork not unlike the French cassoulet, and a lot of Brazilian dishes have their origin in Portugal. Pork and beans tended to gravitate toward each other spontaneously and many rather similar slow cooked combinations are found all around those parts of the world where both are available. There is a lot of both in Brazil, only the beans are black or brown. This is the historical, culinary fact. The Brazilian myth is that the slave dish feijoada was first made from scraps from the big house kitchen, bits and pieces graciously conceded, or filched or rescued from the trash. The meat ingredients of a feijoada are various enough to imply a Saturday night special of hoardings made over the week. There are about a dozen kinds of beef and pork, fresh, smoked and salt, in a feijoada. The pig provides the animal's salted ears, sliced up and salted tails hacked into inch-long lengths, its trotters fresh and split down the middle, smoked bacon, salt bacon, pork ribs, pork loin, *paio* blood sausage and sweet seasoned linguiça sausage. The beef is jerky—*xarque*—and rump, chuck and smoked tongue. The meat components are endlessly variable. Even the beans vary by region. In Rio they use black beans and in the Northeast and São Paulo they use brown. The large fat black *feijão*, with its deep, deep, almost purple gloss—a shining aubergine black when cooked—and its firm consistency, is to me much more beautiful and tasty than the nondescript and somewhat mealy brown, which disintegrates more easily with cooking into a reddish paste. I believe that this day the Bangüê served a *feijoada carioca* with black beans rather than a northeastern feijoada with brown. This would have been odd and it may be a trick of memory and predilection that I recall it thus, and the room was shady.

Whenever I think of feijoada now my mind returns to this emblematic day. The deep earthenware pot that Jorge set down contained, under the lustrous nearly liquid shimmer of the cooked beans, pieces of pork and beef in a rare equilibrium of fresh, dried, smoked and salted in all their various tastes and textures, cooked long enough and carefully enough for each to have lent and borrowed something and reached a complex harmony in which all of the single components retained their own identity. This intimate reciprocity of the different elements is what a good feijoada is about. It is a curiously light dish whose subtlety belies the list of its own gross ingredients. It is a great instance of that transforming principle enunciated by Huck Finn, about to become a runaway boy in the company of Jim the runaway black slave, and escape among other things the miseries of poor white Anglo cuisine in which *everything was cooked by itself.* Always attentive to what he eats, Huck notes that *in a barrel of odds and ends . . . things get mixed up, and the juice kind of swaps around, and the things go better.* Stews are the great thing in Brazilian cooking—the delicately spiced inland stews of chicken and kid, the vividly African *moquecas* of the coast, made with anything from the sea, golden with palm oil and soft with coconut milk—but none of them enacts better than a good feijoada the magic that can happen in *a barrel of odds and ends*.

On the table, the glistening dark velvet of the feijoada shimmering in its pot was flanked by the deep emerald of the kale greens, shredded and sautéed in a little oil, hardly cooked and reeking of just warmed garlic, the big-grained Brazilian rice, the pale yellow of the farofa—farofa came into its own here, in dealing with all the densely laden juice, and the coarse roasted manioc flour was even more intrinsic to a feijoada than to all the other Brazilian dishes it enhanced—and the golden jewel of a many faceted fresh orange on its own plate, peeled with a sharp knife and looking, as its crystalline orange and whiteness glowed in the penumbra, like part of a Dutch still life. The white, the cream, the gold, the vivid green, the deeply purply black of the foods and the roughly glazed brown bowl and the tiny blaze of scarlet glowing from each of the tiny chilies forced into the narrow necked bottle of powerful pimenta made a profoundly harmonious whole to the sight. It was rich and various—the orange and green, and the elements they added in the way of mineral depth, ascorbic tartness, rough fibrousness to the complex whole was something usually missing in a Brazilian meal. Jorge brought a shot glass of neat cachaça and lime juice to go with the meal. In São Paulo they put orange juice and cachaça directly into the feijoada. I liked it like this.

———

New editions of the Bangüê's bill of fare were starting to appear more and more frequently. The list of dishes and drinks was printed and it always stayed the same but the spaces for the prices were left blank and typed in at each new updating by Dona Lia on her ancient manual typewriter. By September of

1990 the price updatings were almost weekly and the fiscal stability promised by the new president already forgotten. The printed words naming the dishes were becoming more familiar, and I realized that most of them were items of outback cuisine. Recife was on the sea, but apart from the reliable fried needlefish and a perfunctory *piece* of fried fish in the evening and a rather good fish stew, or *peixada,* for lunch on Friday, the produce of the sea did not figure in the normal offerings.

Recife itself was greatly populated by people from the interior. To people living through droughts that lasted for years on end the city on the coast was powerfully attractive. Unlike São Paulo in the south, Recife had almost nothing to offer the people who gravitated to it, beyond being easier to reach and less likely to destroy them. Even the temporary visitors who arrived with a truckload of produce for sale had a hard time flogging what they had grown for a street corner pittance, and were always being moved on by truckloads of council guards wearing baseball caps and armed with truncheons. Those who came with nothing, or with their children, found nothing, and these were the people I saw huddled in the church porches or around fires they had made in the public squares at night, and sleeping on flattened cardboard cartons. Sometimes when it rained at night, walking home and sticking to the covered pavements and arcades, you would see a thin hand or a dark foot protruding from under a piece of cardboard in the darkness as you were about to step on someone's bed. People brought their children here and left them, when they thought they were old enough to fend for themselves on the street. Other children came on their own.

In the worst times of the inland drought of 1970, the starving people who arrived in Recife from the interior had been helped by Dom Helder Câmara, the bishop of Recife, and he remarked, when he grew notorious as a friend of the dispossessed, that *when he fed the poor people called him a saint and when he asked why they were poor people called him a communist.* But Dom Helder was forced to retreat into silence and inaction by the new pope, John Paul II, and by the end of the eighties was in any case very old. After its great last stand with the people against the military in São Paulo, the engaged and human Roman Catholic Church in Brazil had become shrunken and inert under Wojtyla's deadening hand. Its influence was fading fast, although Brazil was still called the largest Catholic country in the world. The church of the first colonizers was ridiculed or ignored among the middle classes for its harangues against contraception, abortion and divorce and everywhere else it was being supplanted by proliferating evangelical sects.

Some of the Protestant churches were modest, austere and old-fashioned Baptist chapels where the ladies wore long dark dresses and hats, the men wore dazzling white shirts and dark jackets and the children had brilliant shoes and all clasped the Gospels bound in black leather. The newer ones celebrated fancier rites in temples the size of aircraft hangars and were run by organizations on the North American model, rich and powerful, highly organized, politically demanding and followed by millions. Unlike the Brazilian Catholic Church these offered prospects in the here and now as well as a hope of redemption in the afterlife, and for any candidate for government in Brazil it was more important to get the mass evangelical churches on one's side than to be limply endorsed by the Catholic hierarchy. African religions kept their powerful following in the old slave port cities of the Northeast and had a stronger hold on the minds of European Brazilians than outsiders found easy to realize. In the interstices Brazil pullulated with the adherents of every imaginable belief. Astrological determinism, New Age babble, self-help vacuities and psychologism of all kinds invaded the minds of those many millions of Brazilians who had neither a good education, strong cultural ties nor any immediate hopes in the real world. The land was full of crazies. I met a boy in Recife living in an abandoned house. *Are you a Believer?* he asked. His mother and father had been Believers, in some other city, and now they were dead. *Another Believer killed them.*

Vavá had no discernible religious interest—and was scathing about the church when I asked—and Lia prayed most days. It was a common enough division in marriage. They were themselves both from the interior of Pernambuco, and had gone south to São Paulo just after their son was born. Alexandre had grown up in São Paulo and was already a teenager when the family came back to the Northeast and settled in Recife. Vavá was intensely interested in other people, but years after being transformed in the Southeast from a shy northeasterner into a big city bookseller and art dealer, he still had to overcome a deep personal reticence. It took me a while to realize that the reticence had to do with his being not just a northeasterner but an inlander in origin, from a town on the edge of the high vast drylands where people were dry and laconic and tough. Somewhere inside, Vavá was still a *matuto,* a boy from the bush. He had been around a lot and knew a lot of people of all social conditions, but retained that modest reserve, and an economical social style that identified him as a drylander. That his was the best bar in town had everything to do with the kind of person Vavá was, combining Brazilian cordiality with northeastern reserve.

————

The interior drylands took up well over a million square kilometers, three-quarters of the entire territory of the Northeast. One in three Brazilians lived in the Northeast, but nearly all stayed in the lush littoral. The people of the drylands were a smallish minority, distinct in their appearance and their culture. The Brazilians' name for their drylands came from old Portuguese—my massive dictionary of Brazilian Portuguese described the name of the *sertão* as being *of obscure origin,* but it wasn't really. A *deserto* was a desert and a *desertão* a big desert, which was how the seafaring settlers saw the dry and scary interior. In time they dropped the prefix and often they made the word plural into *sertões* to match their sense of the new continent's endless hinterland. Beyond the green and well watered coast with its temperate sea breeze, and a higher middle zone that was good for grazing, one stony drought-ravaged wasteland receded into another, marked out by ranges of dry hills and waterless riverbeds. Like the name of Australia's outback, the word *sertão* was freighted with the sense of a world elsewhere, beyond human settlement and like the *never never* in some ways beyond understanding.

It was strange and bleak to the maritime people who settled Brazil and *clung to the coast like crabs.* Gradually it was sprinkled with human inhabitants. The índios, retreating from white disease, white weaponry and white projects to enslave them, retreated from their coastal forests to the highlands out of Portuguese reach. They were followed by the settler military, looking for slaves, and the settler priests, looking for converts. By the end of the seventeenth century the índios were gone even from the drylands where they had taken refuge. Índio Brazil remained strongly present in the Northeast and especially the drylands through sexual contact. The indigenous people mated first with white Portuguese settlers and later with the black slaves from Africa. The Africans, when they escaped, headed for the thinly peopled wilds of the interior as the índios had before them, and like the poor whites who were looking to stake a claim and make a living. The intermarriage of the three races was unusually complete and long lasting in the drylands and the people developed quite early into a distinct physical type as the compact, sharp featured, mahogany skinned northeasterners.

The slave hunters on their inland treks—sustained and fortified by manioc, which they planted and harvested as they went, and carried with them as the índios did on their war parties as *war flour*—were on the lookout for gold, as well as what Antônio Vieira, the índios' great champion among the Portuguese, called the *red gold* of indigenous slaves. Toward the end of the seventeenth century they found it, but farther south and not in the Northeast. They brought cattle with them as well as manioc, food on the hoof for long expeditions, and the cattle stayed. Stock trails were worn into the landscape and the interior was parceled into huge cattle properties, some of which were bigger than entire nations in Europe. The owners of these endless properties, the *colonels,* were the only embodiment of the state in this wilderness and they decided what the law was.

The colonels as individuals might or might not formally hold that rank in the national guard, a rank that back in the time of the empire had represented the formal authority invested by the state in the biggest landholder of any given part of the interior. Eventually they gave their name to the whole play of force by which people in the remoter parts of the Northeast were kept compliant. It lasted for a hundred years or more and after a while Brazilians in the south started talking in the newspapers and universities about *colonelism* as if it were a system of government rather than the arbitrary use of power by those who held the land and the water, people who had clout in the coastal capitals and in the south. Judge and police chief in any district each owed his job to the colonel, who was *lord of life and death.* Like their children who died of sickness or hunger, most of the men shot dead at the wells or in front of their mud huts by the colonels' armed enforcers on horseback had never legally existed in the first place.

The overweening power of the colonels went back to the first days of the colony. Some of them, in a contorted and attenuated way, could trace their property rights back to the very first days of settlement. It was 1530 when Dom Manuel of Portugal determined that his sailors and traders would have to push inland from the little enclaves they had dotted along the coast. Fortified coastal trading posts like these had given Portugal wealth without responsibility all along the African and Indian coasts, but they were useless in the densely forested Brazil of hunter-gatherers. In Brazil there were no trade routes, no manufactured goods, no middlemen. If the Portuguese wanted to make a go of their *new world in the tropics,* they would have to settle it.

The coastal Tupi had been more than ready to trade brazil-wood, the tree whose trunks yielded a red dye that was a hot item in early-sixteenth-century Europe. Red was the glamorous color that century, and brazilwood was particularly sought after in France, even though the dye it contained was thin and not very stable. The Tupi used to cut the trees down and bring them to the ships. They would have traded anything for metal cutting tools and firearms. But the trees soon thinned out and nothing else offered quick returns. Even gold was going to have to be mined. There were no Incas or Aztecs in Brazil. Dom Manuel or his advisers divided the newfound land into fifteen horizontal strips, starting at the coast and ending wherever Spanish rights began. He offered perpetual rights in each such captaincy to a selected member of the aristocracy having the will and the resources to develop a colony. One of the strips was Pernambuco, inland from Olinda, and the next one south was Bahia, inland from the city of Salvador on the Bay of All Saints. Only two captaincies made a go of it in the early days, the investment was so heavy and the returns so slow. The colonies never seemed to get started. Pernambuco was one of the two that did, and the secret of its success lay in Europe's craving for sugar.

The most productive of all the sugar growing areas in coastal Pernambuco was the part called Alagoas in the south, just above the mouth of the mighty São Francisco River, which wound for thousands of kilometers through the inland and as it neared the coast became the border that separated Pernambuco from Bahia. For a long time Alagoas, so called for its lakes and lagoons, produced more sugar than almost anywhere else in Brazil, although it was a very small region. Its productiveness of sugar promoted it to the status of a province and it finally became the second smallest state in the federal republic of Brazil. The only smaller state was Sergipe, just over the river, chipped out of the huge state of Bahia. Alagoas was not all coastal sugar estates. It had its inland component of dryland whose landowning colonels ran cattle and disputed power in the state with the sugarcane plantation bosses of the coast.

———

Pernambuco's interior was where Lula came from, which was why he looked so at home in the streets of Recife. But Lula's identity was formed in an utterly different world and it was a long time before he looked back to the place and the people of his origins. Luis Inácio da Silva—*Lula* came years later—was born in a tiny shack in an indeterminate area the locals called *Varzea Comprida,* or Long Plain, in a shallow river valley outside the town of Garanhuns. He was the seventh child of a dirt-poor farmer and he was conceived and born on the edge of the drylands during the bitter drought of 1945. The child Lula grew up fed by his mother on a little manioc meal mashed into some remains of cold coffee.

Aristides Inácio da Silva, being unable to feed his wife, Euridice, and the six small children who were about to be seven, had walked out on them a fortnight before Lula was born. Aristides traveled three thousand kilometers to the south on the back of an open tray truck in search of work. He found it as a dock-worker loading coffee sacks in the port city of Santos. Just south of São Paulo, Santos was one of Brazil's first European settle-ments and São Paulo's outlet to the sea. There Aristides took up with a new woman, who happened to be his wife's cousin, and together they had two children, four by some accounts. Some years later he took his newer wife and the new children back to Long Plain for a visit. Euridice now learned about the new southern branch of the family, and the five-year-old Luis clapped eyes on his father for the first time. Aristides stayed in Long Plain for three weeks and then went back to Santos, taking Euridice's two eldest children with him and leaving Euridice pregnant with their eighth.

A while later, Euridice had a letter from down south, inviting her and the other children to join Aristides in Santos. At the end of 1952 she loaded the six remaining children onto the back of a flatbed truck driven by a neighbor from Garanhuns—one of the locals who made a living transporting the migrants to the south—and they spent the next thirteen days on the back of the truck traveling down to Santos. Trucks like this, with their tray perimeters finely painted with brightly colored lines, were called *parrot perch* trucks and all the passengers traveled standing on the tray, clustered together and clinging to a wooden support in the center. They can be seen at a distance on the dirt roads of the drylands, kicking up a cloud of red dust as they transport little knots of laborers to work, guests to weddings, buyers and sellers to markets.

This particular truck's arrival in Santos caused some conster-nation. Aristides had sent no invitation. The letter to Euridice had been forged by their eldest boy, who was missing his mother. Aristides intended to go on living with Euridice's cousin, although he also made Euridice pregnant again another couple of times. He had more children by her cousin too. By the time he died in 1978 Aristides da Silva was the father of twenty-three children, ten by Euridice and thirteen by her cousin. The domestic situation in Santos became a little tense or messy after four years of the extended family's presence in the same city, and in 1956 Euridice broke away and took her children to São Paulo. In the great city they lived in a single room at the back of a bar, and shared its toilet with the customers. Luis, who was eleven when they moved, had been working on the streets since he was seven, like millions of other small children in Brazil, selling oranges and peanuts and homemade tapioca sweets. He had got some schooling too, and learned to read the year before. In São Paulo Luis got his first full-time job, working for a dry cleaner. It didn't last, and the boy then worked as a shoeshiner, again like millions of young Brazilian boys, treading the fine line that separated subsistence from indigence, lugging a heavy wooden implement box and customer footrest on a shoulder strap around the hot and polluted public spaces, working the bars and the restaurants and the bus stops and the park benches. He got some casual work in an office and felt the first pangs of embarrassment about inviting any of his friends to the room where they lived at the back of the bar. There was no chair for the friend to sit on and Luis realized his family was poor.

Then he got a real job, in a factory that made nuts and bolts, which was something for a thirteen-year-old northeasterner. The migrants from the Northeast soon discovered that they were not much liked in the new industrial Brazil of the south. Like Sicilians in Milan and southern blacks in Chicago at the same time, they aroused obscure feelings of shame and resentment. Brazilians still ignore the history of these internal migrants. Nobody recognizes what they gave, and what they went through—or what they still do, because the Northeast still provides the labor that fuels the growth in the south. The lives of Brazil's earlier immigrants from Europe are recorded and celebrated in histories and soaps as part of the national epic, but not those of the newcomers from within Brazil itself. A new life for the huddled and suffering masses from *elsewhere*, such as Brazil once offered, is one thing, but to recognize the hunger and desperation that drove the internal migration from the Northeast, and the human cost of that displacement, still causes unease. Yet the northeasterners who went south were tens of millions and the public and private glories and horrors of Brazil today are founded on this vast movement of people.

At the end of his first day Luis ran home in his rusty grease smeared metalworker's overall and showed his mother his dirty worker's hands. He recalled this many years later. The general record holds little about Luis's mother. Like the earlier fact that her seventh child had managed to snatch a basic literacy from the least promising of circumstances, the image of the thirteen-year-old in his work clothes is a picture of the skill and determination that Euridice, the woman from the northeastern bush who came south by mistake, deployed to pilot her ten largely fatherless children through the new industrial jungle of São Paulo. And given her silence and his reticence, the image may stand for a great deal. The factory shift was from seven in the morning until seven at night, or from seven at night until seven in the morning. It was during the night shift once that another apprentice worker who was holding back the blade of a lathe while Luis changed a bolt fell asleep at the machine. The blade slipped forward and sliced off the little finger of Luis's left hand. But Luis trained over three years as a lathe operator himself, and got work at one of Brazil's biggest engineering companies on the outskirts of São Paulo, where the car assembly plants were. That year Luis was twenty and it was 1966, two years after the military coup.

He was now a fully paid up member of São Paulo's industrial

working class and his interests were women and football. The military coup in Brazil did not heighten any sense in him that he belonged to a class of people the military had in its sights. Neither did it change his vague sense that the industrial unions, the government run unions set up in the thirties, were run by crooks. Luis was still a boy from the bush, with a deeply conservative rural northeasterner's wariness of the social ways of the industrial south. He clung to his past for a long time. His whole family was like that. The Northeast was like that. *We thought . . . they were only crooks . . . all the leaders were crooks.* An elder brother called José was a unionist and belonged to the underground Communist Party, but he was the only one in the family like that. They called him Brother Chico because he was like a monk with his pudding basin haircut and his devotion to the cause. The others argued with José when they were drinking cachaça. *We thought . . . my brother was crazy to belong to the union . . . we didn't want to hear about it.* It was four years before José convinced his younger brother to take out a union card. Luis dragged his feet. *I was a lathe operator. I was getting good enough pay and I had a girlfriend. I wanted to play football. I wanted to go out dancing. I didn't want to know about union things.* This was in 1968.

This was the year murder and torture became routine in the government of Brazil. Luis went on happily. He married his girlfriend, who worked in one of the textile factories, and she was soon pregnant. At the end of her term she went into a local hospital to give birth, with such attention as a factory girl could expect, and she and her child both died while she was in labor. Nobody had noticed that she had hepatitis, which killed them. The other thing that happened in 1969 was that José put the hard word on his brother again. This time José wanted him to join his slate for the elections to the local leadership of the metalworkers' union. Luis at length and reluctantly agreed to stand for the union directorate. He won a place and won it again in 1972. But he didn't follow José into the Communist Party. Luis was not a political person.

Luis kept his head well enough down for the president of his union, a labor boss who was very much a company man, to nominate him as a candidate for the succession three years later. The workers called the union boss a *pelego,* or saddle blanket, for his situation under the rider's rump and on the mule's back. Sociologists called a corporatist union boss an *urban substitute for the colonel.* The boss candidate Luis had not yet spoken at a big meeting, didn't even know how to use a microphone, and was sufficiently self-aware to suspect the departing president of wanting to shed a retrospective glow on his tenure by having an incompetent follow him in office. Nevertheless, with such an imprimatur the candidacy was bound to succeed and it did. The untried new man won ninety-two percent of the vote.

One of the early perks of office was a union trip to Japan. On his way home, stopping over in the United States, Luis learned that the military had arrested his brother José as a *subversive.* A union lawyer advised him to stay in the States until the heat went off. But Luis didn't like American food, which lacked rice and black beans and farofa and was in any case disgusting, and went straight back to São Paulo. He seemed galvanized by José's arrest and abruptly shed his anxieties about his own security, his job, his family. He said, *I lost my fear.* Charged up, he and some other young activists set out to kick some life into their cowed and compliant union. To get the metalworkers involved, they organized union football championships—factory teams against union leadership. Before the matches Luis talked for five minutes and after the game there was beer and a barbecue. They transformed the leaflets they gave out to factory workers, adding cartoons and comic strips and things people wanted to read. The handouts stayed in pockets and were no longer crumpled up and chucked away at the factory gates. The leaflets named names when factory supervisors started victimizing workers. They talked about the here and now in a lively concrete way and were different from the grimly programmatic clandestine leaflets José the communist had earlier pressed into Luis's hands.

Over the Andes in Chile, South America's oldest parliamentary democracy was destroyed in 1973 by the conspiracy of generals whose *caravan of death* was now picking out and exterminating the leaders of organized labor. It is not clear how far knowledge of the tortures and killings going on in that other world of the exterior penetrated São Paulo's industrial belt. Brazil was still isolated in its own vastness, a strangely self-absorbed and self-referring universe of its own, cut off from its Spanish-speaking neighbors by its different language, its different racial history, its different culture. Even in 1976 when Videla and the Argentinian generals, even closer to home, began their *dirty war* on workers and students, Luis and his mates went blithely on, unaware or unafraid of the danger that Brazil's own generals might decide to follow suit and go for broke.

What changed in the union being led by Luis was that the workers now took their claims straight to the labor tribunal and ignored the government's union federation. In 1976, for the first time ever they won a small wage raise. The new young union leaders were still benignly treated in the closely censored media, since they were assertive and unorthodox but not *communists*. When Luis stood for reelection in 1978 he ran on his record and won a slightly improbable ninety-eight percent of the vote. He *was still very thin and wore flares* and his thick black curly hair hung in long waving ringlets like tentacles and people started calling him *Lula,* which meant *Squid.* Lula put on a suit and tie and invited the regime's state governor and the army commander to his inauguration, both of which moves upset his union friends.

If Lula's awareness of the way Brazil worked seemed to have its radical inconsistencies, it was because he contained multitudes. He was not predictable. He was not sectarian. He was not an ideologue.

————

Sugar had run in the blood of Fernando Collor's family, but the sweetness was long gone. As the nineteenth century turned into the twentieth, more and more of the old sugar estates of north-eastern Brazil were bankrupted and the big houses lay abandoned by their masters. The owner of the Little Waterfall plantation in Rio Largo, not far from Maceió in Alagoas, was ruined at the end of the Great War in Europe. His eighteen-year-old son, who had grown up on the sugar estate, went south to Rio with the money left from the sale of his father's land sewn into his underpants by his mother. Arnon de Mello studied law until the money ran out and then he worked as a journalist in Rio until his paper's offices were burnt down when the dictator Getúlio Vargas took power in 1930. He was smart and rose fast and in 1939 married the daughter of the dictator's minister of labor. When their second son was born ten years later, Arnon and Leda called him Fernando. Fernando's maternal grandfather, Lindolfo Collor, was the son of an immigrant German shoemaker. Brazil's very first labor minister, he had drafted the laws that created the government's industrial trade unions. The Brazilian government realized rather late that labor matters could no longer be left to the ministry of agriculture, and the corporatist—or fascist—labor laws drawn up by Lindolfo Collor in the thirties would last until the metalworkers' strikes in São Paulo at the end of the 1970s. Encouraged into politics by the example of his wife's father, in 1950 Arnon de Mello went home and ran for governor of Alagoas. Fernando was one year old.

The Northeast, unlike the Southeast, was not industrializing. It was falling further and further behind, and was still ruled by colonels whose understanding of politics was that when it was election time you took your peasants to the polling station and told them what to do. The current governor belonged to another family of ruined sugar planters, a wild and brutal clan who had become a political dynasty. One of them had been the dictator's war minister and his siblings ruled the state one after the other and expected to go on forever. Arnon de Mello arrived with a snappy jingle and the state's first ever election posters in full color; meet and greet and baby kissing in country towns where once the candidates went with bullwhips; a comic strip campaign bio with a brightly colored cover. He handed out campaign calendars, campaign pencils, signed campaign photos as the loudspeakers belted out the campaign jingle. He was in the papers, he was on the wireless. He ran campaign film shows in the sharp dry open air of the outback towns. He bought votes with spades, hoes, knives and the promise of the Singer sewing machine which went around with the candidate on the back of the campaign truck. Arnon won handsomely and the loser was shot four months later by a former congressman whose parents had been murdered. It was nothing new, and there would be another nine hundred political murders in Alagoas while Arnon de Mello was governor. The killings went on all over the state. A colonel in his seventies was stabbed to death by the military police. A former governor's grandson was shot in an ambush. A big landowner was killed by the police chief. A religious leader giving trouble was murdered by landowners' men. Arnon bought up the main opposition paper and set the police on the others. There were no public works. Six years later Alagoas was back in the hands of the defeated rivals and Arnon went back to making money in Rio.

Business was good and Arnon moved with the smart and the

very rich. He did property deals with Roberto Marinho, who owned the newspaper *O Globo*. They built Rio's first shopping mall together in Copacabana and it was opened by the president. In Alagoas Arnon kept his paper and added a radio station. In 1962 he was elected to the Senate in Brasilia. His old and hated rival was already installed and threatened to *fill his mouth with lead.* The new session in January 1963 opened with a shootout between the two senators from Alagoas. Arnon missed his target and killed another senator but he was imprisoned only briefly, and the movers and shakers in Rio still did business with him, and greeted him affably in the Jockey Club. Behind his back they raised their eyebrows and called him *the gunman,* which always got a laugh. The son of the ruined sugar planter, after his brilliant early days in Rio, his socially consolidating marriage and his lucrative property deals, was now marked as a northeasterner. The man *who had once shone in looking good in Rio was dragged down to the brutality of the land he came from. His social rise was stopped in its tracks.*

He concentrated on business. In the twenty-one years after military dictatorship began in 1964, the number of Brazil's television stations went from 14 to 150 and most of them belonged to Roberto Marinho. Arnon opened the first television station in Alagoas and transmitted Globo's programs. He became the media boss of Alagoas. His three sons and two daughters were now grown up. The sons were grossly indulged in the manner of rich boys in Brazil. The eldest soon showed himself dishonest and unreliable as well as incompetent, and dynastic hopes devolved on Fernando. He had much in common with his elder brother, but was more personable and more intelligent and in 1975 Fernando made a brilliant marriage to eighteen-year-old Lilibeth Monteiro, whose father owned one of the biggest industrial conglomerates in Brazil. The wedding party was held in the art deco splendor of the Copacabana Palace hotel, where the beautiful people of Europe and America came to holiday, and Fernando started being seriously noticed in Brazilian high society. *Baby* Monteiro de Carvalho was delighted with his stylish new son-in-law. The Monteiros had the newly elected governor of Alagoas to lunch in Rio and the governor made Fernando Collor de Mello mayor of Maceió. The family idyll soured when Fernando needed money and tried to sell his father-in-law some of his own family's real estate for a lot more than it was worth. *The kid's trying to take me in. I'm an experienced businessman and old enough to be his father,* Baby said. The marriage broke down into ugly domestic violence and Lilibeth flew off to Paris.

Fernando promoted Maceió as a tourist destination, which involved building a lot of hotels on the beach and fixing some of the terrible roads. Beautiful people from the south passed through town as freeloaders almost as often as Fernando flew south to the greater glamour of Rio. His last act as mayor in 1982 was to take on five thousand new municipal employees. *All votes for me,* he said, looking down on the endless queue of newcomers from an upper window. *Employment for electoral ends* was forbidden and Fernando, who was standing for the federal Congress, got in serious trouble with the military dictators in Brasilia. His successor as mayor had to ask for federal help to fix the mess he found in the city's accounts. *This boy ought to be in jail,* remarked the minister as he went over Fernando's financial records. But Fernando was elected to Congress easily and within a year his father, Arnon, was dead.

At a coming out ball in the remote interior of Alagoas Fernando had met fifteen-year-old Rosane Malta, daughter of the colonel who owned the cattle land around Big Scrub, high in the bone-dry inland where cattle and goats wandered through the town streets. The Maltas were the impoverished remnants of a dynasty that a hundred years before had run the state. In 1950 they had backed Fernando's father when he ran for governor and on the morning of the vote three of the Maltas were clubbed down and shot dead in the street by the opposition's hired killers. Fernando was linked to the Maltas by spilt blood and he liked fifteen-year-old Rosane enough to overlook her uncouthness. She was nineteen when they married in 1984. Fernando's family despised Rosane, who dished out as good as she got. In 1987 Fernando became governor of Alagoas and they lived in the Palace of the Martyrs in Maceió, built a hundred years before by Rosane's great-uncle, a governor who was twice chased out of it by howling mobs. PC, who was already in charge of the financial side of Fernando's life, made sure all their personal expenses were charged to the state government. While Fernando was governor, a candidate for mayor of Rosane's hometown displeased the Malta family and was shot dead in the back of the head by Rosane's younger brother and her uncle, and a young cousin of Rosane's killed someone else in Maceió the following year. Fernando finessed both of these awkward moments, and soon there were more than fifty Maltas on the government payroll.

It was Fernando's younger brother Pedro who had introduced PC Farias to Fernando. Pedro's wife was the daughter of one of the biggest sugar refining families in Alagoas and João Lyra was about to transform his economic power into political clout. Yet even the Lyras could be embarrassing in the way of the Northeast's ruling families. When a sergeant of the Alagoas military police was shot dead in an ambush some years later, João Lyra was named as the man who ordered the murder. Lyra had put a tap on his wife's phone because after thirty-six years of marriage he thought she was having an affair. He played the family a recording of her conversation with the sergeant. *Just look what your mother's planning to do,* he told them. The sergeant's killing caused some indignation locally because João Lyra himself was known to be having an affair of his own at this time with his nephew's wife, who was twenty years younger than he was.

When Pedro married Thereza Lyra toward the end of 1980, at a little wedding which brought together five thousand of the two families' very closest friends—a further list of two thousand people Fernando wanted to impress politically having been rejected as compromising the intimacy of the occasion—the bride's father invited PC to be the bride's sponsor. The beautiful young bride was startled by the sight of her godfather—who *was* this little bald man with the gold identity bracelets and the sideburns?—but João Lyra wanted to do PC a favor in return for services lately rendered as political bagman. He was helping PC raise his social profile.

Fernando so admired PC's way with money that he was prepared to overlook the white suits and silk shirts when he ran for governor in 1986. PC kept the campaign money pouring in. Salaries were paid, planes were hired, the TV ads went out— PC got Fernando elected governor of Alagoas and João Lyra senator in Brasilia at the same time. Fernando had significant and growing lifestyle requirements and the wonderful thing about PC was that he looked after the money without ever wanting to explain what he was doing, or how or why. Fernando began grooming PC into an acceptable associate, or at least a presentable one, just as he was grooming Rosane to be a presentable wife.

V

Below the Equator

An English traveler in eighteenth-century Brazil recorded in amazement and exasperation that every time he asked one of his Brazilian hosts about the way things worked in the New World, a black slave would be summoned to provide the explanation. The indolence and ignorance of Brazil's plantation masters in other than sexual things matched the sexually repressed indolence of their wives. In few places in the world was working your way so little valued as in Brazil. In the continent's original times it was natural. What else could you expect in a country which filled all human needs so gloriously? The warrior hedonism of the hunter-gatherer peoples who lived in the great river basins and the coastal forests flowed from nature's invitation to a prudent improvidence.

Then the Europeans landed and in the sixteenth century the idea of a golden age again gripped the European imagination, as strongly it had in antiquity. News of the people who inhabited the *brave new world* and were *only wild in the sense that we call fruits wild when they are produced by nature in her ordinary course* delighted Shakespeare and Montaigne. The idea that people might live with no constraints other than nature's was overlaid with tormented Christian notions of life before the fall, of sexual innocence and natural plenty, life defined by the absence of war, guilt, money, work, and the newfound world sowed the intellectual seeds of a newly non-Christian life. The freedoms of the New World's native peoples were, however, strictly a conceit for distant Europe. In Brazil itself the índios were more practically seen by the Portuguese colonists. The women were seized as marvelously available sexual partners, the men as a great source of slave labor. Hopefully the locals would also lead the colonists to the gold that would make a golden age for Portugal.

The Portuguese were doing well at overseas trade with African and Asian countries but making anything of the utterly different Brazil was going to be a long haul. As traders they had never planned to do the work themselves, or live permanently at the supply source. Portugal had a tiny population and Brazil was a huge territory lacking transport, communication or housing, even a reliable food supply. To colonize Brazil the Portuguese needed labor. The hunter-gatherer peoples of Brazil were not the answer, though the Portuguese did their best to make them change their ways. A quarter or half a million indigenous people were enslaved on the sugarcane plantations of the Northeast that replaced the forests where they had freely lived. In the first two centuries of the sugar industry, one in three of the slaves being worked to early death was índio. On the sugar estates the índios were then annihilated by the infections the Portuguese had brought from Europe, Asia and Africa. Epidemics of plague and smallpox and the common cold wiped out the tens of thousands of índio slaves on the sugar plantations of Bahia, and then the sicknesses moved north into Pernambuco and killed off the workforce there. The foreign diseases penetrated deep into Brazil's forests, and uncounted índios died out of sight. The dying gasped for breath for burning lungs as respiration failed. Stinking worm-riddled flesh fell from the bones of those who had lately seemed the handsomest and healthiest and maybe the happiest people in the world. The dead were too many for the living to bury.

Survivors were converted and herded into the Jesuits' fortified villages, Christians of a kind and slaves of a kind too, forced into calico smocks, sexual abstinence, hymn singing and an unpaid regime of crop raising and domestic service, rented out by the Jesuits to the lay population. The missionaries attenuated the suffering and prolonged the death of a people. They fought with the landowners and slave owners and imposed their own miseries in the name of saving souls. Demographically and economically, the indigenous Brazilians quite suddenly ceased to count. Their great defender among the Portuguese in the seventeenth century, the eloquent Jesuit Antônio Vieira, was so appalled by their enslavement and genocide that he came—like Las Casas in the Caribbean before him—to be an advocate of enslaving Africans and shipping them to Brazil. It seemed the lesser evil. Africans were tougher.

The transatlantic slave traffic was already under way. For the colonists African slaves were the perfect solution to their labor problems. Portuguese traders were already doing business with African slave dealers and slaves shipped from West African ports were being landed in Brazil within fifty years of Cabral's arrival. Over the next three hundred years four million Africans, maybe more, were shipped across the Atlantic into slavery in Brazil—seven times the number of African prisoners sold into slavery in North America. Millions of others died at sea before they reached Brazil. Most of the Africans were young men and boys who would die before they were thirty. The slave owners of Brazil were universally pleased with African strength and the African capacity for hard labor, but since the slaves died young and had no children, their owners were in constant need of replacements. For the Africans disease was not the main cause of death. It was the way they were made to live. It was the work they had to do.

The shipping of slaves from Africa to America was such good business for so long because in Brazil it was cheaper for sugar plantation owners to work young Africans to death in a few years and then buy new ones. A new slave, in the great age of sugar, earned back his cost price in a little over a year, and from then until he collapsed and died or was killed by design or accident he represented pure profit. The world's craving for sugar was insatiable and Pernambuco was soon the richest producer in the world. Maintenance costs were minimal, though the Africans were not a docile workforce on the Brazilian plantations. They knew they had little to lose. Their owners, as the Jesuits complained, at the slightest annoyance *threw their slaves alive into the furnace or killed them in various barbarous and inhumane ways.* Some of the slaves sabotaged the sugar production machinery. Others just ate dirt like the índios and waited for the end. Sometimes a plantation's Africans rose up together, hacked their overseers and owner to pieces and torched the place. And fled into the forest. They were without women for the most part. Imports of African women were as slow to start as the settlement of Portuguese women in Brazil. After a time the master's big house became bigger and children arrived and female slaves were needed to breast-feed them and clean and sew and cook the big meals the master's family consumed. Slave women themselves were almost useless for breeding. Their fertility rate was low and in any case breeding slave children made no economic sense, even when the children survived childhood. It cost far more to keep a black child for its first ten years than it did to buy a freshly unloaded healthy adult male ready to be put to work. The increase in Brazil's population of African slaves came entirely through imports, and the profit margin for the traders kept imports well ahead of the attrition rate as the economy expanded.

Brazil's was by far the largest system of slavery in the New World, and slavery lasted longer in Brazil than it did anywhere else. The British pressed to end it for years and finally got their way through the naval power of their empire. British control of the oceans and British control of the Brazilian economy made it relatively easy to ensure that the transatlantic trade in Africans was shut down in 1850. Final abolition within Brazil came in 1888, without a civil war of the North American kind or indeed any obvious social or economic trauma at all because slavery had lasted until the massive free emigration from the poorer parts of Europe. Arriving from Italy, Spain, Portugal and Germany, the newcomers were often so shocked by the conditions they found— slave owners took time to learn how to relate to free labor—that some European governments banned immigration to Brazil until things improved. The new immigrants nearly all settled in the south—it was the time of the coffee boom—and it was they who created Brazil's urban commerce and its late industrialization. Their immigrant hard work and their commercial expertise created the concentration of wealth in the city and state of São Paulo, but they never transformed the country's politics in a comparable way.

Power in Brazil stayed in the hands of the landowners, the exporters of sugar, gold, coffee, beef and rubber. Each state in Brazil was run by a small group of intermarried families. They were the people who a few years earlier had run their estates on slave labor and they still, in the remoter parts of the country—the coffee estates of the south, cattle runs in the drylands of the Northeast and the rubber plantations of the Amazon—kept the people working for them dirt poor and serflike in their dependence. Most of the northeasterners who went south left rural misery for the urban poverty nesting within the Southeast's huge industrial wealth. The landowning families dominated the military high command, and even the career officers who rose through the ranks identified with the ruling caste and were ready to step in with guns whenever its interests seemed threatened. As they had, with a big nudge from the United States, in 1964.

The way Brazilians lived was transformed in the middle of the twentieth century and nothing changed in the patterns of power. The landowners' club let in the new industrial wealth, but Brazil remained a society in which most people lacked representation. Whether it was old money or new money whose voice was currently being heard in the capital made little difference to most Brazilians. Neither the agricultural nor the industrial working people in Brazil were able to form their own workers' organizations, nor did they ever form political parties to represent their interests in government. The absolute newness of Lula in Brazil, so easy to miss from outside, was the more amazing for being twofold. He led the making of Brazil's first free and autonomous workers' union movement and he then led the formation of the first ever mass political party to articulate the larger needs and hopes of those working people—and of Brazil's tens of millions of dispossessed—in representative government. There was a lot of ground to make up. Brazil was still a rural slave society when such rights were being hard won in the industrial societies of North America and Europe, and nearly a century after the end of slavery, labor in Brazil was despised because it was still so cheap.

––––––

Slaves who escaped in the early days found that the forested vastness of the Brazil lying beyond the narrow coastal strip which was being cleared and cultivated afforded great refuge away from roads and settlements. The cost of pursuit and recapture of individual slaves weighed against the owners and the state, and laid bare the weakness of the masters' forces of control.

They could hardly send their slaves after the fugitives. Quite early, the dreadful fear of a mass revolt by the African slaves began to lurk in the minds of the Portuguese landowners. The fear lasted for centuries. There were so many Africans, and so few Portuguese. By 1600 there were already twenty thousand African slaves on the sugar estates of the Northeast, and in the next fifty years their number more than doubled. Precautions were taken. Slave owners mixed members of as many different ethnic groups as possible on their estates, people from different parts of Africa, with different languages, beliefs, traditions. It was much better for the owners if the only language the slaves all understood was the basic Portuguese in which they took their orders. Soon there were so many slaves and so many Portuguese slaving outposts along the African coast that the ethnic mix was easy. Consumer preference played its part. Some Africans were more docile, some harder workers, some more disease resistant. Toughness and troublemaking unfortunately went together. The sensible landowner preferred a blend of *pieces,* or *items,* as the Africans were called in the account books, and the high attrition rate among the *pieces* allowed for fine-tuning of the supply flow.

When slaves did escape into the wild, one African fugitive was likely to have no more in common with his fellow than an Englishman on the run might have with a Russian in a country foreign to both. There was also this difference for the Africans, that while the índios, fleeing forced labor and Christianity, headed deeper into a country they had known forever—every animal and bird, every plant, every fish, every insect, the flowing of the water and the tremors in the skies—the Africans were as far out of their element in Brazil as the Europeans were. But they did escape. Surviving in the wild was easier than surviving on the sugar plantations. Enough Africans escaped to form communities in the bush, and these communities became a pole of attraction for the Africans who remained enslaved on the plantations.

By the early seventeenth century the Portuguese were doing so well out of sugar that the rising Protestant Dutch, in the form of the West India Company, were drawn to the synergies of the African slave traffic and Brazilian sugar production on both sides of the South Atlantic. The British, French, Dutch and Spanish sugar plantations in the Caribbean, all likewise worked by slave labor from Africa, were about to end the sweet times for Brazil's northeastern landowners, but nobody knew this yet. The Dutch landed in Bahia in 1624 and occupied Salvador, but they were driven out after a year. Five years later they took Olinda in Pernambuco and started a seven-year war that left them in control of the whole coast of Brazil's Northeast from Fortaleza in Ceará to the São Francisco River South of Alagoas.

For seven years the Dutch ruled most of the Northeast from Recife. They were enlightened rulers, compared with the Portuguese. Dreaming of Amsterdam, Prince Maurits of Nassau built Recife's canals, brought out scientists and painters to record the wonders of the New World in the tropics, encouraged Amsterdam's Jewish business community to emigrate. He founded synagogues in Recife while the Inquisition was trying to exterminate Judaism on the continent. In Africa, Nassau seized Portugal's slave trading entrepôts on the coast of the Gulf of Guinea and Angola. The big Portuguese landowners of Pernambuco fought back from the interior with a guerrilla resistance and the Dutch were forced back on Recife. By midcentury, the Dutch had their new war with England to constrain them and the West India Company was in deep financial trouble. In 1654 the Protestant invaders withdrew altogether. The costs for the colonial powers had been nearly ruinous on both sides.

For the African slaves of Pernambuco the disturbances of the

Dutch grab for the Northeast were an opportunity they seized. A lot of fugitives had already been gathering in a forested and hilly inland area to the south, a range running parallel to the coast between Recife and Maceió, about seventy kilometers inland. It was called Palmares after the forests of wild palms that were dense in those hills—palms which afforded the fugitives *wine, oil, salt and clothing . . . their leaves serve as roofing, their branches for supports, the fruit for sustenance . . . and the fibre in the trunk makes string and rope.* A network of nine *quilombos*—an African word for a warrior brotherhood gave the settlements their name—grew up in the hills of Palmares, and by 1612 the *republic* was enough of a threat to the slave owners for an armed expedition of six hundred men to be sent to destroy it.

All the expedition realized was the size of the difficulty. The rugged, trackless and densely forested hills were almost impenetrable and the quilombos were spread widely. Palmares went on growing while the Portuguese colonists fought the Dutch invaders. Not only African slaves settled there but índios and even whites who were in flight from the law or the Inquisition. The Dutch in their turn saw the quilombos as *a serious threat* in 1640. There were now six thousand people living in the capital, Macaco, a fortified town built on the Serra da Barriga, the highest ridge. The Dutch mounted a raid in 1644 and killed a hundred of them, and another the following year.

Ten years later, when the Portuguese regained control of the colony, Palmares was bigger than ever. A white man who had lived there told the Portuguese authorities the quilombos were armed with guns and bows and arrows for hunting and self-defense, the towns well fortified and their houses laid out in streets with chapels, statues and *palaces.* The people grew crops of corn, manioc, sweet potato, beans, bananas and sugarcane, raised chicken and pigs, ran foundries, workshops, potteries and carpentry shops. The índios taught the Africans pottery, fishing, hunting, netmaking. The Africans passed on the technology they had learned on the sugar estates. The women were relatively few, but their numbers were boosted by raids and they shared themselves around in a system of polyandry and before long there were many children in Palmares, as there never had been in the slave quarters. The children grew up. The settlement was more than a generation old. Its king had a wife and two young concubines; the other men made do.

For the colonists it was terrible news. The Africans and their allies were occupying the richest agricultural land—the valleys between the fortified hilltops were marvelous for grazing—and the next most accessible after the narrow coastal strip. The Portuguese seafarers had always been lazy and rather scared about penetrating the interior of the South American continent. Now the government was getting sterner. Settlers had to push inland. Cattle were being raised and cattle needed land. The fertile hills and valleys of Palmares were earmarked for Portuguese expansion and had to be cleared of rebels. The Portuguese were more rawly conscious than ever, at the almost accidental end of twenty years of Dutch occupation, that their own situation in Brazil was very precarious. Soon after the middle of the seventeenth century the population of Palmares reached twenty thousand. This made it, along with Salvador de Bahia and the Recife-Olinda settlement, one of the three biggest urban centers in Brazil. What if some other European power—France, England—wanted to move in after the Dutch? What if they did a deal with Palmares? Palmares also had a stable leadership and its leaders necessarily had a sharp understanding of political realities. The great leader of Palmares at this time was Ganga Zumba, the *great lord,* whose

name was partly African and partly Tupi and who lived in the
main settlement on the Serra da Barriga.

Palmares had to go. The first thing the Portuguese did on
regaining power in 1654 was to send another armed raiding
party against Palmares, since *these internal enemies were just as
harmful and more barbaric and dreadful than the {Dutch}*. They
sent expedition after expedition. All failed. In 1670 the government of Pernambuco, alarmed that the landowners were now
negotiating directly with Palmares, planned its total destruction. Every year there were military attacks on its fortified settlements. In 1676 the military razed a fortified town of two
thousand houses after a fierce two-hour battle. Nearly all the
inhabitants escaped and built a new and less accessible town in
thicker forest. This was the first appearance in war of Zumbi—
a Bantu name for a military and religious leader—who was
Ganga Zumba's young son-in-law. It was also a breakthrough
for the colonial forces. And later that year Ganga Zumba's
forces, retreating from a new expedition, torched one of their
largest quilombos, *a city* the Portuguese judged it from its
ashes. Ganga Zumba fell back on another quilombo of a thousand houses, but this was taken at the end of 1677 and several
of the leader's children and grandchildren were among the
prisoners. Another son and several African leaders were killed.
Ganga Zumba was wounded but escaped.

The governor of Pernambuco now sent an emissary who knew
the area to Palmares. The governor made an offer. The escapees
of Palmares had seen how vulnerable their free society was to
the force of the settler state. The governor would grant them
land for a settlement and the release of all the women and children taken as prisoners. Africans who had fled from slavery
would be returned to their owners. All who had been born in
Palmares would remain free under Ganga Zumba as their leader.

If the offer was rejected he would destroy Palmares entirely and kill all its tens of thousands of inhabitants.

On a Saturday afternoon in June 1678, settler society in Recife was startled to see a dozen black warrior *barbarians* enter the city. *They came naked, with their natural parts alone covered. Some wore their hair in braids, others wore false beards and moustaches, and others were shaved, and nothing more. All were husky and powerful, armed with bows and arrows.* Two of them were Ganga Zumba's sons—one of them, wounded, riding a horse—and ten were military leaders from Palmares and they were suing for peace. They prostrated themselves, *striking their palms in sign of surrender,* before the governor, who *ordered them dressed and adorned with yellow ribbons.* A mass was sung, the warriors were baptized and swore allegiance to the king of Portugal. They set off back to Palmares with a treaty document and the deed to a forest *where there was no lack of palm trees to provide them with food.* The barbarians were seen by Recife society as impressed by the sumptuousness of the church, the size of the crowd, the greatness of the governors and the *friendliness.* Everyone was mightily pleased. Slave owner property rights had been reaffirmed, and Palmares would no longer be a haven for escapees. In time, it would be almost a normal settlement.

Only Zumbi was not pleased, back in Palmares. Neither were the other quilombo leaders, who now made Zumbi king. The irreducibles repudiated the treaty. Nobody was going back into slavery. Overthrown, Ganga Zumba disappeared. Maybe he was killed by Zumbi and the new Palmares leadership—what happened on the Serra da Barriga was less well recorded than the public spectacles of Recife. The governor set about the promised extermination. A series of *bush captains* led locally raised armies against Palmares in 1679, 1680, 1682, 1683 and 1684. Every year they were driven back. The placid agricultural settlement of Ganga Zumba had been transformed under Zumbi's leadership into a society on permanent war footing, and Zumbi's Palmares was unbeatable.

In 1685 a man called Domingos Jorge Velho came to Pernambuco. He wanted the governor's authorization to enslave the índios of the interior. He was a *bandeirante,* a *flag bearer,* leader of one of the armed raiding parties who had been heading inland toward the north into unknown territory from the new settlement of São Paulo in the south. The bandeirantes were the first Europeans to penetrate the interior of Brazil in a search for slaves, gold, precious stones. They were private entrepreneurs who lived off the sale of the prisoners they took among the índios while they hoped for a big mineral strike. A small party would spend months or years up country and come back with thousands of índios in chains. In the fragile order of Brazil the bandeirantes, who were numerous, experienced and hard as nails, soon became a de facto army. It was natural, when Jorge Velho heard about Palmares, that he and the governor of Pernambuco should do a deal. After two years of raiding in the Northeast and a good harvest of indigenous people—all the more appreciated by Pernambuco's landowners in that sugar prices had fallen sharply while the cost of African slaves had soared—in 1687 the governor and the bandeirantes agreed on an expedition against Palmares. The deal was payment in kind. Domingos Jorge Velho would destroy the quilombo and take most of the prisoners for himself as spoils of war. He took some time to deliver. It wasn't until six years later that he had a siege in place around the quilombo on the Serra da Barriga. The main quilombo of Palmares, the *royal stockade,* was surrounded by snares and protected by wattle and daub walls topped with iron spikes. It was known as Macaco—*Monkey* in Portuguese and how the settlers thought of it, though the name came more likely from a Bantu word, *mokoko.*

At the end of 1693 the bandeirante siege of Palmares began. In

February 1694 the redoubt fell after forty-two days. Two hundred fighters were killed when it was overrun and two hundred more threw themselves to their death over the cliffs. Five hundred prisoners were sold back into slavery outside Pernambuco. Zumbi himself and others escaped and fought on, and it took the bandeirantes another two years to hunt him down. On 20 November 1695, however, they took him, executed him and displayed his head on a spike for the edification of the African slaves of Pernambuco. After nearly a hundred years, Palmares was over.

The republic of Palmares had opposed a community of the oppressed, under African leadership, to the power of the Portuguese oligarchy. In the eighteenth century Brazil became more settled, and it was impossible ever again to defy the slave owners on the scale of Palmares, which had the size and permanence of an alternative state. Uprisings and revolts continued all around Brazil for the next two hundred years, and the communities of the fugitive were numberless. In 1835 the slaves—tempered by Islam—briefly commanded the city of Salvador de Bahia. The quilombos never again grew as big as Palmares, but around Brazil smaller settlements of escaped slaves, a few dozen or a few hundred people, were inextinguishable. The larger cities were ringed by them, like the favelas of today, and many of them lived, by necessity, off livestock theft and extortion. Most of the outer suburbs of Salvador today began as communities of escaped slaves. Quilombos perceived as dangers were suppressed by fire and slaughter. Others, smaller or more remote, were ignored and many lasted for a very long time. They outlasted the news that slavery was ended and are there, folded away into the remoter parts of the country, today.

———

Below the equator there is no sin. Nothing could have been better judged to attract enterprising male inhabitants of a Mediterranean country under the screws of the Inquisition, or to empty their minds of the fact that there were no quick and easy pickings of any other kind in the newfound land of Brazil. All of Portugal's overseas trade was conducted south of the equator in the spice and textile trades with Africa and Asia, but these offered their own rewards—for a shipload of black pepper, cinnamon, ginger and cloves, the Lisbon market offered a twentyfold return on cost price—and there was no need to bring sex into the equation. Brazil was different.

The *Holy Office* was not unaware of Brazil's erotic appeal. The new city of Salvador had been going less than fifty years when an inquisitorial *visitor* and his investigating committee arrived in 1591, very seasick but determined to see how far the spiritual life of the new colonies of Bahia and Pernambuco was falling short of the rigorous new counterreformation standards lately enforced in Europe. The interrogation records showed the Inquisition wanted to check specifically on backsliding by the *new Christians* in Brazil. Portuguese Jews had converted under pressure at the time of the great expulsions from Spain and Portugal and since the middle of the sixteenth century had been immigrating in large numbers to Brazil to escape the new persecutions of the Holy Office. Now anyone who wore a clean shirt on Saturday or refused to eat rabbit or octopus was under dire suspicion. The old Christians were also a great worry. This was the time of the mass enslavement of the Tupi, to provide the colony's labor force and drive the labor-intensive sugar production. The Tupi, though ready to sacrifice tribal enemies and prepared to go to great lengths for the sake of metal technology and weaponry, were proving refractory to mass enslavement and a future as industrial forced labor. They had withdrawn from the areas of coastal settlement, and the Portuguese slave traders were having to press farther and farther into the forest to round up new prisoners to enslave.

The whites were also having to enter into arrangements with the índio leaderships, mediated by *mamelucos,* sons of Portuguese fathers and Tupi mothers, already quite numerous, who moved between one culture and the other. Dealings were greatly complicated from an ideological point of view by the fact that the Tupi had developed a new religion since their disastrous encounter with Europeans, and it was a marvelous mirror image of the whites'. It was called the *Sanctity,* its leader was called the *pope* and he was backed by a pantheon of índio saints and a battalion of índio bishops. They prayed to a stone idol and exalted themselves smoking *holy grass.* They foretold the death of all whites or, failing that, their enslavement by índios. One of the inquisitor's first and most difficult cases concerned one of the colony's biggest landowners and slave dealers, who was sheltering the Sanctity on his land and was accused of revering their stone god when he went to deal with them. That the landowner had caused a pregnant African woman—from one of the first shipments of African slaves, who was eating dirt in her despair—to be thrown alive into a furnace was by comparison a venial offense. The landowner had only done it to frighten her and the other African slaves and was sorry.

After Judaism and the Tupi heresy, the inquisitor was determined to root out Protestantism and blasphemy and the idea that fornication was acceptable behavior, and anyone who had had contact with the French was particularly suspect. Sex being an ideological matter too, and the inquisitor having held out the promise of leniency for colonists who spontaneously made frank and full confessions, there was a rush to recount the details of sexual life. The rush was to get clear before sexual partners named names, and there was a certain studied vagueness on the part of those under interrogation about the identities and numbers of people with whom they'd had sex. Only a tenth of the

Inquisition records were ever published, but the first revelations
from Bahia suggested that from the start the colony was the
theatre of vice it was called by an observer a couple of hundred
years later. One sin was reading the erotic novel *Diana,* which
was on the index of forbidden books. Thereafter things got
worse. The *unmentionable vice* was rife in the colony and the visitor found himself devoting a lot more attention to penetrations
of *the rear passage* than to those of *the natural front passage,* though
the activity of the male *dishonest member* was ubiquitous. There
was a lot of sex between young boys and between young girls
but also among married women as well as the usual suspects.
First up to depose was a white bearded priest notorious for his
activity among the local boys and for his passivity and *dishonest
touchings.* Penetration or not? Ejaculation or not? the inquisitor
always wanted to know, and whether the women had made use
of a penetrating instrument. Some of the male penetrators were
far too young—nine, ten—to have ejaculated, and others, clearly
worried about the possible additional sinfulness of ejaculation
following penetration, insisted they couldn't remember if they
too had come as their partner most certainly had.

Married women wrote love notes to younger women and shot
them longing provocative glances in the kitchen, older boys
turned younger ones over in bed and mounted them, pubescent
girls clutched and caressed each other nude. The inquisitor
uncovered a relentlessly repeated scenario of lifted dresses, lowered breeches, creaking hammocks and movements from bed to
bed under cover of darkness. Married women coupled passion-
ately *like a man and a woman,* young brothers similarly. A man
was charged with making love to a female donkey, and a herd
boy on an island, perhaps lacking human companionship, *between
the ages of eight and fourteen years . . . slept carnally, very often and
in many different places at many different times, with many animals,*

sheep, donkeys, cows and mares ... as if he had been an animal of the same kind. Bahia was a riot of polymorphous perversity.

Distance makes it hard now to know what came out through ingenuousness, what through panic and what through a determination to conceal the greater by confessing the lesser crime. Was the woman who told on her husband for eating a slice of pineapple just before taking communion thinking only of the pineapple? People were right to take precautions, since the inquisitor followed up and cross-checked obsessively, especially the sexual charges, and other *confessions* were simply denunciations of personal enemies. The thirteen-year-old wife who claimed that her Greek husband only ever entered her by *the rear passage*—adding that he had *threatened to cut her tongue out with his knife* if she spoke—turned out to have been put up to it by her family, and the Greek was acquitted at his trial. The seventeen-year-old schoolboy who refused money for sex with his spiritual mentor changed his mind when the offer was doubled and promptly fucked the priest. Another man, recalling twelve years later the erotic crimes of his adolescence, evoked a pastoral glimpse in the memory of his sexual friendship with a boy who lived on the same street when they were both fifteen. Through the dire bureaucratic filter of the inquisitor's registrar he recorded that

> in this way they alternately committed the said unmentionable sin, each one being sometimes agent and sometimes patient ... very often, at different times and in different places, now at home, now in the forest, now on the river banks, and this friendship and this low relationship lasted for the space of more or less a year, with the said sodomitic couplings taking place thrice in three days, twice in two days, from week to week and sometimes twice a day, such that there is no way of recalling how many times said carnal coupling occurred, but

they were many, as were many the times they joined their car-
nal natures and took their pleasure frontally, the said compan-
ion reaching ejaculation but the one confessing not stating that
he himself did.

The other boy, he remarked, and whether with regret went
unremarked by the scribe, was now married. The inquisitor was
doubtless soon banging on his door. Yet like most of the illicit
liaisons it had happened long ago and in the carefully given
evidence the details slipped away. Endless frenzied couplings
seemed to have been initiated by a young stranger passing
through, sleeping overnight, gone the next day to another town,
name long forgotten.

Yet in this fascicle of Inquisition reports of sexual crimes,
there is no adultery, no simple fornication. For the church, this
was a serious matter, so much that a score or so men were
hauled before the visitor for defending fornication as no sin.
Either the visitor tacitly realized his work would never end if
he included simple male with female sex in his brief and put it
at the bottom of the list, or else the inquisitors simply failed to
impress on the colonists that even ordinary sex was a crime outside marriage.

The inquisitorial visitor spent four years, from 1591 to 1595,
probing the illicit private life of the Brazilian colony. His sexual
obsessions—How did the women copulate? How many times
did the boys reach orgasm? Did anyone *see?*—and his minutely
punitive preoccupation with rooting out Judaism and all traces
of Judaic domestic culture punctiliously documented these hidden corners of life in Bahia and Pernambuco. Oddly, the Protestant heresy seemed less of a worry. The Tupi, who a few years
earlier had flourished along these opulent coasts, had already
been driven farther and farther back into the forest, and appeared
in the records—which were skewed toward life in the more

densely settled areas—only as occasional domestic slaves and already mainly present as mixed blood mamelucos, the first children of multiracial Brazil.

Gilberto Freyre said the early Portuguese settlers in Brazil fell into a kind of *sexual intoxication* as they had elsewhere, yet the sexual welter of Brazil was quite different from the distance and wariness of Portugal's erotic encounters with Africa and Asia. Beautiful and willing though the Tupi girls were, they were never the whole story. The sexual enthusiasms might have been spontaneous but at every point they were encouraged by the Portuguese authorities. Little underpeopled Portugal had to occupy coastal Brazil at almost any cost and start drawing on whatever riches its interior held. It had to populate Brazil or perish, and the Portuguese men threw themselves into the task with a will. They killed or enslaved the men and slept with the women and informal polygamy was the norm. Against natural inclination and the connivance of the secular powers, the church never had a chance. The church, moreover, as the inquisitorial records made clear by omission, had no interest at all in either the Tupi, the *blacks of the land*, or Africans, the *blacks of Guinea*, until they had been baptized. And in the face of the colony's sexual life, all the inquisitor could do was worry at the edges. The murder, rape and enslavement of the Tupi people by the church's flock found no reflection in the records of the Inquisition. What did concern the visitor, and very minutely, was whether a landowner or slave trafficker had bared his head before the stone idols of the índio Sanctity while he was up-country, or smoked índio tobacco, and whether the slaving parties when they were off raiding in the forests had eaten barbecued meat on Fridays or during Lent. It was not that a young Portuguese sailor raped a Tupi girl seen on a riverbank that disturbed the inquisitor, but that he had called out to his shipmates, as he leapt from the dinghy, that fornication was no sin. For the church, the local or imported blacks, unless and until they were baptized, were not entirely human.

The church had not got off to a good start in Brazil. The pope had appointed Brazil's first bishop forty years before the Inquisition arrived, and the bishop had found his flock hard to stomach. He was outraged when settlers took up the índio habit of smoking, and fought with the governor about the criminal license of life in Bahia. After five years of mounting indignation, in 1556 he set off back to Europe with a boatload of right thinking colonists to complain directly to the Portuguese king. They had barely left when their ship went aground in shallows just north of the São Francisco River and was wrecked. The bishop and the others waded ashore and were met by warriors of a tribe implacably hostile to the Portuguese invasion of their lands. In vain the sodden prelate's spiritual authority was explained to them by the other passengers. Brazil's first bishop had his skull ceremoniously split open and the warriors ate him, and proceeded to eat another hundred of Bahia's first citizens who had struggled ashore with the bishop onto what would later be the state of Alagoas.

———

On Friday nights Vavá's exuberance swelled with the crowds and the noise. I used to think it was his social nature taking off and fueled by the extra drinks he grabbed on the side as the work got more frenetic. But it was the thought of leaving it all behind that made him fizz. The Bangüê closed early on Saturday and stayed rigorously barred all through Sunday. You would have thought Vavá was having the time of his life each Friday evening, and he was, but what made his spirits soar was neither our company nor the good business he was doing, nor even the extra drinks. It was getting out of there. Late on Friday night, when the last client—usually me—had tottered off, and the chairs and tables were stacked, the floor swept, kitchen cleaned, accounts done, the waiters paid and the last glass washed, Vavá vanished into the dark and he never reappeared until halfway through Monday. The secret of Vavá's elation was his house at the beach.

Sunday was always a problem. The Savoy did a good *salada de bacalhau* and the company there was always a hoot. The Bangüê almost never offered bacalhau, at most the odd *bolinha de bacalhau*. There is nothing better with beer than bolinhas de bacalhau—small balls of shredded salt cod mixed with potato, egg and garlic, deep-fried and eaten with squirts of fresh lime juice and pimenta—and you could make a meal of them. Coming from the North Sea, bacalhau was enormously expensive and the most insanely illogical of Brazil's imports, but so it was even in Portugal. Taste, as always, transcended logic.

Quite why salt cod from the North Sea became such a strong presence in the cooking of the Mediterranean seaboard I never understood, and still less why bacalhau—whose Mediterranean name seemed to be a scrambling of the Dutch—should have been even more popular in Portugal than in the coastal cities of Italy. Portugal had access to the fish of the Atlantic as well as the Mediterranean's. Yet Lisbon had shops selling nothing but bacalhau and offering about twenty different qualities and cuts. In Naples the shops sold salted anchovies and olives as well, and offered nowhere near Lisbon's variety of *baccalà*. Taking salt cod from the North Sea via the Mediterranean across the Atlantic and across the equator to Brazil was an even greater improbability, and the farther the bacalhau got from where it started the less cheap it became. As a preserved food it was just as resistant in the tropics—but who, living on the tropical South Atlantic, needed to preserve fish for more than a few days?

There was a parallel here. Australia's early colonial life and its insecurities, later but not unlike Brazil's, offered some clues. A genteel visitor to Sydney in the early nineteenth century was struck by never being served fresh fish or seafood, amid a plenty like Brazil's, only salt cod or smoked salmon. The meat was fresh, from her landowning hosts' own livestock, the fish never. Fresh meat was a landowner's luxury—convicts ate salt beef and hardtack or *xarque*—but anyone could throw a line into the waters of Port Jackson and take home a splendid fish dinner. Not to mention the oysters covering the rocks. The only way of asserting your social standing when it came to eating fish was to stick to expensive and inferior preserved fish shipped across the globe from home. I think it was the same in Brazil's Northeast. Whites liked to remind themselves they were Portuguese and fidalgo, and clung, after centuries, to the old ways. The common forms of meat in Pernambuco were dried xarque and carne do sol. Fresh beef or kid was costly and unusual. Fresh fish was everywhere, but bacalhau was imported and recherché enough to count as extracivilized, and far too expensive for most people to afford, especially the descendants of slaves. Discriminations in the kitchen matched the vaster ones in the streets.

On Mondays the rest of the world went back to work and normal life resumed. Vavá was never forthcoming about his other life. He brought back crayfish and pitù and fish wrapped in banana leaves, and I asked him where it was he went. *Porto de Galinhas,* he said. Porto de Galinhas was *Chicken Port,* and fifty kilometers south of Recife. It was where African slaves were landed in Pernambuco after British pressure had ended the trafficking in 1850. It was around this time that a phrase became current in Brazil about keeping up appearances and being politically correct. You did things *para inglês ver,* for the English to see. Through their bank loans and investments the English controlled Brazil's economy and had to be accommodated, and a show was put on out of respect for their human rights concerns. The prison ships now arrived clandestinely, with a nod and a wink and a leer and the necessary cash passing among captain and agent and the customs officials of the Brazilian Empire. Ships bringing slaves no longer docked in Recife. Shiploads of *chickens* were unloaded more discreetly down the coast at the *chicken port,* and when a new load of *chickens* arrived down the coast the landowners and people dealers in Recife knew what they would find. Business in the port of Recife was *para inglês ver.* Business at the *porto de galinhas* was business as usual. There was no real town in Porto de Galinhas, just a good beach with big natural pools in the rocks at low tide, and good fishing. And a random agglomeration of weekend houses kept by people from Recife.

When summer came, and I was back in Recife, the air in the streets was heavy with the fragrant smoke of festive herbs being burnt. The sky was a blinding blue day after day. No more murky turbulence of winter, not a trace of the inky clouds that had sometimes rolled in from the ocean. A permanent high pressure had settled over the Northeast. The air was at thirty, thirty-five, forty degrees. Inflation was running at twenty percent a month. At the Bangüê in the evenings Cândido dipped his cheese in pimenta and talked about the Northeast and the years he lived in Bahia. When Cândido had headed home with his bulging briefcase and his gently swaying gut, Lia finished the accounts and came over for a drink and a talk while Vavá worked. Vavá himself passed on pungent pieces of information about some of the unremarkable looking figures who came and went in the evenings. José plied me with questions about Italy. Sometime between Christmas and the New Year, Vavá inquired with a studied casualness whether I'd like to come down to Porto de Galinhas with him and Lia on New Year's Eve. Alexandre would be driving them down in the huge old Chevrolet. Vavá said it offhandedly, barking a few words out of the side of his mouth while seeming to scrutinize something on the far wall. I said I would, with a nonchalance to match his own. But I was conscious of having passed a threshold.

VI

Stuffed Goat

Lula later claimed that he and his friends *achieved in three years things that normally would have taken thirty in this country,* but in the late 1970s Brazilian workers were already starting to think hard about their situation. They had more than Lula's sprightly leaflets to stimulate them. The military had been riding the Brazilian boom for years and now it was dying under them and workers who had been eating started to go hungry. After a decade of no strikes at all, in May of 1978 the metalworkers in the Saab Scania truck assembly plant rejected the wage rise they were offered and stopped work. They wanted not only a pay raise but the right to deal directly with the company, and the idea of cutting out the government's union structure was the more dangerous demand. The strike spread to workers at Volks-wagen, Ford, Mercedes-Benz, Chrysler, all the other big foreign owned car companies, and within ten days a hundred and fifty thousand workers were out. The military was caught wrong-footed. The workers got their raise and they got it directly from the carmakers. The striking workers were nearly as shocked as the army generals to see how strong they were.

The military responded by putting a decree through Congress

which outlawed strikes in *essential categories,* which included the metalworkers. In response Lula's union called a general strike for March 13 of the following year. The day came and Lula found himself that afternoon trying to speak to ninety thousand metalworkers in a football stadium that lacked a sound system or even a platform to speak from. There was only a little table, and Lula stood there, as he saw himself, *like a clown on top of the table.* His unamplified harangue was passed from mouth to mouth in Chinese whispers through the stands, rippling out in waves from the man on the table until it reached the farthest part of the stadium. *The strike may not be legal,* Lula said. *But it's just and legitimate . . . the laws were not made by us or by our representatives.* The meeting lasted four hours as tropical rain poured down. Two days later the government's labor court outlawed the strike. The day after that a hundred and seventy thousand metalworkers were on strike in São Paulo's industrial belt.

Everyone remembered the wet afternoon in the football stadium. *We realized that if we pooled our courage we became a giant,* said Lula. He had become a compelling speaker. *People listened to him for half an hour and thought he had been speaking for two minutes . . . they wanted more.* He worked from a few notes he'd scribbled on the back of his hand and he was drawing on something he'd absorbed as a child, maybe through his mother, on memories of the wandering preachers and ballad composing troubadors who worked the northeastern interior, men who knew their audience, knew their lives, knew how to transfix a crowd and make time stand still.

A week later, when the strikers refused to go back to work, troops of the military police surrounded the union offices and closed them down. Workers were banned from the stadium. Then Lula disappeared. There were days of alarm and disorientation among the metalworkers. Nobody knew where Lula was, or why he had vanished. Even later, it was never quite clear.

Without Lula, and menaced by armed troops, dogs and water cannons, the strike meetings dwindled. After days of panicky search the other strike leaders found Lula hiding out in a house, playing with his children on the floor. The army commander had telephoned and threatened to arrest him and he had lost his nerve. The other union leaders didn't know what to say. Lula didn't know what to say. The movement had got too big for him. But he got off the floor and went back to the striking workers. He went into the room where two thousand people were waiting to hear him and when he got to the head table he broke down and sobbed. People started cheering him, and it went on and on. *He recovered and made a wonderful speech. For the first time he aligned himself politically with the opposition. He'd never done that before.*

But the opposition, or at least the politicians who feebly opposed the military in the Brazilian Congress, did not return the support. Lula was in a weak position and got a poor deal and the strikers were badly let down. The workers felt betrayed and jeered their leaders, who wept. They were exhausted and badly scared. *Workers left the stadium that night calling me a traitor,* Lula remembered, and it was worse later when the employers broke the agreement and sacked the strike leaders in reprisal. Like the workers' gains, Lula's standing seemed lost forever after this defeat. But *he was born again out of the ashes.* Another strike was called in São Paulo six months later, but the military were ready and repression was swift. A union activist was shot dead outside a factory. Troops invaded churches which offered support—the Roman Catholic Church in São Paulo had an incomparably brave history of defending the people in the worst years of military rule—but something had started that was unstoppable. By the end of 1979 more than three million workers had gone on strike around the country. The Brazilian military had been in power for fifteen years. Enough was enough.

The restiveness among the industrial workers of São Paulo was always about living standards. For years the military had been cooking the books on inflation, and the earnings of Brazilian workers had been eaten away far more than the regime's economists revealed. But what made them so determined and so resilient in the car factories of São Paulo, after years of submission to the military, and what made workers all over the country act on their example, was something more. Their young leaders may have been groping for their tactics, but the people who filled the stadium were asserting their presence as working people, as producers of Brazil's wealth. Like the Polish workers in the shipyards of Gdansk who at the same time in another hemisphere were challenging a whole system of tyranny in demanding their rights, they wanted a voice in the running of their country. The São Paulo strikes of 1979 were about democracy. The regime's readiness to call out the troops against workers, and the failure of the regime's Congress to defend the workers' rights, led the young strike leaders ineluctably to see that union action on its own was not enough. Brazil's workers needed a voice in Congress.

The generals too saw in 1979 that Brazil was changing in ways that the military could no longer control. Military rule had begun its own long disintegration, which the military itself announced as *a process of slow and gradual opening.* It began with an amnesty for Brazil's political exiles who had fled arrest under the National Security Law. The politicians came back and started talking, the old hands, about forming a broad front against the military. Lula and the others found what they planned was far too broad, since it found room for some of the regime's old allies, people who were no friends of the workers. They were not going to play the old game. There was no going back now and in February of 1980 the Workers' Party came into being.

It might not have been a broad front, but it was a mixed

enough bag. At the core of the Workers' Party were Brazilians tough enough to have lived through terrible things and young enough to respond to the changes they were living through now. Compared with some of them, Lula was untested. One of them was a student leader who had been imprisoned early by the military. When the American ambassador was kidnapped in 1969 he was one of the prisoners freed in exchange and was flown to Cuba. There José Dirceu had his face altered and trained in guerrilla warfare techniques, ready to take up the armed struggle in Brazil. He was back in Brazil and organizing resistance when the amnesty meant he had to have himself made recognizable again. Others had already taken up the armed struggle. In the tragic wake of Che Guevara, another student leader, José Genoino, who was the northeasterner son of peasants from Ceará and knew life in the other Brazil, had been one of a few dozen creators of a guerrilla *foco* in the Amazon jungle. They were destroyed by a military offensive of fifteen thousand troops and Genoino, almost the only survivor, was tortured and imprisoned until the time of the amnesty.

The union struggle gathered new life after the near defeat of the year before. A hundred and forty thousand metal workers stopped work at the beginning of April. The government's labor court pronounced the new strike led by Lula illegal. The army and the military police came out again. A hundred thousand workers, with their women and children, who were gathered in the football stadium, saw the army helicopters hover overhead. The helicopters' doors were open and the people below could see the soldiers' machine guns raked above the crowd. The din of the rotors drowned the speakers' voices; the crowd stayed still and sang the Brazilian anthem against the noise. Lula and the other union leaders were arrested days later under the National Security Law, and held incommunicado by the torturers and killers of the Department of Political and Social Order. The strike went on without them and after a month they were freed. At his later trial Lula was sentenced by a military court to three and a half years in prison, but Brazilian justice was slow and by the end of 1981 things were moving irresistibly against the military's justice. The Workers' Party already had nearly half a million active members and by the end of the following year eight members of the federal Congress. Lula's trial was annulled.

The Workers' Party led the great campaign around Brazil in 1984 for DIRECT ELECTIONS NOW—this was the time the TV Globo news, showing the hundreds of thousands in São Paulo, claimed they were celebrating the city's anniversary. A million people massed in Rio to demand elections. When Congress voted against, the Workers' Party alone rejected the controlled congressional election of a new president allowed by the military in 1985. The following year the Workers' Party doubled its number of federal deputies to sixteen, and Lula won his seat in Congress with the biggest vote of any candidate in Brazil. In the local government elections of 1988 the Workers' Party won control of thirty-eight city administrations around Brazil, São Paulo's among them. The Workers' Party was unstoppable. The year after that was 1989, which would see the first direct election of a Brazilian president in twenty-nine years. In Lula the Workers' Party already had its candidate.

On New Year's Eve the Bangüê closed early for the usual reason—Vavá was leaving town—but first he had some regular customers to look after. A group of students always spent the last afternoon of the year at the Bangüê's outside tables, and while the rest of the city was visibly closing down and getting ready to party, this happy group stayed on and there was no way Vavá was going to hurry them off. I came back later and they were gone.

The Bangüê was closed and almost dark inside, but Lia and Vavá had made a clearing in the forest of stacked tables and chairs and were having a last cold beer. Alexandre brought the car around and we set off into the night for Porto de Galinhas.

Recife was not big on nocturnal illumination, even in the main streets, and we drove through a shadowy low-rise urban sprawl. We were making a detour because Vavá decided he wanted to drop in on a university professor he knew who had once bought a lot of wood sculptures. The professor was some kind of technocrat and a high adviser to the Brazilian government. *Part of the cúpula,* Vavá said. In Italy the *cupola* was the governing body of Cosa Nostra, but it seemed not to have a bad sense in Brazil. We got to a part of town where there were trees, and bumped along a narrow, deeply potholed street—the Chevrolet's suspension was almost gone, and you could see why—and stopped outside a pair of iron gates that made an opening in a high white wall. This was the professor's villa and ours was a surprise visit. We weren't out of the car before a couple of giant Doberman pinschers hurled themselves at the gate. In the dark they looked like small black racehorses with long pointy teeth. They seemed to want to tear our throats out. A barefoot youth in shorts appeared and grabbed their chains and wrestled them into a cyclone-wired compound beside the swimming pool. Silently, they hurled themselves toward us again and again and the cyclone wire pinged and hummed.

The Dobermans weren't the only dogs around. From inside the house came a frenzy of demented yapping by many dogs. The house was a curious stone construction that was part modernist and part Middle Eastern. Its blank outer wall made a second barrier against the world, and inside the rooms opened onto a courtyard with a garden of white river boulders and cactus. The courtyard was glassed in and made you wonder whether you were standing in a room or a garden. There were a number of large black wooden carvings from the northeastern interior against the walls and a dozen tiny champagne-colored poodles racing around and barking hysterically. The glass roof, the stone walls, the stone floor, the stone garden all multiplied the noise until it neared the pain threshold.

It took a while to summon the professor and his family, who were very much not celebrating the imminence of 1991. He was a stocky, guarded, hostile figure and his wife, who appeared through another door, was pale and hollow eyed and appeared to have been weeping. Eventually a young adult son and a young adult daughter emerged sluggishly from other rooms. The noise of the dogs did not abate and no one tried to quiet them. The poodles seemed to be trying to tell us something, as the Dobermans had outside. Vavá kept up a flow of bright conversation and everyone else kept up a pretense that human voices were audible over the barking. Since we didn't leave immediately—Vavá was irrepressible, and Lia kept her poise—after about twenty minutes someone sullenly handed me half a glass of warm beer. It was fairly clear that the professor had no plans to enlarge his collection of wooden statues. On our way out, I asked the barefoot youth if it was okay to pat the Dobermans. He looked at me as if I were mad. Happy New Year, everyone.

We headed south in silence for a while. On the outskirts of the low-rise sprawl, we passed strings of dark-skinned boys and girls walking along the shoulder of the narrow paved strip, on their way to parties. They were all dressed in white for the arrival of the New Year. The people wore white who sent off rafts of flowers and lighted candles into the sea toward Africa, for Yemanjá, the Yoruba mother of the seas. On New Year's morning the little boats of candles and flowers would be washed up with the bottles on the beach. All you could see in the dark night now was white clothes—white T-shirts, white shorts, white skirts, white shoes floated along in the darkness.

Porto de Galinhas seemed almost deserted, a darkened huddle of low houses on a network of dusty dirt tracks. Their owners were celebrating in town. We bumped along a rough track to a garden gate. A wide path with low steps led to a small darkened house at the top of a rise, but Vavá led us straight to a bower in a corner and set about lighting a fire. It was nearly midnight and time for dinner. Alexandre went up to the house in the dark and returned with a bleeding gash on his foot. He'd fallen, he said, and wandered off in the Chevrolet to find a doctor. But the charcoal on the barbecue was soon glowing, drinks were poured, and Vavá grilled some slices of zebu hump. Zebu were cattle from India—their name was Tibetan—who thrived in the Northeast, storing food for hard times in their hump, and whose meat was tender and delicious. At some point 1990 turned into 1991. We toasted. Alexandre came out of the shadows with his foot freshly bandaged. At some point we made our way up the path and tumbled into bed.

Vavá and Lia were up before me next morning and offered strong coffee and breadfruit. The house, Vavá muttered with more of his elaborate offhandedness, was just a prefabricated wooden thing like most of the other beach houses. The structure may have been prefabricated, but this house was not like the others. It was stripped back to its wooden essentials, which were all finely finished and coated with a uniform dark protective stain. It was like being in a nutshell. There were no false ceilings or wall linings in this hermit's retreat, hardly any furniture or fittings or any content at all, let alone random junk lying around. There was a restful austerity about it, a minimalism that spoke of a discreet but powerful creative will. Well ventilated, protected by a verandah at the front, across which a hammock was slung, a northeastern hammock with a lacy hand knotted fringe, and shaded by trees, it was dark and cool under the summer sun.

All this enhanced the shock to the eyes of stepping outside into the brilliant profusion of the garden. There was lawn on each side of the steps leading down from the verandah, and between the lawn and the high palisade of stained wood that ran around the perimeter was an opulence of flowering tropical vegetation. Vavá and Lia had brought each plant down from Recife, and made this garden. I could now see how carefully the shady bower had been created around the fireplace, which had a chimney to carry the smoke away, and the table where we'd been the night before. Across the path from the barbecue, under the opposite fence and framed by a brilliant purple bougainvillea, was a larger-than-life figure of a bearded Saint Francis carved in wood by a sculptor of the drylands. A garden hose kept water running through his cupped hands, and a flurry of small tropical birds were splashing and twittering there.

This was Vavá's retreat. Materially it was very little. Vavá and Lia had no money to speak of, and this beach house, hardly more than a cabin, was the only real estate they owned. In Recife they lived in a small rented apartment. A quality of mind, however, had been brought to bear on this place over the years. There was something old Brazilian, aboriginally Brazilian, about the austerity of the human habitation and the natural opulence of the simple well-tended garden. The índios would have been at home in this clean-swept space, the simple wood, the exuberant green. Vavá went on being offhand about it, but he was humming with pleasure at my admiration and my own pleasure in what he had made. This was a place of the mind, *Annihilating all that's made / To a green thought in a green shade.* When we walked down to the beach, calling on a couple of neighbors to wish them well for the new year, I saw how far Vavá's green shade was his own doing. The settlement of Porto de Galinhas was an arid, dusty, uncared-for slum. People had planted cottages on their blocks of wasteland and let the wasteland lie.

Rubbish lay in the dusty rutted tracks that ran between them. The green well-watered place surrounding Vavá's, and the look and setting of the house itself, were a single island among the dry and monochrome dereliction.

Down on the beach we met Paulo. He was a tall thin black man with big hooded eyes and was the source of the fish that Vavá had wrapped in banana leaves. He was the source of the fish Vavá grilled later that day and in general kept Vavá and Lia supplied at Porto de Galinhas. They had an arrangement. Vavá had invested in a *jangada* for Paulo to do his fishing from and Paulo, who had no other work, would supply fresh fish when Vavá and Lia came down with friends. We went out into the bay on Paulo's jangada and I dived into the clear water and struck off some distance, then floated and looked back at the handsome boat. It was a modern catamaran—jangadas were no longer made of logs lashed together—but it still had the beautiful uplifted triangular sail like an Arab dhow's that the Tupi called *cutinga,* the *white tongue.* Cabral's men had seen jangadas off the coast in 1500 and described them to the Portuguese king. Countless of them were still licking the waves of the Northeast's coastal waters.

We had a beer with Paulo on the beach, and from Vavá's sharp allusions I picked up a notion of Paulo's laid-back life in Porto de Galinhas, of the child he had fathered on a local primary-school teacher, a small daughter he took no responsibility for and in no way helped to raise but of whom he was nevertheless very fond and of whose infant exploits in music and arithmetic he was proud. Then Vavá asked after the *Swiss gentleman,* and I learned that Paulo had taken the Swiss gentleman, lately returned to his mountains, for an outing on the jangada and that the visitor had been greatly taken with Paulo. A little dalliance may or may not have ensued aboard the raft. Vavá clearly thought it had and Paulo didn't bother to contradict him.

The Swiss infatuation was well known around the water's edge and Paulo had clearly gained some cachet as an object of desire and maybe a little short term boost to his income.

Vavá talked a lot on the beach about the people we met and the people back in Recife. Cândido had a beach house nearby. I had never found out quite what the enigmatic Cândido did— was he some kind of economist? Vavá's eyes glittered. A relative working in one of the banks in Recife had yielded information. Cândido, said Vavá in a low voice, was the chief of military intelligence for the Northeast. We both had to remember not to let Cândido know we knew this. The news reminded me of the day I had been walking down one of Recife's main avenues by the river. A large American car had tooled past. The driver wore mirror shades and his elbow was resting on the door, and it was only when he gave a lazily economical salute as the car slid past that I had recognized Cândido. The memory of that odd moment, and the sense of being watched, came back now. But you never knew with Vavá. Back in Recife a few days later the chief prosecutor of the state of Minas Gerais dropped in for a drink with Vavá, who introduced me as a gold medal swimmer from the 1956 Olympics. *Goodness,* spluttered the chief prosecutor, slopping beer on his tie and shaking my hand. *What an honor.* I wondered how many other of the Bangüê's regulars knew what Cândido didn't know they knew about his work, and realized Vavá had been looking at my Italian papers while I swam.

———

If Roberto Marinho found something a little unreal in Fernando's announcement at the end of 1988 that he intended to be Brazil's next head of state, it might have been that Fernando— who had once modeled designer clothes at a charity do promoted by the wife of one of Brazil's dictator presidents—put him in mind of someone out of one or another of the Globo soaps.

Marinho had already noticed that Fernando adored the good things of life and tended to overdress in what he saw as a European manner; and he knew that Fernando's family belonged to that tiny number of Brazilians who might have found in the telenovelas' handling of dynastic conflict and family secrets among the very rich not an escape into fantasy but a kind of gritty realism.

Fernando was already better on TV than in real life. He had lost interest in being governor of Alagoas almost before he was elected. The results were barely in when he took off with Rosane for a two-month holiday in Europe. He came back in 1987 to a triumphant and carefully orchestrated landing in Alagoas. Bands played, flags waved, fireworks exploded and Fernando spoke from the back of a truck at Maceió airport. The crowd that had been ferried to the airport was dark skinned and short. Fernando was athletic, white and six feet tall, with longish black hair and a born-to-rule nose. He alone, in the stifling heat of that late summer afternoon in Maceió, wore a suit and tie. *All of us here,* he told his listeners, *are the children of hope.* The crowd went wild and film of that sunny afternoon was useful later, especially the aerial footage of the motorcade. The actual inauguration was washed out by a crushing tropical downpour.

He called them *my people.* The people of Alagoas were the poorest, state by state, in Brazil. They had the lowest literacy level, the shortest life expectancy and the highest infant mortality rate in the country. While Fernando was governor they stayed that way. Fernando did build the Virgin of the Poor Housing Estate on the outskirts of Maceió, which was still unpaid for when he resigned to contest the presidency, and a church dedicated to the same Virgin. She was his own invention, an image of the way he saw his people. Fernando was quick to pick up on popular resentments, and good on sound bites. He tapped into anger at corruption in the Brazilian bureaucracy, and since he had a vicious tongue when he was whipping up a crowd, his attacks on the president were much enjoyed. Fernando was young and modern. He was a *modernizer* and the visuals showed it. Suddenly, amid the dreary array of aging and compromised figures from the past, he was the second most admired politician in Brazil.

Early in the presidential year of 1989, Fernando had three very expensive television programs made about himself, each an hour long. He made deals with three small political parties which got the films transmitted free throughout Brazil as the electoral law guaranteed. Fernando and Rosane and the two children of his marriage to Lilibeth were seen heading up the Amazon in a small boat and looking concerned about ecology; Fernando was shown pointing at rice left rotting in government warehouses while the people went hungry. Fernando spoke vibrant lines against corruption in government and inflation of the currency, and each change of theme was punctuated by a chorus of young people shouting, *We want a new Brazil.* The first program took his approval rating from nine to fifteen percent, and the next two more than doubled that. By the middle of 1989, a few months before the vote, he was at forty percent and no one else came near him.

Now Roberto Marinho began to have second thoughts. He invited Fernando to the great mansion in Cosme Velho overlooking Rio. He and Lily had lately redecorated the whole house, and in the garden Marinho kept a flock of pink flamingos, flown in from Africa. He kept another flock of pink flamingos in the garden of his island home off Angra dos Reis, a beautiful cove on the coast an hour's drive south of Rio. Fernando looked down on Rio and the world at dusk as Marinho's pink flamingos performed their twilight dance, and he was deeply admiring of what he saw. He still nursed a secret rancor about Marinho's earlier dismissiveness but he didn't let that show, and Marinho was deeply appreciative of Fernando's awe at the Globo kitsch. *Brizola's been here half a dozen times,* Marinho said of the aging demagogue who was still Fernando's main rival. *Unlike you, he's never once remarked on the beauty of the view. A man who can't appreciate this view hasn't got the sensibility it takes to govern Brazil.* Roberto Marinho could not get his mind off the old demagogue who was in the lead, and hadn't noticed Lula's steady rise. He offered to fix things with any Brazilian TV channels that weren't already supporting Fernando for president. *Let me know who they are and I'll have a word with them.* Not everyone shared the new enthusiasm for Fernando. His hosts at one lunch thought Fernando was *clinically mad,* locked into his own fantasies and lacking all sense of the world around him. Some journalists noticed how brief his displays of youth and energy were at each campaign stop, how very short his *raucous and exalted* speeches, lacking range and tone. He scrambled back into the plane, slept through the flights, seemed gaga, never speaking with the press or his advisers, never reading. He looked like an actor, wrung out and empty. All these hardened political observers were remarking that a wider gap than usual lay between Fernando's words and the reality of him.

From September, a couple of months before the first vote, all the candidates got free TV time. Fernando and Lula each had ten minutes a day. The time was free but production values were not. PC made sure Fernando was constantly followed and filmed, and their campaign had $4 million worth of equipment, a hundred hours of footage already cataloged into forty themes and a six-thousand-square-meter TV studio. Their first effort opened with Fernando surveying Brazil from Monte Pascoal, the mountain overlooking the place of the Portuguese landing in 1500. His long black hair flapped in the wind. Then viewers saw Fernando defying the sugar growers under a tropical downpour, hair plastered to his scalp. It looked like a shampoo commercial. This was not necessarily a bad thing. Lula's hair was as dense and wiry as the outback scrub. But 1989 was not about hair, and Lula's team faced problems of a quite different order.

The Workers' Party had no money. Lula arrived to make his first campaign film wearing a borrowed suit too big for him. The studio was a rented room in São Paulo and the set was a desk against a beige wall. Lula looked around and asked, *Isn't all this going to cost too much?* There was also the problem of approach. In Brazil TV meant Globo and Globo meant soaps and managed news and the Fernando candidacy. Lula, some in the Workers' Party thought, needed a *people's TV* utterly unlike Globo's. The pragmatists replied that this would take years to evolve. There was an election to win and a style to use—the only style people knew. The conflict grew bitter. The conflict was resolved. Lula's first TV spot began with something strangely like Rede Globo's little logo symbol, the shining sphere that hypnotized Brazilians every night. The little translucent Globo ball came on bouncing and spinning until it froze in midscreen and people heard *Rede Globo, plim plim*—*Rede* was *Network.* This time the little sphere bounced, spun and froze firmly on the left. *Rede Povo, plim plim. Povo* was *People* and this was the People Network. Lula told viewers that *now they could see the truth on TV.* The Workers' Party program went on to parody all the Globo staples. *Globo Reporter* was answered by *Povo Reporter, Globo Gold* by *Povo Gold.*

Regime TV had never been laughed at before, not like this, on the medium itself. The Workers' Party shoestring shows led the ratings. Lula surged. TV Globo made plans to sue. Fernando, who was relaxing on a Caribbean beach when Lula's surge began, berated his team for not doing more of the gritty newsreel-style stuff that had produced his own spurt earlier. Lula's new jingle kept running through Fernando's head. *Lula la. Lula there.* Ooh la la. *A star was shining. Hope was growing.* It was insipid but infectious. That month Lula picked up in the streets. While Fernando lay on the beach with a forty-three percent rating, Lula worked the crowds. Sometimes, around Brazil, he spoke to seven meetings a day. In September fifty thousand people went for Lula in São Paulo, the biggest crowd yet. Sixty thousand in Belo Horizonte and there was a month to go until the vote. Brizola, the honey tongued old rabble-rouser, faded on TV. Lula, the week before the vote, drew crowds of a quarter of a million in Rio and São Paulo. Television, however, still had a part to play.

———

Lula pushed out Brizola. They were both well behind Fernando and there was almost nothing between them, but Lula came in second in November and now the race was between Fernando and Lula for December. The left had been divided. If you put Lula's vote and Brizola's together, there was a clear edge over Fernando. Nobody could feel confident. Fernando lunched with Roberto Marinho a week after the vote in Lily's Copacabana apartment, and the Globo patriarch came out after coffee talking happily about *modernization.* Elsewhere it was panic time. Fernando saw that Lula scared some people and that he had four weeks to work on that fear. In São Paulo, the head of the industrialists' organization announced that *eight hundred thousand businessmen would leave Brazil if Lula won,* and this was a good start. Fernando told the nation that the Workers' Party was heading for *a blood bath* in Brazil, which raised anxiety levels. But he was floundering until a society friend of his mother's told Dona Leda that her servants were threatening to occupy her apartment *when Lula won.* Fernando told a TV talk show that Lula would confiscate people's life savings. That families would have *their front doors broken down* and rooms seized to house the homeless. *You'll have Workers' Party militants living with you,* Fernando said, staring into the camera lens, his shirt drenched with sweat.

Lula went on closing the gap. Five days before the final vote, one poll showed Fernando four points ahead of Lula. Another had him only one point ahead, and the Workers' Party was famous for its dazzling electoral finishes. The artists from TV Globo did a TV program for the Workers' Party and sang *Lula la,* while *O Globo* printed a front page editorial on Lula called THE ROAD TO FASCISM. Fernando's elder brother Leopoldo, lately sacked from TV Globo and now Fernando's campaign manager in São Paulo, gave twenty-four thousand dollars in an envelope to Lula's old girlfriend, who went on TV and said *I could never support a man who tried to destroy my life.* She said Lula had tried to force her to abort their child. Lula was shaken by this. *O Globo* printed a front page editorial on THE RIGHT TO KNOW. There was going to be a TV debate just before the vote and TV Globo urged Fernando to look more human—less cold, less hard, less impeccable, less like a model, less like an automaton, less like *a man without a past.* Lula had done better in an earlier confrontation because he seemed like a real man with something to say. Fernando should *look as if he hasn't been resting all day. And not talk so much.* Fernando lay on his bed and stared at the ceiling all day before the encounter. He canceled his appointments and took no calls. Everything was slipping away from him; the whole manic drive for power had been in vain. He felt drained and limp. He had played the statesman and lost the first debate. This time he would act like a real person and go for the jugular.

Four hundred thousand people rallied for Lula in the center of Rio. It was his last meeting before the vote. That night Lula went back to São Paulo for a dinner with his unionists and metalworkers and it was daybreak when he got to bed. The morning before the debate he flew to Brasilia to meet Brazilian bishops and in the afternoon he flew back to São Paulo. He was exhausted, and went home to his wife, Marisa, and his children.

She was still fizzing with rage at the former girlfriend. An army of people was tramping through their little living room. While a barber trimmed his hair and beard, Lula said suddenly, *Tell them I'm not going.* Nobody took any notice. When he got to the TV studio, he said, *They messed with my daughter. They messed with my family.* The debate was about to start and Lula said, *I'm not going to shake that son of a bitch's hand.* Fernando smiled, suddenly energized. *Who wants to shake the hand of that scum?* Lula hoped aloud that it wouldn't last too long.

It lasted nearly three hours and seemed longer. Fernando ranted about *armed struggle* and *chaos* and *life savings* being seized and *apartments requisitioned.* Hunched and defensive and mumbling and standing on a box behind the lectern to bring him nearer Fernando's height, Lula inertly recited the Workers' Party positions. Fernando, who had earlier attacked Brazil's *corrupt elite* in the name of *the little man,* now stood against *rubbish, chaos, intolerance, intransigence, totalitarianism, the red flag.* The drab and useless old Brazilian standoff between wealth and labor, privilege and deprivation was acted out again, and thoughtful Brazilians were mortified. They were watching the past, and the country needed something new. When they turned off the cameras Lula said, *We're fucked. We've lost the election.* Fernando felt he'd won a resounding triumph and sulked for days when others demurred. He stopped speaking to people and lay on his bed and stared at the ceiling again and took no calls. There was a day and a half to go before the vote.

Roberto Marinho saw the six-minute Globo news report on the debate at lunchtime next day and he was not happy with what he saw. He wanted Lula more clearly the loser. A new version was ready for the Globo evening news. It gave Fernando most of the time, and intercut his more lucid statements with Lula's worst moments of stumbling uncertainty. The editor who made the final cut said, *I never did dirtier work in my life.* On voting day the TV news had something different. The owner of a supermarket chain had been kidnapped for ransom. On polling day police took the kidnappers, tortured them and paraded them to the media in Workers' Party T-shirts. Fernando's brother Leopoldo had been calling TV Globo all day demanding they say the Workers' Party was behind the kidnapping, *because Collor's election depends on it.* The kidnappers were not even Brazilian.

Fernando got thirty-five million votes and Lula thirty-one million. The president-elect came out of his sulk. A few days later he said to PC, *Without you, I wouldn't even have made it to the second round.* PC was over the moon. All through the year he had dined unremarked in the finest restaurants and chewed the bitter crust of the éminence grise. PC was too irrepressible to make a good éminence grise, and if he hadn't been such a positive person he might have resented the way he was always being pushed offstage as if he were some kind of embarrassment. He had been telling people all year how close he was to the candidate. Now, during the day, he called himself *the president's best friend.* Sometimes, after a few bottles of French champagne in the evening, he said, *I give Fernando his orders.* This got into the papers and Fernando was ropable. For the first and last time he threatened to break with PC. But PC needed people to know how close he was to Fernando. After the election, PC ran into a senator called Fernando Henrique Cardoso as they both left the Trianon restaurant after long lunches at separate tables, and PC told him, *The president likes you.* The senator wondered who the fat little bald guy was. This was the cross PC had to bear, while Fernando was already taking on the hieratic distance of a statesman. Fernando had his hair freshly trimmed in a more conventional, older style, and was already more formal in his dress and manner, even to his intimates. *I want to bring back dignity to Brazil,* he told them, his sense of himself returning as the votes came in. Brazil was now formally embodied in the person of

Fernando. And Roberto Marinho stood in the garden with Lily and gazed at his African flamingos moving in the dusk. Never had the pinkness of their twilight dance looked lovelier. Never had the view inspired such inner peace. Marinho was looking forward to his eighty-fifth year.

———

The northeastern drylands have a great population of goats. They are larger than billygoats and none of them is merely white. They come in brown, black, gray, coffee, dappled, piebald, skew-bald. They have large, contemplative yellow eyes—quintessentially ruminant eyes—and huge floppy ears, which frame their narrow faces like great flaps of ornamental dark velvet as they stare in curiosity if they meet you on foot. They always know you are an outsider. A goat is a *bode*. Nourished by all the spiky, tough and fragrant drought resisting bushes of the dryland scrub, the bode's flesh is strong tasting. People in the drylands barbecue and eat great strips of it when they can, and when the best parts have been eaten, the entrails are chopped up and stuffed into the animal's stomach, an instance of the culinary resourcefulness of people who can afford to waste nothing. The *buchada de bode* is a dish analogous to the Scottish haggis, only much more interesting, and you never find it outside the drylands where the goats live.

I went to Garanhuns in the interior of Pernambuco looking for a place where the buchada, someone told me, was exceptional. I trudged around for some time before discovering that the place was out of town and next to an army barracks. The proximity of the army barracks was a hopeful sign and I found the place catering to poor boy conscripts and unbelievably cheap. It was barely noon when I arrived. Garanhuns is high above the sea and prides itself on a temperate climate, but I quickly finished a bottle of cold beer and ordered another. A young soldier was eating barbecued goat off a hot plate fired by an oil flame. Eating a lot of barbecued goat. Outside, other soldiers were heading back to the barracks across the square, and then a group of businessmen in white shirts and ties settled in and ordered the buchada. They had big soft waists and looked at home and clearly found the place worth a detour. A faintly ominous cloud of small houseflies and mosquitoes was hovering in the air. We were downhill from the town itself and, it was my impression, above a swamp. The flies kept landing on the rim of the beer glass, and later they dived into the plates. They seemed friendly enough.

Being a ruminant, the goat has two stomachs, and when you order a buchada you get a couple of small grayish bladders, the larger being like a little soccer ball with a distinct honeycomb pattern imprinted on the outside, presumably meaning the stomach has been turned inside out, and another smaller one like a tiny American football. They come with a certain amount of juice exuded from them, some poached vegetables, and the rice, beans and the *pirão,* a kind of heightened translucent gravy made by adding manioc flour to the juices, which no Brazilian dish involving juices ever comes without. The faintly obscene forms of the moist and grayish bladders on the plate, the grayish liquid gently oozing from them, the surgical look of the neatly sewn seams, the dubiously unidentifiable chopped up gray contents that spilled out in a little puff of unnameably flavored steam when you hacked the soft bags open suggested the work of some unmentionable surgeon. The cooking instructions, when I looked them up later, seemed to belong in a mortician's handbook. *Clean and wash well stomach, tripes and intestines . . . Add the boiled blood, which should now be solid, to the pan.* I have rarely tasted anything more delicious. Compared with buchada the haggis is a drab thing. Buchada, whose remote origin is in the inland Beira regions of Portugal, is fragrant with lime, cumin, black pepper, mint and coriander, as well as the tomato, capsicum, garlic and onions with which the chopped heart, lungs and liver are mixed. There is none of the suet and oatmeal that make the haggis the heavy and bulky food of people who live in a freezing rain-lashed place. Just a piece of bacon to enhance the flavor.

A very young woman served it. The proprietor was sitting outside in the big square by the barracks. His big black mustache flowing into a spadelike white beard made him look like Karl Marx in an old pair of football shorts, taking his leisure in a patriarchal way and watching some kids play football. The teams were largely made up of his own children. It wasn't clear whether the young woman serving was his daughter or his wife and it seemed indelicate to ask. In any case, there was hardly time. I had to meet Pedro, who was taking me to Varzea Comprida. I wanted to see where Lula came from.

This was the other reason I was in Garanhuns. Neither of us knew quite where we were headed. At this point Pedro had not even heard of Varzea Comprida and he was a local. But he had a vague idea where the clan lived and we headed out of town and downhill again, along a narrow paved road with scrubby plants on either side. We pulled up beside a middle-aged woman wearing a T-shirt printed with a faded Workers' Party slogan. She was striding along the side of the road, flinging out her legs in the tireless way of northeasterners, but she happily stopped and talked. Pedro asked her where Lula's people lived. Pressganged into the quest, he was now as eager as I was. The woman was unsurprised, and spoke as if Lula hadn't gone south more than fifty years earlier, as if he were still out there in the scrub, and told us about a dirt track that led off the road some way ahead. We overshot it, but I saw an opening in the bushes and called out to Pedro, who braked sharply and reversed along the dirt verge. We swung off the narrow paved road onto a dirt track that we never would have found on our own.

We jolted along a narrow path over sandy soil, with a narrow ridge of green between the wheel tracks. The vegetation was neither dense nor high, but its pale and youthfully eager fronds leaned toward one another from each side of the track, at the height of a tall man. We were bumping along a dappled light green tunnel which from time to time opened out into a little clearing. We saw, at intervals, a goat, a sow, a string of hurrying earthbound little fowl which might have been quail. Once or twice a big lizard crossed the track, rearing up and throwing out its chest like a tiny angry dinosaur. In some of the larger clearings, behind a few large bushes and surrounded by carefully swept and beaten sandy ground, stood a little white-painted mud brick house, roofed with thatch or tiles. Near the houses were people, women and two young girls, moving along a net-work of smaller foot tracks even more closely hemmed in by leaves. These women and young girls were part of Lula's family. One woman, when we asked where Lula had been born, was starting to explain when Gilberto passed by. Gilberto was about Lula's age and size and had a neatly trimmed gray beard like Lula's, but instead of being covered by Lula's scrubby thatch of low-growing hair his head was a shining mahogany dome. Gil-berto was heading over in that direction and if we let him change first he would show the way. We followed him to another tiny white windowless house in another clearing of spotless beaten earth and he hurried into its darkness, scattering a family of small dark hens that were pecking at grains of corn. He reemerged in a fresh polo shirt and a clean pair of trousers and we set off along the track, following the plumy tail of an eager dog. At the point where we turned off onto yet another track that went up a low hill, we met yet another cousin of Lula's, a powerful youth in T-shirt and shorts who lived in a house near Lula's old place.

Everyone here seemed to be a cousin of Lula's, but there were degrees of cousinhood. Gilberto spoke with the authority of greater closeness. He was Lula's age, and the only one who looked like Lula. If Lula had stayed on the land, been fit and active and darkened by the sun, and not gone gray and soft and somewhat paunchy in decades of indoor dealings, he would have looked very much like Gilberto. And Gilberto spoke with a crisp and unassuming directness and a personal weight in his words that made you think of Lula. Gilberto was articulate and forthright, not overawed by his cousin, nor resentful as one left behind, and showed none of the babbling overexcitement of a city person who might claim some tenuous link to a celebrity. He was just pleased Lula had done some good for his people down south. The younger cousin, an amiable but silent youth, nodded emphatically. The family regarded Lula as an exponent of their own values and showed no surprise at his trajectory. They seemed to find it natural that their values had such a powerful voice in the land. It was not, in Brazil's history, natural at all.

Gilberto seemed amused by my visit, and said a journalist from Rio had been looking around a few weeks before. For Long Plain this was a lot of movement. Interest was clearly growing out there in the world. I asked if Lula—who was not formally in the running, though clearly the favorite by far—might win the presidency at the end of the year. Gilberto's eyes crinkled up. *He's already had three goes —.* I mentioned that Fernando Collor was back in public life and planning to lead Brazil again. Gilberto's eyes crinkled again. *You mean that guy who stole it?* We were wandering around as we spoke, passing an animal from time to time. There was one of everything except the chickens. A mule, a goat, a cow, a pig, a dog. Each animal had its own place, its own comforts gathered around it. The pig was particularly well tended, sprawled in a dirt bed under a four-poster canopy of dense fronds, trying to get some sleep in the heat, its head thrust into a gunnysack. Not for the first time, in seeking out someone's distant origin, I wondered why anyone would have wanted to leave. Varzea Comprida on this good day was like a pastoral dream, a magic world of people and animals and tiny white houses hidden in the green. Lula's mother had cooked on a woodstove and washed the family clothes in the river. But they had no food, only bought rice when the children were too sick to digest farofa. The children had no shoes. Even now, the little white houses seemed to have no electricity.

It's not there anymore, Gilberto said suddenly. *It was pulled down a while back.* There was a newer house nearby, where the younger cousin lived. The small buildings looked as though they were always being replaced and never in exactly the same place. A small rectangle of slightly thinner, paler grass, about big enough to park a small car on, was all that remained of the house where Lula was born. The air was thickening, black clouds had rolled along the river flat. A fine rain fell, getting heavier fast. We were miles from the road.

VII

A World Elsewhere

Before Fernando took office, in the first three months of 1990, PC set up in a couple of hotel suites in São Paulo, and there the industrialists of Brazil came to call on him. One suite was for meetings. In the next suite he kept his callers waiting. The waiting dramatized for PC's postulants just how much things had changed. Six months earlier, PC had kicked his heels outside their own offices and it wasn't until only Fernando remained between them and Lula that the business community had responded. Now PC told them Fernando's campaign had ended $30 million in the red. Nobody believed him. Since PC controlled access to the president and the government, he nevertheless pulled in another $30 million in what he happily called *the third round* of the presidential campaign.

In Brasilia PC worked out of two suites in adjacent buildings. One became the office of a company called EPC, set up in his own name, and this was where PC himself worked, protected by security guards and filtering the visitors he wanted to see through a series of remote-controlled anterooms. The second suite became the office of Salles Tourism. The office was perfectly anonymous. There was no sign outside, no name on the door, and no trace of a travel brochure within. It was even harder to reach than the first. You had to go in by a side door and down to the basement, where a security man checked you out and called the office. If your visit was approved, another security man took you up. Here the pilot Jorge Bandeira did business with people PC did not want to meet personally. The two suites housed the parallel government of the *new Brazil,* which was linked to the other through PC's Monday morning breakfasts with Fernando. It was the time of secret planning for the bank seizure. Fernando authorized PC to attend the planning meetings, but the economists hated him hanging around and moved their meetings to a secret place. Before the big freeze PC moved most of the $90 million to offshore bank accounts in the Caribbean. The rest stayed in the EPC accounts to pay the expenses of Fernando and his family. The week before the plan was announced, the EPC accounts were emptied too. Some of the money was converted to gold and dollars and the rest was used to buy up big blocks of land around Fernando's home.

Zelia knew she was unprepared to run Brazil's economy. As the freeze approached she began to lose her nerve. *Mr. President,* she said, *you realize a lot of people are going to suffer and even die because of our program . . . a lot of people won't even have money to eat.* Fernando impatiently told her to go ahead. Then Zelia fell in love with the new minister of justice, who was twenty years Zelia's senior and widely thought *incompetent and unreliable.* The legal provisions he drew up for the bank seizure had to be redone five times. During the long huddles of secret planning he brushed against Zelia's body and stared intently into her eyes. PC paid for the luxury chalet where the two spent their nights. The justice minister's wife, who had cancer, thought her husband was working around the clock on Brazil's economic crisis.

Fernando was sworn in as president of Brazil on March the fifteenth. The next day Brazilians with bank accounts found they had no more than a little over a thousand dollars each. Zelia explained on TV how the plan would work, and stumbled on some fairly basic questions. She didn't know whether the money seized would be adjusted for inflation when it was returned eighteen months later—inflation over the previous month alone had been eighty-four percent. But the freeze did stop inflation at first. Maybe, people felt for a while, the shock was needed. Then two months later inflation was back at eight percent a month and rising fast. Zelia no longer cared. She blamed the *inflationary mentality* of Brazilians and flew away from their ruined lives for a secret weekend assignation in New York with her lover. The minister of justice had become such an embarrassment he had to go. He wet his pants when Fernando's emissary required his resignation and left by the ministry's back entrance. Then Zelia was found taking money from the transport companies to let them break the freeze and increase fares. A bureaucrat was brought in to pick up the pieces. Looking back years later on the damage done, Zelia's successor as minister remarked on the plan's

> great violence against the principles of an established legal order and the working rules of a market economy—unilateral breaking of contractual obligations, freezing of financial assets, disregard of vested rights. [It] corroded the very idea of monetary restraint central to the plan's logic, . . . assaulted the holders of domestic private savings and so alienated a large part of the new middle class which had brought Collor victory at the polls.

What do you want, now we've won the election? PC asked Jorge Bandeira. Bandeira wanted planes, and PC gave him five percent of Brazil Jet Air Taxi and made him its managing director. Brazil Jet had no capital and no planes as yet. The idea was to start an air courier company. A second company, Mundial Air Taxi, was registered in Bandeira's name. Brazil Jet and Mundial operated out of their office in Brasilia and Bandeira took the calls for both. To get the money to get the planes they didn't have, PC and Bandeira sold prepaid air taxi rides to Brazil's big corporations. The planes were bought on installment plans in the United States—in two years, PC bought three executive jets and his own special plane, a Learjet 55 which was repainted in striking tones of dark gray on gray and called the Black Bat.

At the same time PC registered a company called Dupont Investments in the Virgin Islands. The sole function of Dupont Investments was to start another company on the United States mainland which PC called Miami Leasing. At first Miami Leasing didn't even have an address. It was fronted by a Brazilian who was living in Miami on false papers and being watched by the DEA and the FBI. The DEA was curious about the man's illegal dollar remits to Brazil, and thought he was running a cargo operation that carried cocaine. He was a light aircraft pilot and at the time he teamed up with PC he was also being investigated for trafficking in stolen aircraft parts and the illegal export of planes being used for drug drops. Under PC's patronage he became the director of a conglomerate consisting of Parts Express Corporation, Miami Leasing Aviation Company, Air Trading Inc., Interglobe Enterprise, Avtat Trading, Interglobal Trading, Nevada Trading, Pompano Jet and SCI Financière Albert Premier. Six of these had no address or telephone at all, and Miami Leasing operated out of the Brazilian's home in Miami. The last company on the list was registered in Paris and was the financial nerve center of PC's operation and its link with the Swiss banking system.

PC sent the dollars he made in Brazil off to Dupont Investments in the U.S. Virgin Islands. Dupont Investments sent the money on to Miami Leasing and Miami Leasing used it to buy planes. PC's Brazilian companies leased the planes from his U.S. companies and that way he got the planes into Brazil duty-free. The first was the Black Bat at the end of 1990. The second plane arrived with its papers so crudely forged that the plane's American dispatcher, who was already under DEA investigation for laundering money for the cocaine cartels, went down for some time. That was his problem, not PC's. The beauty of the arrangement was that PC could now send money regularly and legally to the United States as the fee owed to Miami Leasing on these two leasing contracts. He remitted $1.5 million from Brazil to the States every month.

While Brazil's largest real air taxi company was nose-diving into debt, Brasil Jet and Mundial made millions. Brasil Jet logged nearly five hundred flights with the Black Bat and Mundial recorded nearly four hundred with the other plane. In reality, the only person who flew in the Black Bat was PC himself, and the occasional special guest. PC made a quick trip in the Black Bat from Recife to Lisbon and Paris and back over a few days at the end of June in 1991, and that flight cost an imaginary client over half a million dollars. Another of Brasil Jet's biggest customers was OAS Construction, a real corporation which was winning more public works contracts from the Brazilian government than any other. Odebrecht Construction was a similarly big spender with Mundial, and the receipts for the millions it paid to Mundial bore the dates of public works contracts Odebrecht had signed with the Brazilian government. A lot of the real flights being logged by Bandeira in PC's planes were along the drug routes of the Americas, from Brazil to the United States, Venezuela, Bolivia, Cuba and Guyana. And in the first year of Fernando's presidency there were dozens of flights to Caribbean islands offering special offshore banking facilities. The Black Bat made twenty-one flights out of Brazil in this period. In April 1991 Fernando issued a presidential decree ending all federal police checks on the passengers and cargoes being carried by private aircraft. It was part of his drive to modernize the Brazilian private airline sector and make it internationally competitive. PC had already come to a more informal understanding with the customs officials at Brazil's major airports and none of his planes was ever inspected. Things ran especially smoothly out of São Paulo, where in 1990 one of PC's friends, who also represented Dupont Investments and Miami Leasing in Brazil, was made superintendent of the federal customs. It was not the only high government post PC filled with one of his people.

Rosane had no intention of being merely decorative as first lady. When she began to make her own way in the world, Globo's viewing public was bemused to find a new soap playing in the news slot. It might have been called *First Couple,* or *Rosane Takes Over.* It was immensely popular, and as in other soaps the content of each new episode was decided by audience ratings for the one just shown. Earlier in 1990 Rosane had concentrated on shopping. *Madame is spending a lot,* PC said with professional awe. He wondered about the solid gold Rolex, a man's model that nobody ever saw on the president's wrist, when he released the funds to buy it. Sometimes PC sighed, *Madame is spending too much.* The first family's personal expenses were far more than Fernando's income. In two and a half years PC paid out $6.5 million dollars to Fernando, and also financed his private secretary and his press secretary, who was running up credit card bills for double his salary and lighting his Havana cigars with hundred-dollar banknotes. PC transferred the money discreetly from several accounts in the name of several imaginary people in several different banks. Fernando's personal secretary used three different identities, holding three different accounts in three different banks to receive the money. Bandeira too invented another identity, who opened another account.

As first lady Rosane was president of the Legião Brasiliera de Assistência. The LBA was a government charity which spent a billion dollars a year. Its presidency had always been an honorary thing, but Rosane flew around Brazil visiting offices and projects and arriving home at night later than Fernando. Soon she was thinking of standing for Congress herself. Fernando was not pleased and made her promise to be home by seven-thirty every evening. She promised, but she hardly ever was. She was particularly active in Alagoas at election time. The October elections of 1990 for state governors, congressmen and senators was a busy time for Fernando and PC too, who wanted to build up a core of solidly indebted voting allies in Congress. PC raised and spent a lot of money and most of his people got up. The money came from Brazil's big carmakers, banks, contractors and credit card concession holders, and not a cent of it from the $90 million he already had. Again PC pulled in far more than he spent. In Alagoas, the two candidates for governor were both allies of Fernando. One had played an important part in projecting Fernando on the Brazilian scene and was the leader of his party in Congress. The other was a friend married to a cousin of Rosane's and backed by the whole Malta clan. PC spent $22 million on Rosane's cousin's husband, and maybe $1 million on Fernando's old ally. Rosane's cousin's husband won. Maybe PC wasted the money, since Alagoas hadn't changed all that much. An old colonel from one of the interior towns told a visitor up from the south, *None of this TV stuff works at election time. You just stick these country people on a truck and send them off to vote for the one you want.*

The loser assailed PC as *a gangster, an Al Capone dressed up as a public figure.* It was worse that Rosane, as the busy bee head of an enormous charity, had spent $11 million of public money in Alagoas in the month before the vote. Rosane had been to Canapi, Inhapi and Big Scrub, the three specks on the map of the interior where her family lived, and these towns got huge sums for dressmaking and goat breeding with no tenders called, all paid to firms belonging to people called Malta and largely imaginary companies. A firm of tanker trucks supposedly taking water to drought stricken towns was located at Malta Construction, whose workers had never seen a tanker truck. The registered address of the Pro Needy Association was an abandoned shed. No courses in dressmaking or goat breeding were held. Emergency food aid was used to elect Rosane's cousin's husband. Rosane had discovered a vocation.

During the year all this took to emerge, Fernando's and Rosane's relationship plunged into crisis. They were fighting about everything, including a magazine photo of Rosane in a bikini taken on a Maceió beach. Rosane gave a birthday lunch for her best friend at the charity—eighty guests, an orchestra, lobster and French champagne, and all paid out of charity funds. Rosane was taken to court. Three weeks later there was an ugly scene between Fernando and Rosane at a private dinner on their seventh wedding anniversary and they didn't speak for two weeks. One night Rosane came home late again, and Fernando hurled his wedding ring onto the bed. *Send your lawyer,* said Rosane. *You know I'm not afraid.* Fernando started coming home at midnight and they slept in the same room without speaking. *Why haven't you sent your lawyer?* she asked finally. *I'm going to tell my family.* The Maltas flew into Brasília from their outback homes. There was a televised ceremony for the president's birthday, in front of family, ministers, governors, senators, judges, heads of church and diplomatic corps. Rosane went to shake

Fernando's hand. He turned away and left her arm outstretched in the air. It was on TV Globo that night and the pictures were everywhere. Everyone noticed that the president no longer wore his wedding ring.

Then Fernando heard Rosane was having an affair. He was white with fury and she responded in kind. *You believe this story? Just tell me. You believe this story?* Rosane shouted back. *I never believed the stories about you.* The young man, who worked on protocol for the Federal District government, was twenty-seven, well over six feet tall and known in Brasilia as *Handsome.* Someone had recorded Handsome's phone calls to the first lady and he had already left town, warned by the governor that *there were people out to get him.* Handsome avoided the airport, where his enemies were waiting, and left under cover by car and he stayed away from Brasilia until well after Fernando was gone for good.

A solemn mass in the cathedral of Brasilia marked the anniversary of the LBA, a few days after people heard about the $11 million of its funds Rosane had spent. Fernando stayed away, and while the choir sang Gounod's "Ave Maria," Rosane broke down and sobbed. A former first lady lent her a hankie to mop up and these pictures too were everywhere. It was the opening shot in Rosane's counterattack. The Maltas pumped out rumors about Fernando. *I'll be first lady until the end of the presidency,* Rosane said, *and if Fernando wants that to be tomorrow, he can go ahead.* She called a press conference and came with her father, brother, male cousins and an army of drylands heavies. Fernando had been known as *Ferdy Powder* in his student days and the big news at the press conference was apparently going to be that the president was now taking his cocaine through suppositories. *We'll see how macho he is,* Rosane said. Suddenly there was no more talk from Fernando of separation and divorce. Rosane's father had sent a message to the president that in the Malta family there were no divorcées. *A daughter of mine is single, married or a widow.* The Maltas owed a lot to their daughter, like the handsome new villa with a swimming pool where they now lived in Canapi. Rosane resigned from the LBA, and under the cameras Fernando kissed her and hugged her and they walked out hand in hand. Experienced viewers found it about as convincing as Rosane's tears in the cathedral. Fernando was resigned to his fate. He never wore his wedding ring again, however. The ring had disappeared.

One late afternoon in Rio, nineteen years after meeting the little march of bearded and bespectacled Workers' Party members and at almost exactly the same point on the Avenida Rio Branco, I saw another group of demonstrators marching stoically through the black exhaust smoke of the buses. They were different from the earlier knot of frail looking intellectuals—younger, more robust, darker skinned and more of them were women. There were some children marching too, and at least one young woman was marching with a baby at her breast. They carried a flag but no banners and I realized who they were. They were people of the Landless Movement and they were marching on the anniversary of a massacre. Five years before, nineteen unarmed members of the Landless Movement had been shot down by the military police on a country road at Eldorado dos Carajás in the northern state of Pará, south of the city of Belém. Fifty-one were badly wounded. The soldiers shot the farmworkers on the order of their two battalion majors, who were acting on the order of the military police colonel who was leading them, who gave the order to kill on the order of the state commander of military police, who was acting on the order of the state governor of

Pará, who gave the order to the military police commander on the order of a person or persons nobody ever got around to identifying with any precision.

The workers were not simply shot down as it were by panicky police. The police greatly outnumbered the landless. The police first surrounded the peasants and then fired from both sides of the road. Only some of the dead fell in that moment. Autopsies showed quite clearly—beyond the testimony of the people present, who were not taken much notice of—that most of the dead had been shot in the head or the back of the neck at point-blank range. And those who were shot in the back of the head had first been clubbed down and beaten to death—hacked to pieces—with scythes or knives. And a number of those who had been clubbed, hacked to pieces or shot in the back of the head were the leaders of the landless workers caught in the police cross fire. One of them was Oziel Pereira, who was seventeen years old. When the workers dispersed after being fired on, Oziel was handcuffed, led away by the military police, beaten more or less to death and then shot in the back of the head.

The people who were marching through Rio on the afternoon of 17 April 2001 were not simply commemorating the dead of 17 April 1996. People were marching all around Brazil that anniversary afternoon to mark the fact that none of the killers had been brought to justice. Charges had been laid, it was true, but the soldiers charged with murder were still on duty, and two sets of deeply flawed proceedings had been aborted. It was more than a year later, in 2002, that a third trial began of 120 soldiers, eleven sergeants, one captain, two majors and a colonel of the military police of Pará. After 120 hours of hearings many parties claimed were gravely compromised, the colonel and one of the majors were convicted. They were immediately released pending their appeal. Nobody was surprised. In fifteen years more than twelve hundred country workers had been murdered in Brazil, either by hired gunmen or the military police, and almost nobody had ever been brought to justice. It was an old story.

———

When slavery and empire ended, there was a spasm of denial in Rio's governing milieus of Brazil's brutal past and a sudden horror at the black and colored masses that four hundred years of slavery had left behind. The *scientific* literature of racism, which the theorists of the European empires were producing in such abundance at that time, thrived on these anxieties. Cranial measurements were all the rage among the intellectuals of a country that was trying to pull itself up by its racial bootstraps. Brazil—or at least Brazil's leaders—wanted to be like North Americans, like the British, like the Europeans. Brazil wanted to be modern.

The capital had to be made worthy of the nation, for a start. People were driven from the crowded center of Rio, their houses razed and replaced by avenues and squares, libraries and theaters, all copied from Paris and competing with Buenos Aires. The new Avenida Rio Branco was tens of times wider than the Rua do Ouvidor, once the smartest street in town. There was a campaign to suppress yellow fever and remove the tropical taint, the reminder of Africa, so that transatlantic shipping would include a call at Rio as well as temperate and European-seeming Buenos Aires, which was getting most of the immigrants and all of the overseas investment. There were mass vaccinations for smallpox. Most of this was window dressing. The modernizing *order and progress* was a matter of wishful thinking. Brazil got neither.

Landowners got nothing in return for losing their slave labor, but they quietly won a far greater prize. They had so

finessed more than fifty years of political struggle over slavery
that the question of land reform had remained entirely overlooked. Their labor force would now have to be recruited on the
free market, in theory at least, but the vast landholdings were
intact in the hands of the handful who had held them throughout the centuries of slavery. The million and a half newly freed
slaves, without work, family, social connections, education,
training, land—even a home—were left to make their own
arrangements. This number of slaves in Brazil had stayed the
same, through steady attrition and replacement, since the eighteenth century. What had changed was Brazil's growing number of free blacks and colored people. Even in 1870 these free
dark people, all poor and unskilled, outnumbered whites. After
abolition the whites were an even smaller minority, which
enhanced the anxiety the white masters felt about securing Brazil's place in the civilized world. The poor immigrants from
Europe, originally brought out merely as one more form of
cheap labor, to replace the disappearing slaves, were now valued
breeding material. Brazil's elite had convinced itself the new
republic needed to *whiten* to survive. Immigrants poured in
from Italy, Germany and Portugal, and they all poured into
Brazil's Southeast. Nearly all of them went to São Paulo. There,
Brazil did whiten, and the economic center of gravity moved
south and stayed there.

Times got bad in the Northeast. In the early days of the
southern coffee boom in the 1870s, the living standards of
northeasterners had been much like the southeasterners'. But
soon coffee was earning considerably more than everything else
Brazil produced put together, while in the Northeast sugar and
cotton, which had been earning half of Brazil's entire income in
the 1820s, were ninety years later earning three percent. Growers
were getting less for their sugar than they paid to get it to the
ports and everywhere plantations were going bankrupt. Cacao

and tobacco were doing no better. In the last decade of the nineteenth century the Southeast and the Northeast of Brazil became two different countries.

The Northeast was not a good place to be released from slavery into the free market. It was not a good time to be a person of mixed race at all, and the Northeast had four hundred years of mixing among índios, Portuguese and Africans behind it. No landowners in the flourishing Southeast wanted *dark, backward, lazy* Brazilian northeasterners on their payroll when they could get fresh, smart eager white labor from Europe. For an elite yearning for *gringo* efficiency and French style, the Northeast was now an embarrassment and a liability, with a dying economy and a bastard people. This was how people thought. The Northeast's cotton boom had come in the sixties and gone in the seventies, lasting no longer than North America's Civil War over slavery. It had lured many thousands to the interior in time for a terrible drought. The newest hope was the Amazon rain forest and its rubber plantations. Rubber was the very latest growth spurt in the endless history of Brazil's boom-and-bust commodity economy. The Amazon was a long way away and a rubber tapper's life was a new kind of slavery but hundreds of thousands made the journey from the northeastern drylands to try it.

Others stayed on the bleak dryland of the Northeast's interior, trying to do sharecropping on little land and less water. The land was utterly unsuited to agriculture and desperately unproductive, nearly exhausted by centuries of overgrazing and further depleted now by the slash-and-burn practices the new people brought from the coast. Half a million people of the interior died in the *great drought* that finally broke in 1879. It was followed by a worse one ten years later, just as slavery ended and yet more people were driven to scrabble a living from the stony waterless ground, and lasted four years. None of the Northeast's big landowners, having held on to their estates through the rocky days when the slaves were freed and the empire vanished, offered them anything.

The landowners of the interior were doing quite well, though less well than the planters on the coast. They controlled the water sources on the ground and were paid off in *drought relief* for supporting a state governor who had his ties to the prosperous government in Rio. The hungry landless people of the interior made a convenient pool of docile casual labor for the cattle stations. In 1889 the British consul in Recife reported to London that labor was cheaper in Pernambuco than anywhere in the world outside Asia. And the dire condition of the Northeast was starting to impinge on the rest of the country. Brazil's growth was slowing, in spite of coffee, in spite of rubber. The Northeast's second great drought broke briefly in 1890, but returned worse than ever the next year, and then the coffee boom broke and Brazil's currency started losing value fast.

The people of the interior were tough and persistent, and they had to be. Silent and uncomplaining, they got by on almost nothing from dry ground that yielded unimaginably little. *A person who has to die doesn't cry,* they said. Fewer than one person in a hundred owned any land at all. Only one in ten could read or write. Their troubles were manifold. The physical bleakness of their lives—the hunger, thirst, disease—was matched by social absences. Government sat in the pleasant and populous coastal cities and left the interior to the colonels. The church was no more present than the state—lacking other consolations, the people of the interior held hard to their religion, but rarely saw a priest. They had some resources of their own. The landowners' bands of armed enforcers faced *social bandits* who stole cattle and horses, raided transports and homesteads for food, guns and farm tools, held up tax offices, stole what gold and jewels they found, then lost themselves in the thorn scrub. The church's negligence was answered by the wandering penitents and mystics of the outback, whose relation to the doctrines and institutions of the established church went from fairly orthodox to wildly heretical. These preachers and penitents were hated by the absent church, which they undermined without particularly meaning to. People listened to the itinerants when there was no one else to listen to, glad to feel there might be some larger order and meaning in their lives, glad when births, marriages, deaths became more than knots in a string of personal disasters. Hallucinations born of hunger, isolation and the austere intensities of the environment made the people's religion fiercely penitential, its visions millenarian and sometimes wildly apocalyptic.

———

Antônio Vicente Mendes Maciel came from a line of drylands cattle drovers who had gone on to do quite well as smallholders, until they had been almost wiped out in a long blood feud with a family of powerful landowners. Antônio's father had made and lost some money keeping a general store. Antônio taught children on the homestead of a big estate and then he went through a bad marriage and bad times making out as a salesman working the outback routes, and living through another relationship that went wrong. His troubles made him one of the drylands' solitary penitents, given to long fasts and little sleep and living on charity. He rebuilt abandoned churches and cemeteries, and preached in the evenings in the small towns of the interior on the need for penitence and devotion. He knew how to hold a crowd and had a way of lowering his voice at crucial moments, so people leaned forward, not wanting to miss a word. In a little town in the middle of nowhere, two or three thousand people would appear to hear him speak when night fell, from a makeshift platform under a canopy of leafy branches. His listeners vanished back into the thorn scrub the moment he stopped. The church and some of its priests on the ground tried to silence him because he was not ordained. It was, as ever, a question of control.

He was dry as a stick, sleeping on the ground and sometimes near death from his fasting. His personality had been obliterated, but his energy and his seriousness and his compelling voice drew people to him. He was neither a fanatic nor an impostor, though people who never knew him later called him both. People came to him for advice about the problems in their family, their money difficulties, trouble with the law, all the unfairnesses of their daily lives. They called him Antônio Conselheiro, *Antônio the Counselor*. People like him had been wandering the back trails of Brazil since the seventeenth century, but the need was greater now of someone to listen and advise and soon he seemed to be the only one. The Counselor was on the road all through the great droughts of the seventies and eighties. He walked the trails in his sandals, dressed in a dark blue buttoned canvas tunic, with a staff in his hand and a broad brimmed hat against the searing sun. Over twenty years he visited dozens of towns around the interior of the Northeast—in Bahia, Ceará, Pernambuco, Alagoas, Sergipe. As times got harder, landowners and police shared the church's unease at the Counselor's growing crowds. The institutions of property, order and the spirit were already under stress. Landowners were wondering how they would get along without slaves, and how they would get along with the military republicans who had so abruptly replaced the emperor; the church was being disestablished by the atheistic military; police were no longer sure where their loyalties lay. The lines transmitting power between Rio and the states, and between the state capitals and the remote interior, were all, during the years of the second great drought, tangled or broken. Financial instability and wild speculation down south made the uncertainty worse.

The Counselor's moral talk cut into the nervously shifting allegiances. He had always been against slavery, and freed slaves came to him now. He had defended the market women against the new taxes that made them unable to set up at the local markets. When riots followed in the market towns the Counselor was blamed. Most dangerously to himself, he was against the godless new republic—not that he had much idea of what it meant, beyond taxes and irreligion. The taxes, he said, were driving people back into slavery. Everything was secular now and the Counselor hated that. Over the door of one of the first churches he built, he had carved the words *God alone is great,* which summed up his feelings about the earth's powerful. The terrible drought, the scourge visited on the land, was an image of the coming end, he said, and his listeners found that easy to believe.

There had been trouble over the years. In 1876 the police officer and the priest in a town of Bahia's northern drylands were put in such agitation by his followers that the Counselor had to cross the state border to avoid arrest. The area's biggest landowner, the future Baron of Jeremoabo—the title a reward for opening Bahia's first industrial sugar refinery—demanded the Counselor be seized. The police chief of Bahia wrote to the archbishop promising to do it. Everyone was worried about *instability.* The charge laid against the Counselor when they took him was that years earlier he had murdered his mother and wife. The Counselor's mother was found to have died when he was a small child and his former wife to be alive and well, but not before the Counselor had been manacled, savagely beaten by soldiers, paraded through Salvador in irons. *Christ suffered worse,* he muttered when they finally let him go. The archbishop sent out word from Salvador that priests were not to get involved with the Counselor. They were to go to the police if he gave trouble and were reminded never to let laymen like the Counselor preach. Most priests ignored the archbishop, who was a long way away, but several years later he wrote again, requiring them to take a stronger stand against the Counselor, and quite a few did. By 1890 the Counselor's peripatetic mission was getting harder and he stopped moving around. He settled on a couple of abandoned properties north of Salvador with a group of followers. They planted crops, raised goats and chickens, dug a well, built a church and the place prospered through the worst time of the drought. Then the Counselor himself moved on.

The archbishop tried and failed to get the Counselor locked up in a lunatic asylum as a *religious fanatic*. The government thought that was going too far, despite the archbishop's insistence that the Counselor was a *subversive* undermining state as well as church and *distracting the common people from doing their daily tasks*. But then the Counselor's opposition to the republican taxes which were crushing the outback people entangled him in a power struggle in newly post imperial Bahia. In 1893 the state government sent a police patrol to assassinate the Counselor on a back road. He had been protected by tough country men—*jagunços,* they were called in the Northeast, in a vaguely criminal sense—ever since his wrongful arrest fifteen years earlier, and several were killed when the police opened fire. The others fought back and the police fled behind their commanding officer.

Antônio the Counselor again decided to retreat from conflict, to an abandoned property in very remote territory whose title was held by the Baron of Jeremoabo's niece. Canudos was in a relatively fertile river valley. It had water, room, good soil, and a steep hill above it called Monte Favella which commanded all approaches. The Baron of Jeremoabo was enraged when the Counselor's squatters arrived. Wherever the Counselor went now he would have found a hostile landowner and his police chief, and an archbishop fanning the flames in Salvador. The trouble was the people who followed the Counselor. A few hundred arrived with him in Canudos in 1893, to build their wattle and daub homes on land bounded on three sides by a bend of the Vasa Barris River, to plant crops and raise goats and horses. About three thousand people *armed to the teeth* were still scratching a desultory living in the neighborhood of the ruined homestead, drinking cachaça and smoking tobacco and maconha in long clay pipes. Most of them joined the new community and a few months later nearly fifteen thousand people had settled there. A year after that the population of Canudos was thirty-five thousand, living in thousands of mud brick houses. In a year and a half Canudos had become the second biggest city in Bahia, which was bigger than France, and Brazil's second most populous state.

Canudos emptied surrounding towns—one lost its entire population of five thousand. Some people brought their herds, others brought money realized on the properties they left. Women from slave owning families, moved by piety, brought jewelery and family valuables. Most came with nothing. Many had been slaves five years earlier, and all were in such a desperate state that they were ready to try anything. They came to live off the land. Men driven to banditry now saw the chance of a settled and productive life, and the índios who still survived in the district gravitated to the security of Canudos. People even came from the coast, and Salvador was seven hundred kilometers of stony track and dirt road away. More women came than men and all were young, since neither men nor women in the Northeast lived much beyond the age of twenty-seven. As livings dried up and withered all around the Northeast, people were already migrating in a driven, random way. Uniquely, Antônio the Counselor offered hope and Canudos its physical location. Soon Canudos was a self-sustaining agricultural community surrounded by rural poverty and drought. The Counselor himself, who was now in his sixties, retired to meditate, and it was the others who built the town. It was a perfectly free community, if rather austere—the Counselor banned cachaça and was severe about informal sex—held together by a strong sense of shared values. When the Counselor came out to preach in the evening they gathered in thousands to hear his dour compelling talk about the true faith and their lost emperor, the vanished well-being of old Brazil, the ills of the republican present, the new enslavement of the people, the coming end.

People planted and harvested, tended the animals, built houses and stores, traded their produce with outsiders. Corn, beans, arrowroot, potatoes, squash, watermelons, cantaloupes and sugarcane were grown along the riverbank. There were even banana trees, which were almost unknown in the drylands, and manioc grew in the valleys. They dug wells, built water tanks, warehouses, a schoolhouse, an abattoir, churches and armories, even a small lockup they called *the dustbin,* and the Counselor started work on a big new Church of Good Jesus. Some worked elsewhere in the district and came home at night. The children all went to school for a monthly fee paid to the several teachers and the Counselor started two other schools in nearby towns. His self-effacing but charismatic presence held people rather apart from their surroundings, and so did some of his fixations. Not only cachaça was banned in Canudos: so was the paper money issued by the hated new republic, which the Counselor refused to recognize, and business was done rather cumbersomely through notes of exchange. When the settlement needed things from outside, like timber or guns, they traded goat hides. Like any local colonel, the Counselor made all the final decisions.

———

Vavá and I were talking and we got around to seafood. Vavá asked me if I'd like to eat some lobster. I said yes. Secretly nervous about the expense—my time in Recife was being prolonged on a tiny budget—I maintained an outward calm. Later it occurred to me that Vavá might have taken this imperturbability as indifference to cost, which raised the anxiety level as the evening approached. Lobsters were a luxury and were outside the Bangüê's usual parameters. *How many? One, two?* Vavá wanted to know, shouting over the Friday evening noise. *Depends on the size,* I shouted back guardedly. *One large or two small.* Vavá was going to get the lobsters over the weekend and I would dine on Monday. Vavá went on using the plural when he talked about the lobsters.

Monday came, and Vavá electrified the quiet evening drinks crowd when he came over waving a huge red newly boiled crayfish in each hand. This was stuff the Bangüê's clients only dreamt about. The crustaceans were great deepwater Southern Hemisphere crayfish, familiar from childhood summers at Cape Otway in Australia. They were not wretched little Mediterranean lobsters after all. Vavá was unfazed when I said one would be enough. It looked even more enormous when it was split open. It returned thus, not much later, as a *moqueca,* and the moqueca was very well done indeed. The red shells were now swimming in a brilliant yellow sauce. The other eyes around the room made an intermittent show of being directed elsewhere, or lowered over a drink. A hush fell over the Bangüê.

Eating the crayfish moqueca was almost as painful at the outset as it was delicious. I am an untidy eater at the best of times, and that Monday I was naturally not going to leave undiscovered pockets of sweet white flesh in the hidden crevices of the shell. Given that the only aids to cleanliness were a few tiny squares of paper, that the whole thing was dripping yellow juice, and that José was prowling up and down in his slippers and never more than a few feet away, his eyes fixed on the plate like a starving tomcat's, and that I had loosened up with a couple of caipirinhas beforehand, it will be understood that the spectacle was not edifying. Further sets of eyes were drilling into me from behind the green coconuts, through the open window, from swiveled heads on the path being beaten to the pissoir and from the ladder rising to the kitchen. At a certain moment, however, the intensity of the pleasure and the majesty of the self-gratification made all else recede. I felt no shame. I sucked and slurped and shoveled rice into the golden puddles. A day's swimming and your appetite is inexhaustible. At last I slumped back, replete, and José hustled the brilliant debris away as from the scene of an embarrassing accident. He was okay. In several ways José did quite well out of this evening. Nevertheless, the look in his eyes stayed with me. The price was bearable. Vavá was thrilled with the unaccustomed drama and asked when we could do it again. Slowly, slowly I turned the pinpoints of stunned eyes on him. In the depth of satiety something stirred. *Maybe next week,* I said.

Next week came. Vavá, sunny and relaxed as he always was on Mondays, came up and rather abruptly said, *Pitù.* I knew what he meant. The word was written across walls and bottle labels all over Recife and the picture on the label showed another red crustacean, sometimes a couple of stories high, waving its huge pincers. In reality the pitù turned out to be not much more than the length of a finger or two, and not much thicker. I heard they could grow to a couple of feet long, but I never saw one anything like that size, then or later. The carapace was paper thin, the flesh tight packed and sweet. The pitù, Vavá said, was not a fruit of the sea but of the coastal rivers, a kind of finer freshwater prawn—a yabbie or a marron—and out of respect for its more delicate flavor, tonight he had it little more than lightly poached for me in coconut milk, though still with its cheerful tinge of moqueca yellow.

The moqueca is African and its real home in Brazil is Bahia, but people eat fish and seafood done this way all over Brazil. Along the northeastern seaboard moquecas recurred in endless fine permutations which tended to be better the closer you were to Bahia. Recife was pretty close and the versions Vavá rang down from the Bangüê's attic kitchen were characteristically subtle. The moqueca's bright yellow color is ubiquitous in African Brazilian food. It comes from *dendê*, the palm oil used in Bahian cooking. In a row of bottles the oil may cover the chromatic reach of a deeply glowing red gold, from cloudy to crystalline, from pale orange to deep mahogany. The finest extra-virgin oil, the darkest and clearest juice of the first pressing, is *flor de dendê*. The colors are a distillation of the glowing red of the ripe fruit, each one the size of an olive, that cluster by their hundreds in huge spiked bunches under the fronds of the dendê palm. The dendê is not native to Brazil but another import from the west coast of Africa. I wondered who first thought of bringing it across the Atlantic, and why—given that the tree and its fruit were of interest to the black slaves rather than their white owners—and it turned out to be a more complicated and uncertain story than I'd imagined. The question was not just who brought the palm to Brazil but who started using its oil to cook with.

In Africa the dendê first meant wine. In the first years of the sixteenth century, at the time of the first landings in Brazil, various Portuguese explorers of the African coast wrote about

the wine made from the sap of the dendê palm. They also mentioned the oil made from its fruit, but only as used by Africans
to soften and protect the skin. Palm wine never caught on in
Brazil and the first mention of dendê oil in African cooking was
made nearly a hundred years later, by an Italian traveler and
writer called Filippo Pigafetta, who in 1591 wrote a curious and
partly fantastical book on the *kingdom of the Congo and surrounding
lands* using information from a Portuguese explorer, which after
describing how the Africans *oil their bodies* with the oil *made from
the flesh of the fruit* added that palm oil was *excellent in food.*
Câmara Cascudo, the author of the monumental *History of Food
in Brazil* in several volumes, claims that before this there is no
record of Africans cooking with palm oil throughout the four-
teenth and fifteenth centuries, and that it was the Portuguese,
makers and users of olive oil at home for many centuries, who
saw and developed the uses of palm oil in Brazilian kitchens,
and not the Africans at all. It would make sense that the Portuguese themselves, in this case, brought the dendê palm to
Brazil. The academic authors of the even more monumental
Cambridge World History of Food state flatly that food has been
cooked in palm oil for three thousand years, but they don't
mention West Africa as one of the places where dendê was used
to prepare food.

These days in Brazil dendê palm oil is a major export from
the Amazon region, but this cooking oil sold to Asia is an industrial product that has been deodorized of its sharp flavor, leached
of its gorgeous color and fiercely clarified to a pale translucency.
In the Northeast the dendê for local consumption is still turned
out along the coastal Recôncavo of Bahia by ancient and labo-
rious means. The huge spiky husks are broken up with sledge-
hammers and the hard red fruits laboriously prized free. The
fruit is cooked in a huge boiler over a fire of dead husks, then

crushed in a circular stone press by the strength of patient oxen treading in an endless circle like the oxen that once drove the cane crushers on the sugar estates. The oil is released by washing, and the oxen's reward is to eat the mash that remains. The fruit's hard kernel yields another oil that in the old days was greatly sought after as a hair softener and that the food industry now uses in margarine.

A moqueca starts simple and can be elaborated using more ingredients into a very baroque dish indeed. To make a moqueca in its elemental form you briefly marinate some pieces of a robust fish, or some crustaceans or shellfish in some fresh lime juice and chili, then add them to a partly cooked sauté of fine slices of onion, red and green peppers and seeded tomato flesh and sauté them a little more—in dendê of course, though modern cooks usually lighten up in part with olive oil. Then you add some coconut milk and heat until the liquid boils and largely evaporates. You sprinkle the dish with fresh coriander and take it to the table with plenty of farofa. You can make a moqueca of almost anything—using steamed meat instead of fish, or gently breaking some eggs into the sauté just before serving, so that they poach with yolks unbroken. A moqueca of oysters was once the most astounding sexual restorative I ever enjoyed, but since the experience was unique it can't be recommended as a general rule. I raced back the following evening for a further treatment, but the oysters on the second occasion were a different lot, much smaller and quite useless. Neither at that place, a tiny restaurant named for a Yoruba deity, nor anywhere else was I ever offered this dish again.

Was the use of African dendê palm oil in cooking developed by the Portuguese in Brazil and not by Africans in Africa? Gilberto Freyre insisted that the name of the moqueca, the dendê dish par excellence, was a mutation of the índio word *pokeka,* which meant a *bundle,* and that the original dish consisted of a fish bundled in banana leaves and cooked over hot stones—Vavá knew how to preserve fish by making a bundle like this and putting it in hot sand. Gilberto wrote that in Bahia and in Pernambuco the *pokeka was deliciously Africanized, or better, Brazilianized* by the African slave cooks working in the kitchens of the plantation owners' houses. This was another version of his favorite insight, that the most Brazilian things in Brazilian culture were a synthesis of indigenous, Portuguese and African elements, and like the Brazilian people itself, new and unique. The marginal history of dendê seemed to be making the point over again. The oil was not African, or not just African, it was Brazilian.

VIII

A Place to Die For

When the emperor was shoved off from the Rio docks in 1889, Machado de Assis was fifty years old and the most popular novelist in town. Born in Rio, he had practically never left the city and was also one of its most popular journalists, commentators and writers of stories for magazines. They were women's magazines for the most part. Brazil's busy new middle class had been accreting around the imperial court in Rio and the traffic of its port for a couple of generations. Now it was enjoying the boom of the new coffee economy and the fruits of its own speculations, and had time for the luxuries the boom brought with it. Men went to concerts, went to the theater, went to the opera—you could see your friends here, make a show, and keep a sexual assignation—but the reading public's private enclave was entirely female. The first place you looked for fiction in Rio was among the new season's hats and frocks and the corset advertisements of the luxury magazines.

The magazines themselves were quite something, forerunners of glossies like *Vogue*. There was the *Family Journal*, for which Machado had been writing until it folded at the end of 1878, and the *Season*, the even more luxurious magazine which took its place the following month and became his outlet for another decade. They were both printed in Europe on the latest presses and had full color fashion plates. Only the literary supplement, the part Machado wrote for, was put together in Brazil. The point of reference was Paris. Fashionable Rio deferred to Paris in almost everything, making only the odd exception for the British when quality manufacture or efficiency of operation really mattered, as it did for gabardine and railways. Elegance in Rio— sartorial, gastronomic, intellectual—always aspired to be French and it still does.

Machado de Assis was not born to the class of leisured consumers for whom his writing catered. His father had been a house painter and his mother a domestic servant. This was about as near the bottom of the social pyramid as you could get without actually being a slave. Rio society, with the emperor at its apex, cultivated its social distinctions with more anxious energy than was ever required in the European metropoles. But the child Machado was taken up by the family his mother worked for—the slack and accommodating households of the Brazilian gentry were always acquiring *agregados,* who were neither quite the servants nor quite the equals of the people they lived with, and who passed their days in an agony of ambiguity. Machado got some education and started young and quickly acquired— getting a break from his printer's apprenticeship and learning to meet the brisk demands of the new journalism and filling the daily and weekly spaces in its papers—a pleasingly fluid, flexible, accessible, conversational tone that flattered and never intimidated his lady readers. A hundred years later Machado would have been scripting telenovelas for Globo. Writing for the illustrated magazines, he developed a style that made it utterly painless to assimilate the things he had to say. He needed such a style. Lolling on hammocks, fanned by slaves, sipping their syrups and juices, the ladies of Rio were not about to have demands made of them.

Only Machado did make demands of them. It was imperceptible at first. He turned out shapely little stories, barely more than anecdotes, on love and marriage, sexual choice. "A Husband's Wiles," "To Marry or Not to Marry," "A Superior Man," "Which of the Two," "Neither One nor the Other" were some of the very early magazine stories. Sometimes the sexual interest lay nearer the surface, as in "Confessions of a Girl Widow." When the first episode of this story came out in the *Family Journal* in 1865, it was attacked in a newspaper for its shocking frankness about sexual behavior. Other readers wrote in to praise the frankness and defend women's rights. The whole thing was likely a plant by Machado himself, an astute publicity move by a young writer who was also drawing attention to the real problems his story raised.

Sex was inseparable from class. It was sexual behavior that caused the deepest anxieties about social class, because sex had a way of cutting across the flimsy social distinctions Brazil's new middle class was trying to erect and threatening to throw everything into chaos. Sex was also inseparable from race, and it was particularly hard for the new bourgeoisie to maintain its civilized standards in a country that was fast being populated by a people who were clearly the product of sexual unions that crossed the lines of color and class, particularly the brutal line that separated the slaves from the free. The sensuous climate and the obtrusive near nudity of the lower classes were constantly inviting you to shed your imported finery. Even a well born white woman might *fall.* The men were falling all the time. The ever present personnel of the service economy were always presenting new invitations to your gaze and touch. The universal susceptibility and the barriers raised to stop your acting on it by the stern rules of family led to nagging suspicions and a pervasive culture of sexual jealousy. It was all the more insidious when you had nothing else to think about.

Racial identification tags proliferated madly as the nineteenth century moved on and the European middle class struggled to keep on top of all of Brazil's permutations and combinations of indigenous, African and European, mixes that kept blurring the necessary distinction between Us and Them. In a delicate and allusive way for the most part, Machado's first stories touched on the realities of class and race that constrained sexual life, but never too much to disturb his readers by reminding them how fragile everything was, or to upset the advertisers of the luxury goods imported from Europe which those readers were buying. The havoc that sex could wreak was always there yet always on the outer edge of the fictional world of the ladies' magazines, which always seemed to have the word *family* worked into their masthead. You had to be really sharp to seize the odd glimpse of the bitterness and violence that underlay the world he wrote about. Nevertheless, these things were in Machado's stories.

After a good marriage and a decade or more of very hard work he was established as a figure in Rio's literary life, and had quite a following among his women readers. He had risen in society. The printer's boy who had published poems at fifteen and made the leap into journalism had since brought out three books of poetry and four novels and seen several plays produced, quite apart from the stream of articles and stories for the press, which were already being collected into books. Machado's was an eminently nineteenth-century career: a talent had found its chance in feeding the voracity of the new print media and then it had transcended its origins. Over the years Machado wrote for thirty-five different magazines and newspapers. In his career he was a later and Brazilian version of Dickens, of Balzac—a prodigy, a celebrity, a social success as much as a literary one. In a

Francophile, Latin and less rambunctious way, Machado was like his North American contemporary Mark Twain. The social dimension of his career through the 1870s had been as remarkable as his output. And Machado the unfalteringly productive writer had for thirteen years also been a fast rising public servant. He had even, much against his own inclination, stood for parliament.

In late 1878, when he was a few months shy of forty, Machado broke down. The medical reticence of the age and his own exceeding discretion meant that the nature of his collapse and what brought it on were never made clear. Had he been driving himself too hard? Balzac had barely survived to fifty. Dickens never reached sixty. In Rio the prognosis was worse, and any man facing a systemic breakdown at forty would have expected death. The *girl widows* of Machado's own stories were a reality that ignored class and race. The deceased had often worn a velvet tie and a black frockcoat and many of the widows sported big hats and bustles. Rio was an overcrowded unplanned European metropolis that had grown in a tropical climate without thought of sanitation or of what, in that latitude, the European models of urban life might mean. Malaria, dengue, cholera, syphilis, leprosy and yellow fever were endemic. *It is impossible to think of Rio de Janeiro in the nineteenth century without being haunted by this mortal spectre,* remarked Fernand Braudel of the yellow fever that had come from Africa with the slaves.

Machado left the busy round of his social and cultural activities, took leave from the ministry, suspended his magazine writing for six months—they would be the only six months in forty years that he was not producing material for several periodicals at a time. He left Rio and went with his wife, Carolina, to a small hill town for total rest. It was his first holiday, the first time they had been alone together. His eyes were giving him worse trouble than usual. He was almost blind, could neither read nor write, so Carolina read to him and took dictation. He had always had a stammer, and had been epileptic as a child. Was it an epileptic crisis? Before the collapse he had told a friend, *I'm heading for consumption of the small intestine with giant strides.* The diagnosis was curiously particular. There was no other indication that tuberculosis was his problem, and the highly clinical suggestiveness of his own account was perhaps intended to throw people off the track. He got over it. And not long after Machado went back to work in 1879 from his six months of social nonexistence, when he was still almost blind, he began dictating a new novel to his wife. Early the next year his disconcerted readers encountered the first fragmentary installments of *The Posthumous Memoirs of Bras Cubas* in their favorite magazine.

————

That they listened at all to this voice from the dead was its triumph. All Machado's art was in the laid-back, funny, disabused and hypnotically conversational tone of Bras—late *homme moyen sensuel* of the Brazilian ruling class, an underachiever even by the lights of that deeply relaxed milieu—speaking from beyond the grave about the events of an uneventful life. This was a great change from Machado's earlier novels and tales about disadvantaged young women struggling for romantic fulfillment and a place in society, a fulfillment they usually and reassuringly found. Bras Cubas took Machado's *pale lady readers* into the male mind. And from beyond the grave Bras is free to speak as frankly and as inconsequentially as he feels like doing, dwelling on tiny details when he likes and skipping what bores him, since *frankness is the prime virtue of a dead man.* Technically, Machado had found in Laurence Sterne's whimsical eighteenth-century protonovel *Tristram Shandy* a way of getting free of the relentlessly external procedures of the realistic novel, and he owed even more to the ruthlessly direct—even cruel and petty—truthtelling of Stendhal's personal writings. But the cruel realities were painlessly assimilated through Machado's lightly insinuating prose.

Seduced by the conversational tone, the lady readers found themselves encountering some unexpected realities—learning that the child Bras at the age of six had *split open the head of a slave because she'd refused to give me a spoonful of the coconut confection she was making.* And that he whipped a black houseboy of his own age, saying when the other child complained, *Shut your mouth, animal.* These glimpses of domestic life in the slave owning households of Brazil were ordinary enough—Gilberto Freyre would document them amply—but disconcerting to meet in a novel. Likewise, the long adultery with a politician's wife which comprises the central fact of Bras's life as a man. Adultery was still an electrifying subject for a novel's lady readers, but in *Bras Cubas* it is neither daring nor tragic nor even a cynical seduction. Bras and Virgilia live a purely sexual relationship which eventually fades from the very lack of obstacles it encounters, an adultery as dull in the end as a bourgeois marriage. Just as Bras's political career—the only career imaginable for a nineteenth-century Brazilian slave owner in Rio who already had more money than he could possibly need—dies from sheer lack of interest. Readers are spared the details.

Along the way, in this unexpectedly recognizable version of life in slave owning Rio, Machado's lady readers kept running into the realities of a woman's life in the capital, since the memoirs are basically the story of Bras's sex life. The child Bras spies on a grown-up adultery in the garden at his father's dinner party, his lubricious uncle hangs around the slave women in the laundry and later leads the adolescent Bras to the prostitute Marcela. The thread of Bras's life links vivid and complex glimpses of women: Marcela, grimly on the make and then obliterated by disease; the ship's captain's wife who dies at sea of consumption when Bras is packed off to study in Portugal; the beautiful lame girl he is briefly infatuated with; Virgilia, who marries ambition but sleeps with Bras; Dona Placida, the desperately poor and pious unmarried mother—seduced in a church—employed to keep the house where the affair is conducted; Sabina, his sister, who marries a rising businessman in the clandestine African slave traffic, whose slaves are thrashed bloody in his cellar; and the young girl Bras is being organized to marry when she suddenly dies of yellow fever. The men are all urbanely sketched nullities of conformity, greed, lust and madness.

The year *Bras Cubas* came out Machado reached the peak of civil service distinction as a cabinet officer advising his minister. From now on his career was a tremendous balancing act. The more truth he showed in his fiction about the higher levels of Rio society in the last decades of slavery and empire—and his intimacy with that world now gave him plenty of material—the more seductively he had to present it. To alienate his audience would be to lose everything. He went on upping the ante until his death, and although his loyal public grew increasingly bewildered, he never lost them. He became the ornament of Brazil's new metropolitan culture. The emperor conferred on him the Order of the Rose and he was the founding president of republican Brazil's new Academy of Letters, whose members wore elaborately frogged jackets and carried swords, in the manner of the Académie Française. Photographs show him transmogrifying from the long-haired dark-skinned sensuously open young artist into the angular close-cropped patriarch of letters, screened by the pince-nez firmly clamped in front of the failing eyes and made severe by its emphatic black ribbon, the abundant and now whitening mustaches combed ever more carefully over the still expressive and generous African lips.

In the papers and magazines of Rio, Machado de Assis spoke first to the European slave owners of Brazil, and then to the

former slave owners, in the confidential tone of one of themselves, and he was valued above all for the worldly assurance and
the relaxed elegance of language he brought to a Brazilian culture that had seemed locked into a permanent cringe. The end
of slavery and end of empire were a time when Brazil's rulers
wanted reassurance about their place in global civilization almost
as much as they wanted to secure their place in global capitalism. Everything they consumed was being imported or imitated
from Europe—of the time when he was alive Bras most fondly
recalls the delicacies of M. Prudhon, formerly in the service of
the cream of the French aristocracy and latterly *the chef at the Hotel
Pharoux . . . He was famous . . . arrived in Rio along with the
polka . . . the polka, M. Prudhon, the Tivoli, the foreigners' ball,
the Casino, there you have some of the best memories of that time.* The
English, who controlled the economy and had forced the end of
slavery, lacked this charm. Bras's second prospective father-in-law
tells him on their first meeting that *the English could go to hell!
Things would never be right until they all sailed away.* In Brazil the
English disapproved of everything they saw except the business
opportunities.

———

Meanwhile, far from Rio and its indulgences, Canudos flourished, and as it grew it drained other settlements of people,
drove the surrounding district's small town commerce even
deeper into crisis and emptied churches of their flocks. More
ominously, the Baron of Jeremoabo and the other landowners in
a now depopulated region found themselves without that res-
ervoir of cheap and pliant labor they had come to rely on. The
people of Canudos had better things to do. The baron had always
found the Counselor a pest. As the conflict over new taxes flared
all around the interior into public burnings of the government's
decrees, the baron saw the Counselor as a political enemy and a

threat to his own well-being. It did not help the Counselor that he refused to recognize the republic at all. In the press and the state parliament in Salvador, Jeremoabo and the other colonels demanded that the state act against the Counselor, who was *either insane or criminal* and had a *sickening* ascendancy over his followers. Choosing the words most likely to disturb insecure new republicans, they said the Counselor was acting like an *absolute monarch* and forming a standing army of *criminals and fugitives* and *índios armed with bows and arrows*. That the last of the region's Kiriri índios had joined the settlement and celebrated their own rites there alongside the Counselor's Christians made Canudos even more the enemy of the new Brazil. The pressure to intervene against a settlement that challenged church and state came to a head at the end of 1896, when a shipment of wood for the new church at Canudos was confiscated at a port on the São Francisco River a hundred kilometers away.

It was a provocation—the wood had been paid for—and a party of five hundred men set out from Canudos to recover it. A hundred state police intercepted them, fired without warning and killed more than 150. The others fought back with sticks, iron bars, tree branches and a few old muskets. They drove off the police, who looted and burnt the settlement where it happened and arrived home after a four-day forced march, *their uniforms in shreds, wounded, crippled, exhausted.* The governor of Bahia telegrammed Rio for the federal government to intervene. The president of Brazil was sick and the vice president ordered five hundred troops to march on Canudos from Salvador. When the troops arrived in the outback in January 1897, with their fourteen officers and two small Krupp cannons, they found ten kilometers of scorched earth around Canudos. Not a building, not a tree. They marched into an ambush and after twelve hours of fighting retreated in confusion, fired on from the surrounding scrub on all sides by the Counselor's men.

Confusion overcame Rio too, where the young republic was being racked by its own troubles. The vice president was trying to force its first civilian leader from office, with the connivance of the military high command, who felt the president was too liberal, too close to the coffee growers. The Counselor had already got entangled in the power struggles of Bahia's ruling group and in Rio the military saw enemies everywhere. Coffee, the republic's main earner and the president's main support, was in free fall on the world commodity markets. Now the rumors of *monarchism* in Canudos set off a panic among the high command in Rio. From the capital, the movement at Canudos looked like an insurrection against the army's republican coup of seven years earlier and the army had just lost its opening skirmish. It was not a good moment to seem to be opting out of Brazil.

Antônio the Counselor was not unknown in Rio. Canudos had been settled barely more than a year when Machado de Assis made the Counselor and his followers the pretext for one of his urbanely inconsequential weekly magazine columns. The drylanders were exotic and remote enough to let Machado fantasize in his gracefully reassuring manner about the glamour—sexual and otherwise—of an outlaw band, which is what he vaguely took them to be. He deprecated by contrast the relentlessly modern metropolitan life of Rio, in a way that was sure to flatter and titillate his mainly female readers. Right from the start Canudos impinged on the mind of the capital, and right from the start the capital got it wrong, though Machado got it less wrong than others. He had kept his ironical distance from the institutions of the empire and he maintained it now from the convulsive enthusiasms of the republic. He wrote again about Canudos and the Counselor in January of 1897, while Rio was quivering with fascinated anger, whipped up by politicians and journalists, at the *fanatics* in the distant drylands who had just routed the nation's troops. As carefully light in touch as ever, but with a barely perceptible edge in his tone, Machado reminded his readers that in Rio they knew next to nothing about the people of Canudos or the Counselor, how they lived or what they believed. Since these people had now been living together—and fighting and dying together—in large numbers for several years, Machado suggested they might deserve some friendly attention. Provocatively—in the name of imagination and inclusiveness—he made oblique fun of the grimly positivist future being mapped out for Brazil. He imagined the Counselor as a colorful new addition to the parliament.

> We'll lose all this by hunting him down. We'll end up over-
> thowing the apostle, destroying the sect and killing the fanatics.
> Peace will come back to the drylands and with it monotony.
> Monotony will come into our own minds again too. What will
> we have left when the law has won out?

Nobody listened to a novelist. Rio was in a political panic. Military and civilian powers turned from fighting each other to confront what they decided was a threat to the Brazilian republic's existence. Canudos had to be crushed. A new force of thirteen hundred men with artillery, cavalry and four cannons was assembled. Its commander was Colonel Moreira Cesar, a bandy-legged martinet who had first shown promise as a young officer when he murdered a journalist who had criticized the army. He had proven himself by crushing dissent in the military republic, and being without scruple he was thought just the man to eliminate Canudos.

Machado tried once again a couple of weeks later. *Yesterday I found out what celebrity is,* he wrote in mid-February. He had been buying a paper when a woman—a *simple* woman who he thought *didn't know how to read*—had asked the man in the kiosk for *a paper with a picture of the man who's out there fighting.* She couldn't recall his name, but she meant the Counselor. Machado didn't insist on the matter, and soon floated off into literary matters, but the terms of the woman's recognition and the fact that she wanted a picture of the Counselor carried their own freight, and so did Machado's reminder to his metropolitan readers that the government's panic over the Counselor was sending Brazilian stocks plummeting in London and New York. A fortnight after that Machado gave up writing his weekly magazine column for good.

One of the things the landowners of Bahia's drylands were always telling each other, and telling anyone who would listen in Salvador and Rio, was that cattle thieves and criminals from all over the interior were hiding out in Canudos. It was a lie— the Counselor had an old-fashioned respect for private property and Canudos did good business around the district—but there were men in the Counselor's personal guard who had been in trouble with the law. Not many people hadn't, in a region where the judges served the landowners and the police were violent, predatory and mostly uncontrolled. Banditry was on the rise all through the Northeast, and former members of big bushranger gangs—one of them wanted for eighteen murders in another district—made the Canudos militia a formidable force. There were eight hundred men in the Counselor's Catholic Guard, led by the man who had fought off the police when they first tried to kill the Counselor four years before. The *street commander* in Canudos came from a *good family* and was a close friend of the richest and most influential of the several merchants who did business in town, a man who always wore a suit and tie and practically ran the economy of Canudos—his notes of credit were its currency. The merchant was also the man who imported, stockpiled and distributed the weaponry. The militia leader and the merchant were both unusually tall and about the only people in Canudos who lived in big houses with tiled roofs. They were dispensers of civil justice and the mainstays of civil order, the lay leaders of Canudos.

The Counselor had chosen Canudos with fine strategic instinct. It was the best place for water—from unseen artesian sources below ground and the river above—for miles around, and a site nobody could take by surprise. Ignoring the rout of the earlier expedition against it, Colonel Moreira Cesar sailed north from Rio in perfect confidence that his own much larger force would have no trouble against a settlement of unruly country people, and hardly bothered with the details of distance, climate, water, terrain in a region he knew nothing of. From Salvador he drove his men at a forced pace through the heat and desert of the drought. The transport wagons sank to the axle in sand, the soldiers tore their uniforms on the dense thorn shrub. At the expedition's first stop, engineers found they had brought the wrong equipment and were unable to sink a well for water. They had to press on.

As they neared Canudos and passed glowing embers from recent fires and remains of meals of roast kid and roast turtle, they realized their progress was being tracked by unseen eyes. They were drenched by a sudden downpour and everything turned to mud. Then the sun was blazing again. A group of horsemen galloped up and caused a panic, but they were guides sent by one of the landowners. They slept uneasily, the officers holding their horses' reins, and set off precipitously at first light. They were fired on near a homestead, but the attackers soon withdrew and the retreat gave the troops confidence. The colonel announced, *These people are unarmed* and urged his men on faster. He wanted to get in artillery range of Canudos. Morale soared. They were about to do what they had come to do. Under the scorching sun the troops scrambled up the slope of Monte Favella and on its peak they positioned the four Krupp cannons to fire on the settlement at its base. The size of the place quite startled them when they caught sight of Canudos below them, its thousands of small houses, the labyrinth of streets, the big square with the churches. The cannons started firing. A church bell below rang an alarm. Then the smoke from the cannons and the fires that broke out in the settlement and the dust raised by the smashed mud brick walls hid everything from sight. After a while the soldiers made out a scurrying of insect figures in the town, men heading into the scrub with rifles, women and children running for cover behind the thick walls of the unfinished new church. Nobody fired back and after a while the labyrinth of alleys was deserted again. The silence was total.

At one in the afternoon, under cover of artillery mounted on the hill across the river and facing the unfinished church, two columns of soldiers came down the slopes with their bayonets fixed. Buglers played as they crossed the river and entered the town, meeting only pebbles fired from ancient muskets. Then everything broke up. Inside the settlement the troops got lost in the maze of narrow irregular alleys. They were no longer a compact body but fighting as individuals against men who ambushed them with rifles, knives, scythes and table legs. The houses were solid. If grenades were used to blow them up, the rubble blocked advance. In the town, the soldiers lost the cover of their artillery, which could no longer fire without killing the men it was meant to protect. Snipers from the Catholic Guard hidden in the church tower picked off the military with impunity as the bell tolled again.

The colonel, who was starting to lose his nerve, ordered a cavalry charge, but the horses were spooked by the rifle fire coming across the river.

Darkness came quickly and after five hours of fighting the troops pulled out of the town. Now they were attacked from the scrub. The retreat turned into a rout. Platoons disintegrated as soldiers fought each other to escape, trampled the wounded, threw themselves into the river. The colonel, who was particularly loathed by his own men, fell from a bullet in the back. The people of Canudos gathered for the Angelus, and the troops could hear the Ave Maria drifting over the water as they hauled their cannons off. There were more than a hundred wounded beside the dying colonel, and they spent the night untreated, surrounded by the others, hidden in the darkness. The colonel refused a general retreat, but he was ignored and dead before daybreak. His men retreated without order, increasingly gripped by panic as the Canudos militia picked them off one by one from the scrub, dropping their weapons, their equipment and their wounded as they fled. They dumped the dead colonel, who was buried later with the others by the people of Canudos. The colonel who replaced him as leader was then himself killed in the retreat. At the end of the rout, the Canudos militia attacked the artillery and seized the army guns. The third expedition against Canudos had ended like the others.

Mud brick houses with one or two rooms, open spaces for doors and windows and dry fronds as a roof were soon rebuilt. Even after the assault by thirteen hundred troops with cannons, and although the governments of Bahia and Brazil were clearly determined to destroy the settlement, new people kept on coming to settle in Canudos. The Counselor was irresistibly attractive to the people struggling to survive in the interior. The balladeers of the drylands sang about him, and mocked the fallen Moreira Cesar. The landowners worked themselves into a frenzy about feared and rumored invasions of their property, attacks on their homesteads which never happened.

The people of Canudos knew nothing of the howling mobs that raged through the big cities after the army's new disaster in Canudos, and torched the offices of the monarchist press. They knew nothing of the national mourning decreed in Rio, the masses for the dead soldiers, the queues of volunteers from the *best families* lining up to join the forces of retribution. Without meaning to, the Counselor's subsistence farmers had shaken the republic to the point where the very future of Brazil was felt to depend on the total extermination of Canudos. As hard and canny veterans of dryland blood feuds, however, and victims of all the local agencies of power, they did know that bad brought worse and worse was coming. Canudos resumed its work on the big church—the Counselor was sixty-seven now, and anxious to see it finished soon—unknowing or uncaring that in the south they were seen as primitives, fanatics, a threat to civilization and the matter of other people's bad dreams. They had no idea that in London, having the benefit of distance, the *Times* sagely deemed the trouble insignificant in itself, but worried about the threat to the future stability of an outpost of the British economy. Brazil was finding itself unable to service its debt to the London banks.

After a while Canudos would have heard of the tumult in Salvador—the city on the coast was swollen now with soldiery and engineers and matériel. And of course the press. Men, armaments and war correspondents were shipped up from the south, banquets were held for the important visitors, Salvador's retail business flourished amid drunken brawls and sexual assaults. The entire Brazilian army was moving toward Canudos: thousands of troops from ten different states, with hundreds of machine guns, dozens of Krupp cannons, cavalry, engineers were gradually assembled in Salvador. Boys of thirteen were pressed into service to exterminate Canudos. It took more than three months to assemble the fourth expeditionary force. Over eight thousand men marched on Canudos that June, led by three generals and the minster for war himself, Marshal Bittencourt. Quite a few of the troops were recruited in the northeastern drylands, men who knew the terrain and its people. The new expedition was not going to make the mistakes of the last.

It was spooky all the same. Along the route they saw the rotting corpses of the men of the last expedition hanging from the thorn trees. The roadside was littered with skulls, and shreds of old army uniforms fluttered tangled in the thorns. One of the corpses they saw was the colonel who had led the retreat after the death of Moreira Cesar. Then a battalion was drawn into an ambush and hundreds of soldiers were killed. It was not beginning well. The expedition was being swept by rumors—reports that the Counselor's jagunços had taken surrounding towns, that foreign arms and mercenaries were getting to Canudos. The republican paranoia in Rio fed reports in the newspapers that the United States, France and Austria were ready to intervene and bring back the monarchy to Brazil. In Bahia, the drylanders' skill at moving unseen and fast around tracts of near desert fed the soldiers' panicky sense that they were facing an unknowable and invisible enemy. They were being attacked everywhere with the captured arms of the third expedition. Hundreds of soldiers deserted and made off into the scrub, and some of these joined the fighters from Canudos.

But the fourth expedition reached the district largely intact and set up its headquarters in the town of Monte Santo, throwing the inhabitants out of their houses to accommodate Marshal Bittencourt and the generals. The assault on Canudos began in July. Fifteen hundred men were dispatched to hold Monte Favella above Canudos, six thousand to surround the settlers and starve them. It took the army more than two months to lay a siege line around the settlement. In its first assault on Canudos the army lost a thousand men. Thereafter hundreds died each day among the army and the Canudos fighters from wounds or sickness. It went on for more than two months, and over time superior technology and the blockade on food and water began to tell. The dead were in their thousands and thousands. The fighters were able to slip out through the siege lines, and the battle of Canudos was fought as a series of guerrilla skirmishes over a wide area, but the center was always the settlement itself. The people never gave up.

Toward the end, some who had more to lose than their lives took stock. The merchant, who had moved to Canudos with his entire extended family, decided it was time to move on. He took leave of the Counselor, who was now sick with dysentery, and took his family away in small groups. He buried four boxes of silver in Canudos, and took with him several kilos of gold back to his home state of Ceará. On September 22 Antônio the Counselor died and was buried and two days later the army finally succeeded in encircling Canudos. Some of the fighters slipped away under cover of dark. The rest stayed. The jagunços counterattacked every night with their rifles—eighteen assaults on the night of September 27. On the first of October the army threw its heavy artillery at Canudos, smashing the mud brick houses where the inhabitants were sheltered and hurling grenades. Fires broke out and the whole settlement began to burn. Nobody cried out, nobody ran in the streets. They died silently in their homes.

The next day, being promised safety, five hundred women, some small children and a few old and wounded men gave themselves up to the army. The campaign photographer was brought over to take a picture of them huddled on the ground. The women's faces under shawls were masks of fear and pain, the children naked, the men grouped less distinctly at the back. The picture he took—unlike the endless studies of lines of tightly buttoned officers and wild eyed ragged soldiery he recorded standing outside their tents—came in close, at least to the women and children in the front, and the image of a mound of humanity was given a depth and strangely expressionist intensity by the flowing lines of the headcloths that framed the terrified fixity of the stares, all fenced in by the line of sticklike standing soldiers and a broken tree at the very back. When the photographer had done his work the military, notwithstanding their promise, cut the men to pieces under the women's eyes. The picture that survived was not technically remarkable, which was hardly surprising in the circumstances. It was greatly overexposed and seemed to obliterate its dreadful secrets just as an observer's ravenous horrified eye closed in on the detail. The foreground faces and figures that remained spoke for the others that were lost in the short distance. The drearily competent war photographer Flávio de Barros was probably unaware that he had caught one of the great images of the horrors of modern war, the first war photograph that registered not the combatants, bearded, male, alive or dead—and Barros brought back from Canudos nothing like the North American Civil War photographs taken by Mathew Brady decades earlier—but the collaterally damaged, the women, the children, the old, the hurt, frozen on their brief passage from one horror to a worse. The bleached out picture cast its shadow forward to certain images caught in Central Europe nearly half a century later.

In Brazil, it would not be matched until Sebastião Salgado published his photographs of the immense open gold mine of Serra Pelada nearly a hundred years later. Salgado's panoramic photographs were Dantescan: as images of an obscure punishment from which there was no escape, no end in sight, they would have seemed monstrous imaginings had they not been so precisely and unfakeably what they were. The mud of Serra Pelada had its continuities with the stone and grit of Canudos. A century on, the desperation of the Brazilian poor in the remotest corners of the country had found a new setting and no solution. Serra Pelada is worse: its miners have not been exterminated but—working their individual claims amid the arbitrary violence of their neighbors and the police—they have never known solidarity, never realized the beginnings of a shared future. Observers at Canudos described from their vantage point how the people died *like ants* under the army's final cannonade, a killing force that came from outside. Salgado's image shows people dying *like ants* without the intervention of the army.

The jagunços made their last stand firing from a trench by the Counselor's unfinished church. Among them were the last two chiefs of the Kiriri índios. The last to fall under the fire of five thousand infantry were an old man, two fighting men and a boy. No male of any age survived the destruction of Canudos. Every male prisoner, man or child, was taken out into the thorn scrub by the republican forces and his throat was slit. Many were treated worse. Prisoners had their eyes gouged out, were cut to pieces, children were smashed against trees. The army counted over five thousand houses in Canudos, and then dynamited and torched all those which had survived bombardment and fire, along with the thousands of unburied bodies of their inhabitants. There was a frenzy to eliminate every trace of the place and its inhabitants.

But there were too many dead. Fifteen thousand or more from the last days. Clouds of carrion birds hung in the air over Canudos and dogs howled for their fallen owners on the ground. For years afterward, whenever rains came, corpses washed up, mummified in the desert air and still dressed, some of them, in their officers' blue republican uniforms with the red stripe. Year after year after year, every little drylands shower brought up skulls and bones that the hooves of the oxen and the mules slowly ground back into the quartz and granite. The frenzy of extermination did not allow the Counselor to lie in peace. Two days after his community was razed, the army discovered where Antônio Vicente Mendes Maciel was buried and they dug him up and photographed the corpse. The picture of the dead and bearded Counselor anticipated the postmortem photographs of the bearded Che Guevara taken in Bolivia seventy years later.

They hacked off the decomposing head with a knife and carried it on a pike in civilization's victory parade through Salvador, much as Zumbi's had been after the destruction of Palmares two hundred years before. Then, this being the age of science, the head was taken to the Medical Faculty of Bahia to be studied for *abnormalities*.

When the troops arrived back in Rio the president went to meet them at the docks, and during the victory parade an ensign tried to assassinate him. The war minister Bittencourt stepped forward to help the president and was himself stabbed to death instead. Whether it was a conspiracy by the military was never known: the ensign's death in prison several weeks later was reported as suicide. Civilian rule tottered on. The nineteenth century was ending and Brazil was deeper in debt than ever to Britain, America, France, Germany. The war against Canudos nearly bankrupted the nation.

———

Traveling to Canudos now from Salvador, you go over paved roads over what seems for most of the way a straight line. The road just rises gently into terrain that is ever more sparsely peopled and trees and grass are gradually replaced by thorn scrub and spiky succulents, the cars by trucks and mules and bicycles. The journey from Salvador that Brazilian troops made over several days I did by bus in eleven hours. The railway was no more but the roads had improved. I left before daybreak and the light was still gray when the roadside monotony was broken by what looked like a vast and very trim military encampment. Hundreds of small structures were laid out in rows and rows of dead straight lines. They caught the eye because they were bright black and yellow. Wooden frames were walled in shiny black plastic sheeting and roofed in fresh straw. I assumed it was the army encamped here, but the big flag on the pole by the gate was not Brazil's: it was the red banner of the Landless Movement with the map in the middle. This was an occupation. It was very early and the landless seemed to be still in bed.

It startled me, not the size and the military order of this great encampment—I knew the organized landless were many millions, and I knew their systematic occupations of Brazil's unworked farmland, which had been going on for nearly twenty years, were formidably disciplined actions—but the thought that it was still going on. Brazil's rural poor at the end of the twentieth century were as badly off as the people who had set off with the Counselor a hundred years earlier to make the abandoned farmland of Canudos flourish. Worse off. Brazil's development had concentrated landowning, not opened it up. Inequality on the land was now even worse than Brazil's wealth distribution overall. It was the second worst in the world. One percent of Brazil's landowners owned forty-five percent of the agricultural land. Three percent owned two-thirds of it. Nearly a third of the farms in Brazil were family smallholdings, but these properties worked by their owners occupied one and a half percent of all the agricultural land. It wasn't, however, just the concentration of wealth. Many families had been dispossessed by the growth of the immense estates owned by Brazilian and foreign corporations—despite the drift to the great cities, Brazil had nearly five million landless rural families—and yet more than forty percent of Brazil's agricultural land was lying fallow. Ninety percent of the land in the big holdings was being left uncultivated. The monstrous waste and the hunger, in a land where nearly a third of the people lived in poverty and nearly one person in five suffered *extreme destitution,* had together triggered the land invasions.

The people who worked the land had missed out on everything. Until they organized themselves as the Landless Movement in 1985 they had no form of representation at all. Even

Lindolfo Collor's corporatist labor laws of 1930 had only applied to the industrial workers in the cities; and the working people's autonomy finally achieved in industry by Lula and the others fifty years later had passed country workers by entirely. And unlike the metalworkers of São Paulo, who could pack a football stadium in hours, the country people were isolated, scattered in all the lost corners of Brazil's immensity, utterly at the mercy of the landowners, the contemporary colonels, and the colonels' agents the hired gunmen and the military police. The violence was anything but random. Most of the dead were the leaders, organizers or spokesmen of the country workers. The assassination of the rubber workers' leader Chico Mendes in 1988 and the savagery of the Eldorado massacre in 1996 caught a flicker of attention from the world, but the rest of the ordinary everyday intimidation and murder went on and on unnoticed because it was so ordinary.

In Canudos it was raining—a fine soft intermittent drizzle rather than actual straight rain, surprising nevertheless—and there was a gray-green fuzz of vegetation on the face of the land. Until a few months earlier, not a drop of rain had fallen for six years. Or so Leandro told me. Leandro was a boy from New Canudos who drove me in his pickup to where the Counselor's people had made their stand. His mother did shampoos and perms from home and a small cousin came along for the ride. It was six months since the drought had broken and the people and their yellow-eyed goats had a sleek contented look. Canudos did not get a lot of visitors and the goats in particular did not try to disguise the intense curiosity aroused by a stranger. They followed me everywhere, swinging their pendulous velvet ears and chewing fast but thoughtfully as they sized me up. The old men were less curious, sitting in the shadows of the windowless farmworkers' club in New Canudos, looking out the door, taking things in, emaciated, observant, leathery as their leather dry-landers' hats, helmets with a narrow upturned brim and a broad leather lace hanging down at the back.

The old Canudos, wiped out, remained a wasteland for many years. Local people buried some of the thousands of bodies and the orphaned children were taken away into domestic service. Bones, bullets, shell cases, all the hard stuff lay scattered all over the district for decades, slowly being broken up and trodden into the stony ground. A little rain always turned up fresh skulls. And since drylanders who do not die young of violence or disease are indestructibly tough and live long lives, until quite late in the following century there were old and then ancient people in the district who remembered the last days of the Counselor's people. An ending of a kind came as a final act of desecration long after the event itself, in the flooding of the river valley in the 1970s to make a dam which covered the cemetery and the unburied remains and drowned the one part of Canudos which remained, the massive ruined hulk of the Counselor's new church. Very occasionally, the water level gets so low that the submerged ruin reappears, like a dreadful memory returning. The irrigation system fed by the dam serves mainly the big landowners, and the smallholders of New Canudos hardly at all, and in that sense is true to drylands history. Leandro and I and Leandro's cousin looked out over the water covering the church, and into a tiny museum into which the rusting relics had been gathered—some pistols, a few muskets and rifles, bridles, horseshoes, a sewing machine, a shoemaker's last, a hoe, buttons, needles, a couple of family photographs. Really, there was nothing, or rather that little that reminds you how easily the traces of ordinary life all vanish. These were the instruments of that daily work that the war of Canudos, on the part of its losers, was fought to defend.

I arrived in New Canudos in the middle of a Sunday afternoon expecting no sign of human life and found it seething with activity. It was market day in the main street and when Leandro brought me back from the old site at the end of the afternoon, when the unsold goods were being loaded onto trucks, and the buyers and sellers from surrounding settlements were standing patiently at the parrot perch on the trays of other trucks, the fine rain got heavier and the ground got muddy and the people clearing up got more impatient and the ones drinking in the bars got more raucous and some of the girls were being cruised by boys and others were on the lookout for more mature men with money in their wallets. There were a fair few of these and as night fell on New Canudos I watched girl after girl climbing into pickup trucks alongside middle-aged men they had lately met and roaring off into the night.

Soon after dark all was dismantled, the respectable people had disappeared and the limited but intense night life of New Canudos unfolded in its weird splendor. I had to wait several hours for the bus that would take me to Salvador, and took refuge from the dark and the drizzle and the sudden chill of the upland night in what seemed a quiet and moderately clean pizzeria. It was quiet, though not clean, but quiet only because the people of the drylands kept talk to a minimum in extent and volume. In this they were like Sicilians, and for similar reasons. The movement of persons in and out of the pizzeria and within the pizzeria was manic but almost entirely mute. Part of it seemed to be that the protagonists of all the permutations and combinations knew each other so well and had done all this so often before that words no longer mattered. It may also have been that they were all coked up. The performance was electrifying and I was trapped there for hours. For this reason my memory of Canudos will not be the place of desolation I expected to find, but a girl in a black lace brassiere, a tiny bolero in tan mock suede that came halfway down her back and halfway across her front, crotch length shorts in purple crushed velvet held up by a single button on a tense and fraying thread, and platform soled espadrilles. She was a girl who would have appalled the Counselor.

IX

Witnesses

The foreign correspondents who covered what was soon being
called the War of Canudos, as if it were a conflict between nations
rather than the extermination of a tiny community within a single
country, were nearly all embedded with the army of the Brazilian
republic. They had been sent up from the south and needed no
urging to take the republic's part against the strange inhabitants
of this lunar landscape. Embedding was taken seriously in those
days. Most of the reporters were military men themselves, or were
made army officers for the occasion. This did not always secure the
right attitude. One honorary army captain and the correspondent
of a big Rio daily was also a northeasterner alert to local realities,
and he noticed how well the people of Canudos kept up their
land, tending their pastures and retrieving strayed goats even as
the war raged. *So far nobody has managed to give an idea of {their}
culture, bravery and fighting style,* he reported in July, and segued
into one of the first accounts of modern guerrilla warfare.
Unwisely, he also wrote south that the fighting in the drylands
had nothing to do with monarchism, and was promptly expelled
from the war zone and sacked from the paper for his frankness.
This was not what the army or the government wanted people

to be reading. This correspondent was maybe the only person present during the fighting at Canudos to understand that he was witnessing a people's struggle for economic survival.

The man reporting for São Paulo's biggest newspaper was Bahian by family and partly by upbringing, but born near Rio and every inch a southeasterner in his beliefs. A passionate republican and positivist from his schooldays, Euclides da Cunha was also very much a military man, though his relations with the armed forces had been stormy from the start. As a military cadet in the last days of the empire he had flung down his sword during an inspection by the imperial war minister and been drummed out of the war college. He later rejoined the army and left again. In 1897 he was thirty-one and working as a civil engineer—but known as an articulate propagandist for the republic—when he was invited to reactivate his army commission and sail north on the staff of the war minister Bittencourt as adjutant and war correspondent for the final campaign against the people of Canudos. Da Cunha did not see all that much of the fighting. He spent most of August in Salvador and then traveled by train and horseback to Bittencourt's headquarters in Monte Santo. He was hardly more than a fortnight in Canudos and didn't file a report directly from there until a week before the army's final assault. He got close enough, however, to be deeply marked by what he saw and heard and felt. His last telegram to the newspaper in São Paulo, before the fall, proclaimed, *The republic is immortal!* The two he sent from Canudos a few days later, at the very end, were notably terse.

Euclides da Cunha spent the next four years struggling to reconcile what he had seen at Canudos with his belief in the future of Brazil. He worked it out in a long book which he called *Os Sertões,* or *The Drylands,* and published in 1902. He was fighting his own mental demons: his obsession with progress and modernity, the scientific racism that told him the people of the northeastern interior were doomed to backwardness by their mixed race. He had been overwhelmed by the wild, bleak beauty of the drylands—even from the front, as the massacre entered its last convulsion, he had been telegraphing south rather more lyrical evocations of daybreak in the desert than behooved a man reporting on the republic's hour of greatest danger—and what he saw of the people too was at odds with what he was reporting from inside the war minister's entourage. He registered their toughness and resilience, their remarkable ability to survive in an unimaginably difficult landscape, the bravery and cunning they showed in meeting a mortal threat. Like all the outsiders who arrived in Canudos he felt obscurely diminished by the jagunços' readiness to die to defend their way of life.

Euclides the Brazilian engineer and republican, violence hating soldier and militant journalist, failed to find a way out of the prison of his preconceptions. *Order and progress* mattered too much. But he could see and feel the otherness of this unknown world of the interior. It fired his imagination and so did the horror that was visited on it by the very forces of his adored modernity. Thrashing about in his mental cage, he wrote a tortured and powerful book. Its talk about *the resurrection under arms of an old society, a dead society, galvanized into life by a madman* was elaborated in the crass and ugly vocabulary of positivism, and Euclides clung to his original view of Canudos, even while his account of the land and its people was lit up by a passionate sympathy. To read it you had to ignore the teller who was so insistently explaining what it all meant and listen to his tale.

Or hold both the story and its interpretation in your own mind simultaneously, as Euclides so uncomfortably did himself. Those Brazilians who read books found that their minds too were able to embrace the radical contradiction Euclides embodied— he whose dark fine índio features were so much more those of a

northeastern drylander than of a Francophile metropolitan from
the south—and they greeted *The Drylands* with a rush of amazed
self-recognition. The book had trouble finding a publisher but
when it came out at the end of 1902 it met with huge and
immediate success, and went on having success for the next hundred years. This weird work of epic journalism became, and
stayed, the great Brazilian book. It gave the feeling of meaning
to the terrible slaughter. Its success was as unlikely as the recognition of *Moby-Dick* as the great American novel, and came
far sooner. *The Drylands* was obsessive like *Moby-Dick* and it had
the same epic remoteness from its readers' everyday lives—there
were hardly more Brazilian readers who knew the northeastern
drylands directly than North American readers with a firsthand
knowledge of whaling.

The tense, nervy, earnest builder of bridges Euclides da
Cunha became a literary celebrity overnight. He was elected to
the Brazilian Academy of Letters. He was also inducted into that
stronghold of Brazilian imperial tradition, the Geographical and
Historical Institute, and the government made him head of an
expedition exploring Amazônia. It was perhaps during the year
he was away from home that his wife, who was the daughter of
a general, began an affair with a seventeen-year-old military
cadet in Rio. The adultery became notorious. Euclides contrived
to ignore it, though the cadet fathered one of his children, until
one afternoon in 1909, when Euclides arriving home saw the
cadet coming out of his house. In a sudden jealous fury he fired
his revolver twice at his wife's lover, missing both times. The
cadet pulled his own gun and killed Euclides with a single shot
to the head. A few years later a son of Euclides tried to avenge
his father and was killed in turn by the same man. The lover
was acquitted once again on grounds of self-defense and later
became a general in the Brazilian army. For a long time people
suspected that the army itself, deeply unhappy that the realities

of its genocidal devastation of Canudos were broadcast in a best-selling book and fearing Euclides planned further revelations in a revised version, had plotted the assassination, but the killing seems to have been an entirely domestic matter, if killings ever are. It was a failed crime of passion.

———

When Euclides was about midway through writing *The Drylands* in his evenings after work, in a wooden shack on the site of a bridge construction job he was supervising, a Polish exile named Korzeniowski, who had become an officer in the British merchant marine and lately turned English novelist writing as Joseph Conrad, spent a month at the end of 1898 writing his first indisputably major work. At less than forty thousand words it had none of *The Drylands'* bulk and none of its awkward portentousness. It was a novella written in a deprecatory conversational tone which slowly, inexorably, in the hundred years that followed, became Conrad's most famous and most read book.

Heart of Darkness, like *The Drylands,* grew out of a working journey made by its author from the metropolis to the remote outer edge of the imperial world. At this outer edge each found horror. Conrad arrived in Africa aboard the *Ville de Maceió* to command a riverboat on the Congo and found the human devastation wrought by Queen Victoria's cousin Leopold of Belgium. The moral annihilation of the Europeans in Africa was a part of the damage done by a rush of mad greed called a *mission civilisatrice.* The company doctor measures the cranium of the departing employee with a pair of calipers; human skulls surround the company agent's upriver hut. What Euclides saw in Brazil was the consequence of an earlier paroxysm of European greed whose victims had also been African as well as índio. New World slavery was an exercise in depredation, enslavement and genocide which preceded the big assault on Africa itself. When the Belgians brought the slave labor system home to Africa—at a time when slavery had been abolished even in Brazil—they made it even more inhuman. Unlike Euclides, Conrad saw the connection between the ideology and its consequences.

Heart of Darkness was published with two other stories in London in 1902, the same year Euclides' book appeared in Brazil. Conrad then began to work the single terrible insight of his African story into a daring and complex novel set in an *imaginary (but true)* country in South America. Conrad made his Costaguana into the most sensuously real country ever imagined, and every detail in *Nostromo* carried its moral freight. There is nothing else like it in English. His Africa and Asia were written out of his own close experience, but Conrad's Latin America was based on the merest fleeting memory from his first ocean voyage twenty-five years before, and on some of the travel and adventure memoirs that proliferated in the imperial metropole toward the end of the imperial century. He also relied on advice from his friend Cunninghame Grahame, a Scottish traveler and adventurer who had contributed mightily to the genre, mainly with books mixing history with his own adventures in South America. Cunninghame Grahame ranged widely over the continent but didn't touch Brazil until he plundered Euclides' book for a quickie of his own which he published as *A Brazilian Mystic* in 1925. This book was little noticed, but in a small way, by taking over Euclides' version into English, Cunninghame Grahame kept the notion alive that the Canudos slaughter had been all about religion. When Samuel Putnam translated *The Drylands* excellently into English in 1949, he misleadingly called it *Rebellion in the Backlands* and made people think the slaughter had followed an armed uprising by the people of Canudos. Mario Vargas Llosa worked the same material into a verbose epic of 1981 called *The War of the End of the World,* and so helped to keep the phantasm of a religious revolt in Canudos alive until a hundred years had passed since the people there were massacred.

Conrad's *Nostromo,* however, a book written in English by a Pole who was working from a twenty-five-year-old memory of *a short glance* at the continent, was the great book about Latin America. It was great for the hallucinatory economy and precision with which it showed the disconnections and the unrealities of Europe in the New World, and the destructive cruelties brought about by the pursuit of *material interests.* It caught the magic beauty of the continent—I can hardly look at Guanabara Bay where Rio stands, at the play of light over its hills and monoliths and water, breathe its sweet air, without thinking of Conrad's Golfo Placido, although Costaguana is on the Pacific coast and overlooked by the snow covered Andes, insofar as it is anywhere at all. Conrad may have only had *a glimpse* of South America, but he could see the British railways and the Italian immigrants of Brazil—*Nostromo* has some further claim to being a great novel about Italy, where it is as little appreciated as it is in Latin America—the torturers and the radical priests, the devotees of progress, the devastated environment. He saw how the British interests, to which Brazil like the whole continent was so deeply indebted, were becoming ever more beholden in their turn to North American interests working out of skyscrapers in *the greatest country in the whole of God's universe,* to men like the fundamentalist Christian who announces in *Nostromo* that *We shall run the world's business whether the world likes it or not.*

When he was in Africa the only European Conrad found to respect was a British consul at Boma near the mouth of the Congo. Roger Casement, who was actually Irish, saw the Belgians come in and the rubber and ivory go out and he caused some difficulties in the metropole the year after *Heart of Darkness* came out as an adventure tale. He made a report to his government on the Belgian regime of slave labor and genocide in King

Leopold's private dominion in Africa. The report was challenged but the consul, who had once been employed himself by King Leopold in the Congo and knew how the system worked, was vindicated and awarded a modest honor for his work against slavery. He was nevertheless eased out of Africa and posted to Brazil, first as consul at Santos for São Paulo in the south and then to Belém at the mouth of the Amazon in the north. In 1908 he was made British consul general in Rio. If the British government had wanted quietly to remove one of its slightly overzealous servants to a place where he would be less of a disturbance to the business of empire, South America was an unfortunate choice. In Belém Casement had heard about atrocities on Amazonian rubber plantations, and in 1910 he sailed up the Amazon through Brazil from Belém and Manaus and on to the Putumayo River region in what is now part of Colombia and was then part of Peru.

He found that the enslavement of the Amerindian rubber gatherers was as terrible as the Africans' had been. In the Congo, aside from the intermittent slaughter of the men, the chain gangs and the death by starvation, the hands of the Congolese women and children were quite routinely chopped off if the gatherers fell behind in their rubber quota. So King Leopold in Brussels made sure they never reached it, as he *sat at home and drank blood.* Mark Twain put it thus, circulating the photos of the children with their stumps. Casement's report on the activities of the Peruvian Amazon Rubber Company, which was based in London, recorded a hideous orgy of flogging, rape, mutilation, starvation, shooting. People were hacked to pieces. It was all too much for the metropole. There was a parliamentary inquiry in London. Measures were taken and Casement came out of it with a knighthood. Abruptly he left the consular service. He lost the knighthood three years later, when he was convicted of treason in 1916 for his efforts to help free Ireland from British rule and hanged. The trial shocked people who knew Casement, but the several efforts to obtain a reprieve were undermined by the British government's circulation to influential people of Casement's confidential diaries recording his sexual activities with a large number of young men in different countries. Casement had two or three parallel records of his activities on the go simultaneously, and the terse, sometimes effusive annotations of his most private record would surprise or offend no one now, but at the crisis of European imperialism, and within the particularly repressed and duplicitous British version of imperialism, they were fatal to their writer. The greatest number of annotations were of encounters with young Brazilians.

———

Fernando Collor never really got over 1990 and the failure of his bank seizure. His end was in his beginning, and the scandals in the airline industry, the oil industry and the road transport industry followed at ever shorter intervals. In Brazil, however, the system was elastic. It stretched and stretched, even when leaders failed to manage the economy, even when they were manifestly corrupt, and the scandals were not generally seen as scandals at the time. Fernando never looked to be in trouble until Pedro intervened. The rivalry between Fernando and his younger brother was complicated. There were crosscurrents of conflict between the brothers and their wives, and rivalry between the wives and conflict between the two sisters in the family, and the role of the interloper PC. There was Dona Leda's anguished matriarchy. The Fernando and Rosane story was only one of a dense mesh of plot lines in the family story, and the others soon followed on the screen.

Fernando's problem with Pedro began in early childhood and took its specific adult form the year before he became president. Fernando had sneakily tried to win control of the family media organization, which he and PC wanted as a platform and a power base in Alagoas. Pedro had outmaneuvered Fernando and PC, to their surprise and displeasure. Now they were mounting a rival media group and Pedro, who ran the organization, was beside himself. Fernando talked about an *unpretentious* little newspaper *in black and white* that would merely *take up some political space* and not compete with the family's daily, while PC quietly spent $5 million on color offset presses and his brother Augusto gathered up radio licenses. They hoped Roberto Marinho might give them the Globo transmission rights, which would leave the family firm without its main income. Business was complicated by sex. In 1987 Pedro's marriage had been rocky. He was overworked and drinking a lot of vodka on weekends. He got back from a business trip to the United States and heard how his wife, Thereza, had been locked away with Fernando in the governor's suite for hours on end and how she came out flushed and disordered from these long encounters. Another person who soon heard the stories was Rosane, who had never trusted Thereza. *I'm thinking you wanted to marry the other Collor,* she said on the phone to Thereza. *My Collor.* Flustered, Thereza denied everything. *I'm warning you, Thereza,* went on Rosane before she slammed down the receiver, *I've got my eye on you.*

The new media group was part of PC's plan for long-term power. Fernando was mainly attracted by the idea of destroying Pedro. At a social occasion in the blazing heat of Maceió at the end of 1991, someone brought Pedro an offer from PC: $25 million to leave Brazil until after the presidential elections of 1994 and give up all business in the media. And never enter politics in Alagoas. Pedro took a slug of vodka and suggested $50 million. The intermediary laughed nervously. Pedro suddenly felt afraid. It occurred to him that there were much easier and cheaper options available to PC if he wanted Pedro out of the way. There were so many contract killings in Alagoas that people hardly noticed and the going price was five hundred dollars. Pedro went home and recorded two videotapes outlining what he knew of PC's activities, of how Fernando and PC split the take and how PC paid Rosane's huge personal bills and had bought Fernando a $3 million apartment in Paris. He described the offer of $25 million to get out of Brazil and preemptively accused Fernando and PC in the case of his murder. Pedro locked the tapes in a small brown leather suitcase and buried the suitcase at the back of his wardrobe. A little later he went to Miami and locked his tapes in a bank safe-deposit box and took out a $3 million life insurance policy. Friends in Miami told him a financial operator of the Cuban diaspora had been bragging about his links to the *immensely rich* Brazilian called Farias who had *enormous influence inside the Brazilian government.* Pedro started working the Miami financial network to find out more.

In Brazil PC attacked. He called Pedro *the Vodka Boy* in an interview. *The kid's got a brain this small and he drinks slugs of vodka this big.* Pedro gave his own interview. He called PC a *walking disease* and said he had material to bring down the government of Brazil in days. Fernando's private secretary was on the phone straightaway. *Pedro, for the love of God—.* Pedro shouted back, *Do you all think I'm a child?* The secretary told him Fernando was going through *a horrendous time with Rosane* and had not spoken to anyone for a week. *And this interview . . . there must be a way . . .* The chief state prosecutor was talking about an inquiry. *You lot planted the pineapple,* said Pedro sententiously. *Now you can peel it. Enjoy Carnival.*

The Carnival of 1992 came and went and a friend of Pedro's in Miami called to say PC was moving enormous quantities of cash that had to come from drugs. Pedro flew back to Miami. He told people he was the covert emissary of the president of Brazil, who was *worried* about the activities of his associate PC Farias. Six months earlier in Brazil the federal police had arrested someone setting up business fronts for the Cali cartel from Colombia—he was carrying $4.5 million and said the money belonged to a person with known links to Fernando and PC. He had also met with the Colombian cocaine people in São Paulo. The president might well be concerned. Pedro found a financier who knew PC and his companies—there were at least nine of them, apart from the air taxi companies. PC had over half a billion dollars in banks around the world and the *intricate meshing* of his companies looked like a drug cartel arrangement. *The president,* Pedro said, *needs details of Mr. Farias's companies and his business dealings . . . He wants me to come back to Brazil as soon as I've got hold of the incriminating material.* Two days later the financier handed over details of PC's companies and photocopies recording movements of around $50 million in the United States, the United Kingdom, France, Switzerland and the Caribbean. One document signed by PC authorized a Cuban proxy to transfer funds from the account of Dupont Investments with Citibank International in Miami to the Multi Commercial Bank in Switzerland. There were a couple of big checks drawn on the BNP in Paris, and a letter to PC's lawyer in Brazil about the registering of one of his companies in France. Pedro left one set of copies in his Miami safe-deposit box and took another back to Brazil. Three days later he started getting death threats.

The messages seemed to come from PC's brothers. The Farias siblings had been moving up in the world with PC. Augusto Farias was now a federal congressman and to Pedro he seemed *the most excitable* of the family and the threats were coming from him. Farias friends and associates told Pedro he should *look out,* because if he went on attacking PC something *very bad* might happen to him. Pedro's wife, Thereza, also got telephone calls and once a male voice called his secretary to say that Pedro might be found one day soon *with his mouth full of ants.* The speaker was evidently a man of the northestern drylands. Down south an article appeared on *PC's tentacles.* PC denied owning offshore companies, denied it was his signature on the proxy document and said Pedro had forged the papers. Then someone got hold of PC's tax returns. For 1990 PC had reported an income of only twenty-five thousand dollars and questions were asked in Congress. PC's nerves were frayed. *This country is a democracy,* he shouted, losing his equanimity for once. *And in a democracy nobody gets hunted down like an animal.* He called Pedro *Cokehead.*

A week later Pedro had a showdown with his mother in the presidential suite of the Caesar Park Hotel in São Paulo. Dona Leda, who told people she *thought in French,* had been spending most of her later years preparing for the life to come in an increasingly eclectic series of spiritual exercises and retreats. She was nevertheless still worldly enough to be pleased to be the president's mother and determined to remain such, and when Pedro refused to stop undermining Fernando she sacked him as director of the family firm. The dismissal fax signed by Dona Leda mentioned *a serious emotional crisis* and it came from *the press secretariat of the presidency of the republic.* Pedro saw it as Fernando's work and felt *strangely calm, wounded by the brutal injustice but unmoved by my own mother's treachery.* He now attacked Fernando openly. *PC is the front man. Fernando takes seventy percent.* TV Globo began wondering what to do. So far they had ignored the gathering storm—Roberto Marinho had told the director, *Nothing's going to come of it. It's just a family squabble. This boy Pedro's worthless.* Now Globo ran its first little story on what was happening, and the next day the Brazilian Congress, urged forward by the deputies of the Workers' Party, announced a parliamentary inquiry into PC's activities. However, the inquiry would not be looking into PC's connection with the president.

Brazilians expected little of their leaders and even less of the mob in Congress, but now the scale of the crimes being alleged was so great and the president's claimed involvement so deep that the crisis paralyzing the government held a vast fascination. And what gripped people, and most of all those people who hardly knew or cared what it all meant for Brazil, was that Fernando was being undone by his own brother's vendetta. The war between the brothers, the war between the wives and the aging matriarch's struggle to revive her dynasty's power and fortune and bring unity to her children, the sinister interloper and the troubles he brought—the drama being played out on the TV screens was following the most rigorous rules of an art Brazilians knew better than any other. Viewers were riveted as Fernando told the nation on TV that he had ordered the federal police to investigate his brother. Audience interest surged when Thereza turned up at the inquiry to give Pedro moral support. She arrived on very high heels and in a very short red dress and a senator of the Workers' Party lunged forward with the offer of a chair. Thereza chose a strategic spot between the commission and the congressional benches, demurely crossed and uncrossed her bare tanned legs and was never off camera.

PC faced down the congressmen through tinted shades and said loudly, *We're all being hypocrites on this,* sure they could prove nothing and confident of what he knew about them. Pedro feared arrest after Fernando's threats and said almost nothing. No industrialist wanted to talk about payments to PC; then one small businessman spoke up, who had been shocked when PC's people demanded forty percent of the value of his contracts with the government. This was far more than he had paid to do business with previous administrations and he had refused and PC's people had locked him out of government business. The businessman directed the inquiry to Brazil Jet's office and a suite owned by one of PC's brothers. The businessman drew a very detailed plan of the suite and PC's brother, who was head of Brazil's health ministry, had to spend all night rearranging the furniture before the commission's visit. Jorge Bandeira was called and remembered nothing about the companies he was a director of, not even their addresses or who his fellow directors were, or why Brazil Jet's planes flew quite so often to Brazil's cocaine producing neighbors. Outside Congress people were less shy. The former head of Petrobras, who had been PC's first victim, spoke about PC and *the man who gave him the power to do what he did . . . Fernando Collor de Mello.* The former head of Fernando's party said, *PC is an extension of the president . . . Like a virus PC is going to corrupt the whole fabric of public administration in this country.* Fernando went on TV again and called his old ally *a loser.* Fernando understood it was on TV that it would all be played out.

———

Plenty of suggestive things about how PC worked were heard by the commission but there was little real evidence and none at all that tied PC to the president of Brazil. The lack of hard proof slowly wore the hearings down. Viewer interest waned with the dramatic tension. The Workers' Party demanded that the commission look into Fernando's role in milking the Brazilian economy, but all the other parties blocked this avenue— the politicians were as nervous as the industrialists about where the inquiry might lead, and those who knew most about PC's extortions had no intention of incriminating themselves. The establishment was closing ranks and Fernando's people exulted. In the end it was not a member of Brazil's industrial or political elite who took Fernando down. Insofar as any single person broke through the president's defense, it was one of those people Brazil's economic and political processes had always overlooked. None of the sleek silk-suited figures who were probing, lobbying, threatening, pleading in those days of uncertainty at Brazil's center of power would have thought for an instant about

Eriberto França. He was one of the army of faceless personal servants who had always made life so easy for Brazil's better off.

Eriberto was twenty-eight and might have been a younger Lula. He was the youngest of seven children of rural workers from the Northeast. Five of the others had died in early infancy. When Eriberto was nine, his mother and father had upped stakes and migrated with their two surviving children to Brasilia, where the child Eriberto sold grilled corn cobs at the bus stops. His father saved for two years and bought a van, and at eleven Eriberto was its driver, delivering fruit and vegetables around the city before daybreak. Later he got a driver's license and drove buses. In 1989 he landed a job driving for Fernando's campaign and so in his twenties he became a driver on the presidential staff in Brasilia. He was entrusted with the more delicate jobs, and drove visitors like Dona Cecilia, the Xangô priestess from Alagoas who led private African Brazilian ceremonies for Fernando and Rosane in their Brasilia home. He had delivered an actress from one of the soaps to a late night meeting with Fernando, who liked the look of her. Mostly he ran errands for Fernando's personal secretary, in two cars rented by PC. Eriberto picked up checks and cash from Brazil Jet and delivered them to the housekeeper at Fernando's home, who used them to pay Fernando's staff. Eriberto was the material link between PC and Fernando and he had checks and receipts to prove it.

After Eriberto spoke to the reporters who had found him, they published an article showing how Fernando's family expenses were paid out of three accounts held by his personal secretary in three different banks in three different names. When Fernando needed money, his secretary called PC's secretary, and the money arrived from PC's accounts. Even Dona Leda, who abhorred the man, got money in this way from PC. Having revealed this, Eriberto was now in danger. He resigned his job and the reporters flew him to Bahia with his wife and children, where they went into hiding on a farm. When Eriberto saw the story on Fernando at the airport in Salvador, and his own face on the cover of the magazine that was everywhere, his arms shook so violently he couldn't read. *You've fucked up my life,* he said to the reporters. On the farm he calmed down. The country and the animals recalled his childhood, before his parents had moved to Brasília. Back in the capital, Fernando went on TV yet again: *I have no business ties with Senhor PC Farias.* But everything was falling to pieces around him. The inquiry got PC's accounts, and records of the payments to Fernando's secretary. *O Globo,* of all papers, published records of all the phone calls made from PC's office to the presidential palace and the president's own office. The armor plated car used by Fernando's sons in Rio was shown to be PC's. PC reached everywhere.

Eriberto lost four kilos in the days before he testified. He couldn't sleep and his gut was knotted. One of Fernando's people tried to lure him to a private meeting with the president while others combed Brasília's police files for dirt. At the inquiry Fernando's loyalists tried to throw him. *You say you're poor but you've just given up a good job. What are you going to live on? Got something put away?* they asked. *No, but I don't lack the will to work,* replied Eriberto briskly. *You mean you're doing it all just out of patriotism?* they asked. *Isn't that enough for you?* said Eriberto sharply. An insinuation about the *diamond jewelery* Eriberto's wife wore at the hearing got an even sharper response. *It's costume jewelery and I bought it at the market and I'll thank you to respect my wife,* snapped Eriberto. He explained how PC financed the president. He remembered a new car he had picked up for Fernando, paid for with a check drawn on one of PC's accounts and signed by Bandeira's imaginary alter ego. It was stunning for the viewing audience to see one of the walk-ons—a door opener, a spear carrier—at the center of an episode and putting the powerful in their place. The powerful were speechless. The script had taken a drastic and unprecedented turn and the public came flooding back.

Fernando's people told the inquiry all his money came from a $5 million campaign loan raised in Uruguay in 1989. They were given three days to prove this. The Montevideo connection turned out to consist of a convicted gangster, an illegal currency trader and a businessman on the run from gold bullion smuggling charges and the Uruguay version collapsed as soon as it was floated. The president had lied and now his back was to the wall. The whole thing was too much for Dona Leda. In a long phone call to her younger daughter the matriarch poured out her terminal exasperation with her favorite son, Pedro. It was a marvelous prolonged close-up moment.

> You think it's right for one brother to go round saying the other's a crook? . . . Didn't he see he was going to lead us all to disaster, that he was going to leave me in the worst possible situation as a mother? . . . I'm at the end of my life and nothing worse could have happened to me. One son's a crook and the other's a snitch.

————

Halfway through July, TV Globo began showing a new drama series. *The Rebel Years* was rather daring. It broke away from the usual soap formula and dealt with the repression under Brazil's military and on the young people who resisted it. Suppression of personal rights of expression and association, arbitrary imprisonment, torture and murder at the hands of the military were not the usual Globo fare. The whole point of the soaps had been not to think about those things. In earlier days military officers had sat in the editorial rooms of daily papers *at risk* to censor the contents before they went to press. Brazilians, even friends or family of the victims, didn't know what was happening to the young people who disappeared. They were never mentioned. The Globo soaps, whose golden age the dictatorship was, had blocked out the sound of gunfire and the screams of the tortured. The past remained a dark pool nobody had yet plumbed and *The Rebel Years,* however timid and anodyne, peeped into the years of exile, of the resistance by students, workers, soldiers. People were reminded of the metalworkers who went on strike and the hundreds of thousands who took to the streets to demand DIRECT ELECTIONS NOW. They were also reminded of the misfortunes, bunglings and compromises that had come with democracy. Was it for Fernando that people had fought and died? For PC Farias? Young people were fascinated by this unknown past. The army ministry was furious at the program's *deformed and tendentious view* of what it called the *Democratic Revolution of 1964.*

One day in August, as the inquiry neared its end, some school students demonstrated in São Paulo. THE REBEL YEARS: NEXT EPISODE. COLLOR OUT: IMPEACHMENT NOW. They were echoing the old, great failed campaign of 1985 for DIRECT ELECTIONS NOW. The students' march began small and quickly grew to ten thousand people. It stopped the traffic in the center of the city and office workers urged the students on by showering them with festive shredded paper from the skyscrapers. Fernando was furious. Speaking extempore in Brasilia, he called on Brazilians to put an end to *disturbance* and support the president by turning out the following Sunday wearing the national *colors* of blue, green and yellow. Now Fernando's remaining powerful supporters in the political establishment were furious. *The man's mad,* thought one. *What's this shit?* yelled another. Fernando had got carried away. Three days later students in Rio gathered outside Fernando's old private school in Copacabana. They wore black armbands and went on a march through the center of Rio, where they were joined by thousands of office workers at closing time. *PC TO JAIL AND TAKE COLLOR WITH YOU,* they cried. Hundreds of PC Farias masks appeared, and PC's bald head and glasses over a thick mustache multiplied through the crowd. A samba school materialized and the march through the center of Rio became a kind of Carnival of revolt. When Sunday came everyone in Brazil seemed to be wearing black.

Fernando and Rosane did what they could. Rosane had a rag doll made of each of the president's enemies, and riddled them all with black and red pins while she prayed for the enemies' undoing. Under the guidance of Dona Cecilia of Arapiraca, as the end approached, she and Fernando sacrificed black roosters and goats, bleeding the animals to death inside their home as they prayed for their own survival and cutting off their heads. The animals bled in vain.

On the Tuesday sixty thousand people gathered in front of the Congress building in Brasilia, waiting for the inquiry findings. Hundreds of thousands gathered in forty other cities around Brazil. In São Paulo universities and factories went on strike, and half a million people demonstrated. In Rio a sea of people flooded through the center. In Recife, I heard a dull roar come floating up from the Avenida Conde de Boa Vista and in through the open windows of my apartment. To thrilling rapid-beaten drums, a hundred thousand young people were marching toward the center of the city, faces painted in Brazilian green, blue and yellow. They were the *painted faces* and Recife's contribution to the upsurge, students from Recife's schools and universities. An indescribable gaiety rose into the air. It was dark when they surged past the Pátio de São Pedro. *Painted faces* came pouring into the Bangüê to use the inadequate lavatory. José huffed and frowned in displeasure at the youngsters who failed to buy a single soft drink and showed disrespect toward the nation's leader. José was out of touch. All around Brazil giant bald bespectacled PC dolls were being paraded down the streets, and dolls of Fernando and Rosane in convict garb. There was music and dancing and rhythmic chanted slogans were heard about Fernando snorting cocaine and Rosane's monthly spending. In the second Carnival of 1992 everyone had the same theme.

The inquiry commission took five hours to present its findings. It found PC had committed seven criminal offenses worth fifty-nine years in jail. Industrialists and businesspeople were seen as victims of an extortion racket. Fernando was found guilty of fraud, conflict of interest, passive corruption, criminal conspiracy and abetting criminal acts—charges worth eighteen years' jail and permanent exclusion from holding public office. The commission remarked how all of Fernando's inner circle had emptied their bank accounts in the days before the freeze. This hit home, because ordinary Brazilians had only lately retrieved their much diminished personal savings and the seizure had done nothing for the economy. For a year and a half inflation had been running at twenty percent a month. *Rouba, mas faz,* Brazilians had always said of their more competent politicians. *On the take but gets things done.* Fernando had got nothing done. Brazil had been in recession all through his presidency. The gross domestic product had fallen nearly five percent in his first year in office and was still falling. Fifteen percent of the active population of São Paulo—the economic powerhouse of South America, with an economy bigger than Argentina's—was out of work. Two hundred and ninety cases of corruption in government were reported during Fernando's presidency. Brazil was sinking deeper into the swamp of underdevelopment.

The honorable president of the republic has been receiving throughout his term of office illicit financial gain in the form both of bank deposits . . . and of material goods and services . . . has failed in his institutional responsibility to maintain public morality and prevent third parties from using his name for personal enrichment without cause or from practices at the outer limits of morality and decency. These, the timid relator said firmly, were criminal matters for the public prosecutor. There were also matters for the Congress to consider. *The above facts are contrary to the principles set out in the Constitution, being incompatible with the dignity, honor and decorum of the office of head of state.* At this point he burst into tears. Brazilians poured onto the streets. The next day the commission voted sixteen to five in favor of the findings against Fernando. Shocked by their own daring, they held hands and sang the Brazilian national anthem, as the metalworkers had done ten years before when they faced the army's guns.

A few days later Brazilians saw pictures of the recent landscape improvements in Fernando's Brasilia home. Thirteen thousand square meters had been laid out and planted with 240 big trees. There were eight electronically activated fountains and an artificial lake of 1.5 million litres in which swam a hundred Japanese carp. The swimming pool was now a hundred square meters and kept at a constant temperature of twenty-eight degrees and surrounded by two suites of changing rooms, a gymnasium and a six-person sauna, all in tropical hardwood. Two hundred lamps and fifty floodlights kept it lit at night. The landscaping had taken three years and cost $2.5 million dollars and PC paid the bill. Roberto Marinho trembled with anger. *He copied my garden.* Marinho's garden in Rio, where the African flamingos performed their evening dance as the Carioca River flowed down to the sea from the peak of Corcovado, was a great work of time, created over many decades as the Marinho fortune grew. Fernando's gaudy copy was an unforgivable presumption. Marinho held a small private dinner on the terrace overlooking his garden. His two guests were Brazil's previous president, José Sarney, and Fernando's vice. Vice president Itamar Franco told Marinho, as they gazed down at the flamingos and the river, that he was ready to take over.

When Fernando took the salute as commander in chief at the national military parade he was booed and jeered by the crowd. His ministers and staff left one by one. Fernando had to write his own TV address to the nation, and it was full of lies and evasions. Dona Leda had a heart attack and went into a coma, and when Fernando and Rosane arrived at the hospital in Rio they were booed and insulted by an angry crowd. Fernando's newest press secretary blamed Dona Leda's terminal coma on Pedro. Fernando himself was hoping a wave of sympathy might be created by the family drama, but Brazilians knew how soaps were engineered. In Recife, Vavá came rushing into the Bangüê shouting, *He's dragging the mother into it now.* There was a kind of admiration in Vavá's voice, the tone a military man might have used at the last-minute deployment of the heavy artillery that could still turn a battle around and save a campaign; or a TV critic's at a dramatic new turn in a soap. In Rio, Fernando's route to the governor's palace was lined by jeering crowds. Black banners hung from windows and outside the palace people banged on saucepans all through the night. Inside the clinic Fernando's two sisters brawled and screamed at each other while beyond the door their mother went on dying. In the São Paulo clinic where they moved their mother, it was worse. *I'm going to rip your face off,* cried Ledinha, sinking her nails deeply into her sister's arms. Then Leopoldo arrived. *I'm the boss in São Paulo,* he said, waving his finger. *I know you're the boss here,* his sister Ana Luisa shot back. *São Paulo's where you do your crooked deals.* Leopoldo slunk off.

At the end of September the Brazilian Congress voted on whether to suspend Fernando and open impeachment proceedings. There were strikes around Brazil that Tuesday and outside the Congress itself a crowd massed. A two-thirds majority was needed to suspend the president. In the end, it was 441 to 38. Fernando sat the vote out alone in his presidential office. He turned the lights out and kept the TV off and stood by the window staring into space and then he heard the roar. *What I suddenly heard was a dull roar, the noise of a mass of people, coming out of the congressional chamber, reaching the demonstrators outside and spreading . . . it was the end.* He rang Rosane and started to weep. She started crying too. *You'll get back on top,* she told him. *Promise?* said Fernando. *I promise,* said Rosane.

Three days later Fernando and Rosane left the presidential palace and walked toward a military helicopter while the crowd yelled *Crook!* and *Search him!* until their angry voices mixed with the roar of the helicopter as it lifted off. Safely inside, Fernando punched the air with his fist. It was nearly three months before the Senate voted on whether to impeach him. On the third-to-last day of 1992, when the Senate was already twenty minutes into the final deliberation on impeachment, Fernando delivered a handwritten note resigning as president of Brazil. The vice president was sworn in. Next day the Senate impeached Fernando anyway. They found him, by 76 votes to 3, *criminally responsible* and banned him from holding public office for eight years. It was a remarkable win for accountability in public life and for social justice in a country which had little experience of either. Yet the achievement of the young Brazilians—the river of young painted faces pouring into Recife—and the briefly steadfast parliamentarians of 1992, unlike their contemporaries' in Prague, Berlin, Warsaw, Manila, Beijing, was hardly acknowledged, even in Brazil. Especially not in Brazil. Slothful, self-lacerating Brazil dismissed them. It was true that their victory was rapid and without cost, yet the rapidity and vigor of their response was its point. They saw, they knew, they struck with great strength and they won. The age of Fernando and PC was appalling, but it was unbelievably brief. Things slid backward after that, but in Brazil things always do.

The Portuguese airliner taxied to a halt at Fiumicino. The airline's director of Rome operations sprang aboard in gold braid. *Welcome home, sir,* he said. *Tanned as ever.* We knew each other quite well. I had spent the greater part of the year of Fernando's fall making three visits to Brazil and always traveled with the Portuguese. The Brazilian embassy in Rome, in its magnificent palace on the Piazza Navona, had on my last visa application expressed the suspicion that I was running some kind of racket between Italy and Brazil. People, drugs, sex slaves, body organs— they never told me what they had in mind. The consular official's attention had been distracted the moment he raised the question by the arrival of a stunning transsexual, dressed down for the embassy visit in braless T-shirt and jeans. In this youthful apparition male and female, African and índio lived with perfect harmony in a figure which seemed to incorporate all the fleshly splendors of every imaginable race and sex. The transsexual was requiring, in a low but animated voice with the softest Brazilian consonants I had ever heard, to be repatriated by the embassy. A sick mother needed attention. Pair by pair the consular eyes lifted from their other work and swung toward their fellow countryperson. One by one and ineluctably the officials were drawn into the transsexual's domestic drama. The transsexual stirred in further detail, flung out tangential plot lines. The rest of us conceded this as natural. We were drawn in too, and wanted to know how it would end. Would the Brazilian bureaucracy be deaf to so Brazilian an appeal, and made so far from home? Distractedly, at some point in the day, the consulate handed out my new visa. The other story, the trade in body parts or whatever it was they had in mind, died in the air.

X

A Used Revolver

Unhappy Itamar Franco's brief replacement presidency lasted less than two years. It was remembered for the photo of the president deep in conversation with a young lady who was visibly wearing no panties. Nobody minded, but poor Itamar's credibility vanished with the knickers and it did not return when Lent followed Carnival.

The Workers' Party, first by insisting on the congressional inquiry and then by driving it forward to the end, had done most in Congress to bring Fernando under scrutiny and then to throw him out. The party went on growing and growing in the country. In the October elections of 1990, even when Brazil was still in the first flush of Fernando, voters had once again more than doubled the number of its deputies in Congress, who were now thirty-five, and elected the first Workers' Party senator. Two years later, in the local government elections held a couple of weeks before Fernando was impeached, the Workers' Party won control of fifty-five city administrations around Brazil. Lula's loss in 1989 had not demoralized the believers. Rather, the nearness to victory and the sureness that Fernando had won only through cheap tricks on TV had energized the militants.

The Workers' Party was the institutional engine driving the impeachment, and Fernando's fall energized them again.

Lula put a plan to the new administration to deal with hunger in Brazil. Nothing happened and he set off on a year of long journeys around the country, visiting its remote and neglected corners and finding out how people lived away from the great cities. His first *caravan* went to the northeastern drylands, which happened to be ravaged by drought and hunger. People from tiny and remote places walked all night, some of them, along fifty kilometers of track through the thorn scrub, sustained by manioc meal wrapped in palm leaves, their way lit by candles, to meet with Lula and his party. They came to speak, not to ask favors, and the travelers were startled by the savagely artic- ulate ironies of the unlettered. And when he later went through the Amazon by boat and jeep, Lula said, *I had no idea . . . some of these people are living in the sixteenth century and watching TV Globo from the twenty-first . . . We can try to listen.* He held talks and meetings in four hundred places and by the following May had covered thirty thousand kilometers by road. There were now five months to go to the presidential election and Lula was get- ting forty percent in the opinion polls and nobody else had even half that.

The Workers' Party had elaborated its plans for Brazil, but through fear or hubris or blindness or mere incompetence they had ignored the trouble that made all their other plans vain. They forgot the old Brazilian disease of inflation. The currency was losing a third of its value every month and Brazilians were again longing for the social stability that only financial stability could bring. Achieve that and anyone would be forgiven a great deal—if Fernando had dealt with inflation he would never have fallen. And three months before the 1994 election Itamar's government launched its economic plan. Brazil's currency had already changed its name three times in the years I had been going there and now it changed its name again. Now it was the *real* and worth one Yankee dollar. Its begetter was Itamar's new finance minister, Fernando Henrique Cardoso, a sociologist who had once thought of himself as a Marxist and written academic studies of slavery and the growth of capitalism in Brazil. He had gone to France during the dictatorship and had studied and taught in Paris and had been hovering on the periphery when the Workers' Party was formed. As academics sometimes do, Fernando Henrique had acquired a taste for power and for policies which pleased the powerful.

Unlike Fernando's half-cocked freeze of four years earlier, the *real* plan bit and held and Fernando Henrique became a presidential candidate. Lula's great lead vanished, and in October FHC, as they now called him, was elected president in a single round with twice as many votes as Lula. The Workers' Party itself went on growing, with forty-nine members of Congress and five senators. The years of FHC in Brazil—which lasted until the end of 2002, since he made some dubious deals to change the Constitution, stood for a second term and beat Lula again in 1998—were the years when the earlier Fernando's promises were carried out. Brazil modernized in a way that delighted the World Bank and the International Monetary Fund. The state enterprises were sold off with only a medium amount of corrupt dealing and millions lost their jobs. The currency kept its value for a few years and then it all started to unwind again. Toward the end of his time FHC's *real* had lost three-quarters of its original value.

FHC brought some calm to Brazilian politics, but the greater monetary stability made life harder for many Brazilians, and FHC had nearly a decade to work in. Many felt as damaged by his measures as they had been by the freeze in 1990. Vavá was eloquent on the hardship he caused, and contemptuous of the maneuvers by which he prolonged his time in power. FHC didn't care. Brazil's creditors in the exterior loved him, and he cared about that. He spent almost more time out of Brazil than in, and adored swanning around international meetings, collecting honorary degrees, speaking French and showing the world how presentable Brazil could be. The exterior was happy to let FHC feel he belonged there as long as the interest payments came in on the huge Brazilian debt. The worst financial crisis came in 2002, when Argentina—the IMF's model economy, which FHC's Brazil had burned to emulate—collapsed in a cloud of dust and destitution, and the IMF's condition for saving the Brazilian economy from its own impending collapse was that all the candidates for the succession undertake to respect the new deal worked out for FHC. Even Lula, who was making his fourth and final run that year, made this promise to the IMF.

———

Like its fashions in food and clothes and music, Rio's ideas a hundred years ago were imported from France. The most fashionable of all the imported ideas was the positivism which had such a grip on the minds of the republic's founders and which made Euclides da Cunha's book on Canudos such a tortured work. Machado de Assis could be particularly cutting about the imported preconceptions and *out of place ideas* on which Brazil's intellectuals were determined to found the culture of the republic, but he dismissed them too slyly and adroitly to offend. His own books were easy to read. Machado had taught himself the several languages he read, and flattered his magazine readers by letting them feel as widely read as he was himself, reassuring the masters of Brazil while he entertained their wives—delicately probing their marriages, subverting their husbands' politics, making nonsense of their ideas and undermining the social values that sustained them. Machado made it very easy to forget he was the grandson of freed black slaves and the son of the poorest dependants of a grand household. He himself never forgot. He was nearly fifty when slavery ended in Brazil.

The stories pressed home savage insights with a beguiling nonchalance. "The Mirror" seemed a slight story about a boy's coming of age, but his loss of identity, in the solitude that follows a mass flight of slaves, reads like Conrad transposed from shipboard to the big house of an isolated slave plantation, written twenty years before Conrad's tales of youth under stress. The lack of identity is a whole society's as well as the young man's. The boy in another story who is saved from the seminary by his uncle's mistress has to watch his rescuer casually and cruelly mistreat her young slave girl, and remain complicit in the cruelty. In "Midnight Mass" an adolescent encounters a lonely and unhappy young wife and is too young and ingenuous, or too obtuse, to understand the nature of her longing or his own. "Father Against Mother" is about a professional slave catcher and forces a look back at slavery when everyone was trying to forget the recent past. After describing some of the iron devices used to punish runaway slaves, Machado urbanely explains that *fifty years ago slaves often used to escape. There were a lot of them and not all of them enjoyed slavery. They sometimes got a flogging and not all of them enjoyed a flogging either.* Machado published his first story at nineteen and his last in 1907, the year before he died. He loved a story's casualness of tone and its economy of means, and part of the breakthrough of *Bras Cubas,* along with its insolent liberties of tone, was that it let Machado call a series of stories a novel.

Quincas Borba was a kind of sequel to *Bras Cubas,* though the tone is very different in the story of a provincial schoolmaster and failed businessman who inherits a fortune and a dog and moves to Rio, where he is taken up by a young couple on the make. The husband is a former seminarian of modest origin who is rapidly realizing his vast ambitions of money and power and

social prestige—a fictional anticipation of PC, an influence trafficker and investor with his eye on ownership of a major bank.
His beautiful and glamorous wife, Sofia, is very much his partner
in all this. The two rise as a couple and Sofia's adultery or two,
which may or may not have been physically consummated, are
more like supporting acts in their joint career than betrayals of
their marriage. Rio in the late empire was a boomtown that
offered a great deal in the way of fast money—the former seminarian tells the new business partner whose fortune he is appro-
priating that Rio is *turning into South America's Paris or London.*
Sofia is especially attentive to their provincial friend, who falls
for her catastrophically. In the end, done over sexually, socially,
politically, financially, the former schoolmaster goes home to
poverty, madness and early death, a victim of Rio's and Brazil's
multiple unrealities.

Who, asked one of *Quincas Borba*'s earliest and most acute
readers, *can say that this character is not Brazil?* The same critic
saw the fool at the book's center as a *stalking horse for the rage of a
philosopher hiding in the bushes,* and Machado's rage lies nearer the
surface here than anywhere else in his work. A street crowd
watches the public hanging of a black man by a black executioner in the center of Rio, in a moment more brutal than anything Machado had dared before, a scene of everyday Brazilian
life normally unthinkable in its polite literature. *The prisoner
kicked, stiffened; the executioner climbed on to him in an agile and skil-
ful way.* Only Machado could get away with this in a ladies magazine. *Quincas Borba* also lacks anything like the earlier book's
prolonged adultery for Rio's lady readers to relate to. Sofia the
career wife is a compellingly modern presence, but since her gift
is to work wonders of intensity with her eyes without going too
unequivocally far in other areas, her role and her interest are limited. Machado saw the problems and reworked the story radically

between its ladies' magazine appearance and its publication as a book in 1891, which was the year the coffee boom broke.

Dom Casmurro was a relief when its episodes started appearing in 1897. It was a love story, and instead of confronting its readers with the adult greed and ostentation of Rio's early gilded age, it opened onto the past. In *Dom Casmurro,* lady readers entered an old-fashioned household of a generation earlier, a world the more mature subscribers remembered well, and the relatively unchallenging infatuation of a fifteen-year-old boy for the fourteen-year-old girl next door, as the elderly Bento recounted the first and last love of his life and the obstacles it had to overcome. Fragments of meetings, interrupted conversations accumulated like tiny stories in the reassuring world of the recent past. As a novel for lady readers, *Dom Casmurro* looked a much safer bet than *Bras Cubas* or *Quincas Borba.* The story of Bento and Capitu's adolescent love and how they eventually married took up most of the book. Bento's family was a cluster of survivor drones living on inherited wealth and served by more slaves than they could use—the widowed mother, the beady eyed widowed aunt and the amiable widower uncle, a barrister with a very desultory criminal practice, a man *brought up for a serene life living off capital . . . {who} spent more than he earned,* and

when he was younger he was very popular with the ladies, and was a fervent political enthusiast; but the years had removed the greater part of his political and sexual ardour, and corpulence had dealt a final blow to his ambitions, both in the public arena and in more intimate spheres.

The low-key domesticity was so beguiling, the adolescent eroticism was so tender and Capitu, the girl with *the undertow eyes*—or, to her enemies, *oblique and sly, like a gypsy's*—so vivacious, smart and resolute, that a lot of other signals coming at the lady readers—about what a scared and passive mama's boy Bento was, and how much an indulged male product of his wealthy milieu—were easily overlooked as the story moved forward in Machado's random, fragmentary and half distracted seeming way. The rapid precipitation at the end—the disintegration of the marriage under Bento's conviction of Capitu's adultery with his friend and business partner Escobar—unfolded with a terrible force of conviction. Only in the madness and destruction of the very last pages—Bento ready to force the poisoned coffee down the throat of the child he thinks is Escobar's, Capitu's exile and death in Europe—might the lady readers have been shocked out of their female trust in Bento. They had got everything wrong, had been reading the wrong book. No other narrator was ever so cunningly, insanely unreliable as Bento, who put his case so subtly that none of *Dom Casmurro*'s pale lady readers seemed to have doubted Capitu's sexual infidelity and the better part of a century would pass before anyone questioned in print the reality of the adultery the novel turned on.

Dom Casmurro is less a nineteenth-century study of adultery like *Madame Bovary* or *Anna Karenina* than an exploration of the psychopathology of jealousy which anticipates Proust. Adultery, as *Bras Cubas* showed, was no great deal in Machado's Rio, but Bento's jealousy still disturbs today, because it entraps the complicit reader. His uncertain sense of the world is in vertiginous parallel with the reader's own uncertain grasp of his story, and its disturbing inwardness makes *Dom Casmurro* unique. The mad self-rationalization comes from the Bento who is a lawyer as well as a slave owner, the first member of a former plantation family to grow up in the unsettlingly mobile city. His psychic and social insecurity in the new metropolitan world of Rio is enhanced by the creeping fear that Capitu has married him as a way of moving up into wealth and distinction, and that his dearest friend Escobar—one of a new business class and yet another former seminarian whose real vocation turns out to be making money fast—has displaced him not just sexually but socially and financially as well.

In his own private life, Machado was personally austere and almost neurotically discreet, which was unusual in the lustful, indulgent and gossipy Rio of the 1890s. His polite reserve was legendary—an extension of the armory of pince-nez, mustache and the impeccable bourgeois dress—and another part of the Machado legend was his long idyllic marriage with Carolina. This sorts oddly with the terribly disabused accounts of married life in his greatest novels. Machado and Carolina had no children, but friends remembered them as devoted to their small dog. An adoring woman biographer did, much later, catch the whiff of a single fleeting *adventure,* in conversation with a friend of Carolina's, but the putative lady lover was lost in the clouds of Machado's discretion, rather like the vague rumor Bento hears of his business friend's tactful affair with an actress. As for Bento, having banished Capitu and her son to Switzerland, for the sake of appearances, he admits, *I lived as best I could, with no shortage of female friends to console me for the first . . . It was they who left me, like people who come for a retrospective exhibition, and either tire of seeing it, or the light in the room fades . . . They didn't come back.*

Machado died in 1908, four years after Carolina, afraid of the unknown, still firmly unbelieving, still seeing further than most of his novel-writing European peers into the shattering of the modern consciousness. Like his Russian contemporary Chekhov, he had shown that a sense of life on the periphery might yield more than most views of life at the center. Perverse, backward, deluded Brazil had produced a world master. Machado was buried with due pomp by the Brazilian Academy. As he lay dying, Euclides da Cunha had come to his house and knelt and kissed his hand. The next year Euclides was shot by his wife's young lover, in a kind of negative image of a situation Machado had once described in a story. In the story, "The Reader of Cards," it was the lovers who were killed.

———

For neither PC nor Fernando was 1993 a good year. They had planned thirty years of power and it was over in less than three. It was worse for Fernando. The insults in the streets of his last months, the saucepans, the slogans, the dolls. All through 1993 Fernando lay on his bed and stared at the ceiling again. He thought of doing away with himself and wondered about his impending trials for corruption and fraud. Rosane was seriously worried. PC had been humiliated too but he was not a public figure and had less credibility to lose. What each of them now did have was a lot of money. The money was not necessarily instantly accessible, but sooner or later it could be parlayed into great things. Resilience was all and PC was nothing if not resilient.

In the months after Fernando's fall he spent a lot of time with his lawyers, and it was a rewarding time because the police had rushed into action ill prepared. Their case against PC was full of legal errors that the lawyers would be able to use in court. Nevertheless, in June 1993 the supervising judge ordered PC's arrest and imprisonment. Jorge Bandeira was also to be held until his trial. *Son of a bitch,* said PC to Bandeira. They had taken the precaution the day before of hiding out in the beach house of one of PC's friends. Now they went into deep cover on a remote property on the border between Pernambuco and Bahia. Here they worked out their plan. They would go to Recife at night, dressed in black, and scale the three-meter fence around Recife's Guararapes international airport. They would make a dash for a small jet which would be waiting at the end of a runway, ready for takeoff.

PC had never walked more than twenty meters in any given day, and Bandeira insisted that he get fit before trying to climb the fence and run across the tarmac. PC was persuaded to start a regime of three-kilometer daily walks through the sand dunes on the property where they were hiding out. He turned up for the first walk in shorts and running shoes and smoking a big hand-rolled Monte Cristo cigar. *Throw it away,* Bandeira told him sharply. *Oh, get fucked,* said PC, but about halfway through the walk he did chuck it into the sand. In the end the commando style departure was called off. They paid a Chilean to get them out of Brazil on a private jet. They stopped in Bahia and Mato Grosso do Sul and flew west out of Brazil along the drug route in a plane piloted by a Paraguayan who ran contraband whiskey. One of PC's associates called one of PC's brothers after putting PC on the plane. *The little bird has flown,* he said. *That's what friends are for.* PC's brother was overcome with emotion. *A new home,* the federal police, who were listening in, heard him sigh. PC and Bandeira first landed in Paraguay. They made their way to the capital, Asunción, and then went on to Argentina.

In Buenos Aires they holed up in a flat carefully chosen in the suburbs. PC couldn't go outside and risk being recognized. Even in Buenos Aires his face was now notorious. Every morning Bandeira woke him with an elaborate breakfast and later took him through his daily exercise. Bandeira was determined to keep his boss fit for life on the run, but it was a losing battle. They drank together through most of the nights, reminiscing and planning their next move. PC felt trapped in the apartment and made contact with a group of Uruguayans who promised to get him across the Atlantic. Three months after arriving in Buenos Aires he left for Montevideo, parting company with Bandeira, who stayed behind in the hope of getting something going in Argentina. Three weeks later PC telephoned Bandeira. He sounded exuberant. *I'm in the kingdom,* he said, meaning England.

It's marvelous here. In London PC had met a girl called Zara Malone. *What about you?* he asked Bandeira. *Fucking anyone yet?*

As Brazil's most wanted man PC went on Interpol alerts around the world and his movements were followed. However *the little bird* continued its flight unimpeded. This was made possible, Italian police learned some years later from a lawyer who was one of PC's people in Buenos Aires, by the million dollars PC had the lawyer withdraw from one of PC's bank accounts in Geneva. The money went, on a strictly informal basis, to the Brazilian and Uruguayan agents of Interpol who had tracked PC while he was still in South America. The Brazilian police got rather more than half a million dollars and the Uruguayans the rest.

It was private enterprise, in the form of TV Globo, which tracked PC down in London. The Globo reporter heard that a Portuguese-speaking Arab prince was circulating in the pleasure haunts of the West End. PC had lost ten kilos through Bandeira's fitness program. He had shed his mustache and dyed his hair a Nordic light chestnut. PC was feeling so on top of things that he did a twenty-minute interview with TV Globo from a Kensington apartment, an interview watched by eighty percent of Brazilian viewers the night it was shown. It led to a British arrest warrant and extradition proceedings and it was time for the little bird to fly again. In November PC flew to Bangkok. He established himself in the Royal Orchid Sheraton and called his wife, Elma, to fly out and join him. While he waited for Elma to arrive, PC spent several days in the company of a person from Naples, a person who was *sick of Italy* and after some unpleasantness with the police and judiciary had gone to make a new life in Brazil. He had barely settled into his new home on the Copacabana beachfront in Rio when he left on a quick trip to Bangkok, on the same day that PC flew there from London. Three and a half years later PC's acquaintance from Naples would be arrested in Maceió as a member of the Naples camorra and charged in connection with $34 million of Italian state railway contracts awarded to camorra companies. When he was arrested the camorrista angrily denied knowing PC and denied having ever been to Bangkok. He hadn't even finished building his new house in Maceió, which was a couple of houses along from PC's on the beach at Guaxuma.

After three days Elma Farias arrived from Brazil, and in the restaurant of the Royal Orchid Sheraton that evening PC had a dispute with another guest over which of them had made prior reservation of the table PC wanted for Elma. The other guest turned out to be a Brazilian who recognized Brazil's most wanted man, and on November 29 the Brazilian embassy in Bangkok revoked PC's passport—something nobody seemed to have thought of doing before—and the Thai police came knocking. PC had been at liberty for five months and used his passport for travel to five countries on three continents. For three days he was kept in a Bangkok jail while Elma protested loudly at the embassy. *PC was carrying out the president's orders,* she said. PC was flown back to Brasilia. There were forty-one charges against him and he spent most of 1994 tracking his cases from his cell in the police barracks. In the end he got four years for tax evasion and seven years and four months for the imaginary bank account holders. There had been seventeen of these phantom accounts; fifty-two Brazilian companies had paid into them and forty-nine members of the Brazilian government had been paid out of them. At the end of the year PC was moved to Maceió and passed the rest of his sentence in a comfortable minimum security regime in the rustic setting of the firemen's barracks just outside the city. A year later, two years and one month after his arrest in Bangkok, he was out on parole, looking after business and spending a lot of time, as he used to say with a mysterious smile, *putting his files in order.* Even after his time in jail, Brazilians counted PC the eighth most influential man in the country.

Fernando was helped by the fact that the indictment against him drawn up by Brazil's chief prosecutor was found almost incomprehensible by the court. By the end of 1994 Fernando had been acquitted of all criminal charges. There was a wild party in his Brasilia home on the night of the last acquittal and at midnight the guests went down to the lake and fired dozens of rockets over the center of Brasilia. Rosane had a narrower escape. *Madame* was sentenced to eleven years for corruption in 2000 but the conviction was almost immediately overturned. Zelia, the architect of the Collor Plan, was sentenced to thirteen years for taking bribes and Fernando's labor minister got two— taking bribes again—but they had years of appeals ahead of them. Pedro, who had brought the whole thing crashing down, was at a meeting of the family firm in late 1994 when he asked for a glass of milk to wash down some pills against the terrible headaches that had been troubling him. The milk ran down the side of his face, which was paralyzed. He had several tumors on his brain and he died a month later in a New York clinic, unvisited by Fernando, who was off with Rosane on a skiing holiday at Aspen which cost several tens of thousands of dollars. Dona Leda, who had never come out of her coma, died a couple of months after her youngest son.

In 1995 Fernando decided to spend his years of proscription in exile. He and Rosane went off to Miami, where they bought a house with gold bathroom fittings for several million dollars and a couple of Ferraris for him and a couple of Mercedes-Benzes for her and a Jeep Cherokee for the two of them. How Fernando managed this was never clear, given that he was unemployed and living on a modest monthly allowance from the family firm.

The house seemed to be in the name of the Brazilian ambassador. Fernando offered himself to American universities, but nobody wanted him, and then he opened some kind of consultancy in Miami called Collor's Office. Over the next few years Fernando and Rosane concentrated their energies on global tourism and visited many countries, Australia among them, in search of new ways of enjoying themselves. Criminal charges still hung over Rosane, and indeed over Zelia, but in the first instance the only people definitively convicted along with PC were a couple of PC's office workers and Jorge Bandeira, who got a year and two months for fraud, which was eventually written off. PC was never one to bear a grudge—he was too irrepressibly an optimist to ever look back in rancor—and he never complained about being the only one to take the fall.

———

I went back to Recife four years after Fernando's impeachment and found Vavá strangely diminished. He was the same compact man with the same strange, compact fierce head on him, still with his nocturnal predator's look, ruffled, still, poised to strike. He never did strike, though, and was the mildest of men. He glanced at me now with his glittering eyes as a couple of silent figures passed under a streetlight on the other side of the square, along a row of colonial houses. In the little circle of light you could see the houses had been freshly repainted in pink and blue and cream, their baroque details picked out in white. Heritage had come to the Pátio, but FHC's new economic plan had dealt another blow to business. Vavá looked out past the slatted wooden window shutters into the hot black summer night above the square, into the velvet mysteries of Brazil. José, who was the last of the waiters left, was stacking the seats. The bar had already closed and we hadn't finished talking. When José had changed out of his working slippers into street shoes and put on a new shirt and gone, Vavá's son, Alexandre, swung the same old battered Chevrolet up to the door, a car the size and color of an old aircraft carrier. This was a permitted intrusion at midnight into an ill lit square that was closed to traffic during the day to preserve its colonial authenticity. It was a security measure that let Vavá bundle the takings away and out of sight of any armed persons who might be present in the shadows. The military police by now were nowhere in sight. After Vavá had spent several minutes locking the newer steel grille that fitted over the colonial wooden door, he and Alexandre rumbled off into the night and I thought about what Vavá had said as I walked back to where I was staying. I could smell the tidal mud as I walked over the brightly painted iron footbridge that crossed the Capibaribe River.

Later I asked Vavá about Porto de Galinhas and his face crumpled. He wasn't going there. They didn't have the house anymore. I gaped. He volunteered no information. There was nothing really to ask him. Vavá, who was forthcoming on any matter you liked to raise, closed the door on this part of his life and changed the subject. Later, when he was working, Lia came over and told me that they had done it for Alexandre. He had wanted to open a shop in a new shopping mall called the Play Center at Olinda, and selling his parents' house at Porto de Galinhas was the only way to raise the money. There was a practical hardness in everyone's voice when they talked about Alexandre's new shop, which sold soft drinks, and the numbers of thirsty people expected to flood the mall. Nobody mentioned Porto de Galinhas. They all stressed the second word and not the first when they named the shopping mall and this started to grate. Not that I ever heard Vavá refer to the soft drink outlet in anger or reproach. Vavá didn't talk about it at all. Now there was nowhere for him to go at the end of the week and his life had lost its shape. No more green shade, no more green thought.

Friday nights were still the busiest of the Bangüê's week, but the sense of a crescendo of hilarity leading to the moment Vavá vanished at midnight was gone. Vavá still vanished, or rather pottered off, but now he went no farther than a tiny rented flat at Boa Viagem. Would the new owners keep up the garden? What happened to the wooden statue? I felt unable to ask. New Year came and went. Vavá brightened a little when Carnival was mentioned, a speck on the horizon as the summer drew to a close, something to hang his expectations on. The long range weather forecast suggested there might be rain, and the thought excited Vavá. A wet Carnival was rare. Tropical wetness made everything more anarchic and more lubricious. Wet bodies were slippery. Wet clothes clung like a second skin. People lost their last inhibitions. *People like a wet Carnival,* said Vavá, his eyes shining for a moment.

It was very subdued at the Bangüê. Cândido no longer came in the evenings, though we managed to do lunch one day. He arrived carrying two plastic bags full of bacalhau. He had resigned from his government job as an economist and was now doing a little consulting work. I didn't ask if he had once been the chief of military intelligence in the Northeast. A lot of the other regulars were no longer around either, and Vavá was no longer surrounded by the agregados to whom he had been a discreet and kindly dispenser of favors—the out of work wood-carvers whose work he could no longer sell, the other figures who were well rewarded for running errands in the car. The car was rarely there to run errands in, because Alexandre needed it and Alexandre was busy with his soft drink outlet at the Play Center and rarely around himself.

Vavá's main company was now a figure from the periphery of several years before, a lugubrious and faintly sinister sergeant of the military police, who had moved up the Bangüê social list as the more brilliant presences fell away, like the poet who had never repaid a loan and now drank in a bar on the other side of the square. The sergeant had lately taken early retirement from the force. He and his amiably blowsy wife lived near Vavá and Lia and the four of them whiled away the weekends in Boa Viagem with drinks and cards and talk about how the soaps were unwinding. The big soap of the moment was an epic saga of an Italian immigrant family making good in Brazil while being racked by almost overwhelming passions of a dynastic and erotic nature. There were a lot of golden landscapes, operatic crises, determined patriarchs with handlebar mustaches, powerful matriarchs with drawn back hair, bronzed young men and raven-haired young women and choral feasts at long tables in the open air. It was like a pasta commercial and I think it was called *Terra Nostra* but I may have been confusing it with *The Cattle King,* which was about an immigrant family making good in Brazil while being racked by almost overwhelming passions of a dynastic and erotic nature and either preceded or followed *Terra Nostra* or ran simultaneously in another slot. Once at Vavá's home I saw a bit of one or the other; otherwise I heard about them over drinks and got the synopses in the paper.

Carnival in Recife was not wet but it was dire. The beauty and imagination of the old Recife Carnival had been swept away by sound system trucks belting out deafening Brazilian rock music, T-shirts, disco dancing. Everything was sponsored by the breweries. I watched part of the parade from a poet's apartment high above the main bridge over the Capibaribe, where at least the company was merry and the booze and food plentiful and the noise diminished by distance. I spent one evening shouting desultory remarks to Vavá and Lia and the policeman and his wife on the deck of a restaurant in Boa Viagem. Lia pointed out an English couple who had come to enjoy the special authenticity of Carnival in Recife. A young girl offered them a souvenir doll for sale, and when the Englishman pulled out his wallet to pay for it she made off into the crowd with his passport, cash, airline tickets, traveler's checks. An evening with a friend in Olinda was little better. Carnival was now entirely orchestrated for television and people stayed at home to watch it.

Vavá had been sick, Dona Lia told me. A sudden intestinal seizure some months earlier had nearly killed him. He'd been out of action for weeks, but was fine again now. He didn't seem fine to me, but weighed down. He had lost his spring. Dona Lia expressed some bitterness toward fair weather friends who in his time of trouble had melted away. Vavá himself mentioned none of this. He did at one point allow himself an angry diatribe against Paulo. Vavá had bought the jangada to let Paulo earn his living as a fisherman and Paulo would provide some fresh fish at weekends to grill on the barbecue. Paulo had never been bothered to work for his living, let alone keep his bargain with Vavá. For several years he had not supplied a single fish. *Not a single fish,* Vavá repeated over and over, in various heartbroken tones of anger, sorrow and amazement. Now Vavá had lost the house and the garden, lost his place of retreat, his work of art, his image of conviviality, his peace of mind and the idea that got him through the week. Vavá had lost his reason for living and the only doubt was whether Paulo might be taking more than his share of the blame. The family who had lost Vavá his retreat was in brazen denial. Depleted though he seemed, Vavá soon brought up the latest on PC. Finding someone so out of touch revived his relish in the telling, and what he told me kept me nailed to the bar until he finished.

———

Suzana Marcolino was twenty-four when she was engaged to keep PC company at night during his time in jail. PC's wife, Elma, had died suddenly while PC was in jail and when he was released, with only four hours a week of community service to

worry about, he went on seeing Suzana. Suzana did not have
entrée to his house at Mangaba Tree Heights, on account of
Farias family sensitivities, but she went to most other places
with him. His beach house at Guaxuma was where PC spent his
private time with Suzana. Then five months after his release PC
met a blond divorcée of thirty-one with blue eyes who unlike
Suzana had some social standing and belonged to a family with
political clout in the interior. He invited the divorcée to dinner
at Mangaba Tree Heights, champagne and Frank Sinatra and
Julio Iglesias on the sound system. *I'd like you to be part of this
new phase of my life,* said PC, who was nearly twenty years older
and looking for a new wife. *With you I know it would have to be
something serious.* Meaning not like Suzana, who had been a great
consolation in hard times but whose resources out of bed were
limited. When someone had asked if he planned to marry Suzana, PC had burst out laughing and said, *Are you joking?*

In a year and a half PC had given Suzana more money than
she had ever imagined having. He had taken her to Europe,
bought her a new car and a little clothes boutique called Lady
Blue which she ran in one of the smarter streets in Maceió. Now
Suzana was faced with going back to the clubs and bars for one-
night stands with mature clients. PC was closing off her lines
of credit and she was already overdrawn at the bank by fifteen
thousand dollars. She was only five years younger than the blond
widow, and not inclined to start over again on the bar scene.
She had bought a secondhand revolver, a Rossi thirty-eight, and
taken a few lessons in how to use it. Or so some people later
said. Things were coming to a head.

PC spent the Saturday afternoon of 22 June 1996 at the beach
house. Guaxuma, once well out of town, was on the northern
edge of Maceió, about fifteen kilometers from the center of the
city. His two children had arrived the day before, home from
school in Switzerland for the holidays, and he spent the earlier

part of the day with them. Then he stayed in the house alone, with the cook and her son the manservant and the housekeeping couple and the caretaker and the two bodyguards who were on duty at that time. The four bodyguards in PC's team were all members of the Alagoas military police who worked for PC in their off-hours. In the afternoon, he drank three bottles of champagne while he went over plans to make his brother Augusto mayor of Maceió. Darkness fell and he had a good red wine uncorked. Two of his brothers dropped in at eight. Augusto, the federal congressman, brought his girlfriend and the other brought his wife. PC opened a bottle of sixty-year-old Johnnie Walker Blue Label, a present from his young daughter. Toward the end of the afternoon PC called the blond divorcée and told her he'd *sorted everything out*. She understood he meant Suzana.

Suzana arrived at nine, in jeans and a red blouse and apparently carrying the Rossi thirty-eight in her handbag. After several days of dentistry and shopping in São Paulo she had arrived in Maceió that morning tired out. After a sleepless last night in São Paulo with her dentist she'd caught an early morning flight home, and it was a long way from the industrial megalopolis of twenty million people to the modest capital of Alagoas. She slept most of the afternoon, showed her sister the new clothes she had bought in São Paulo with a dud check for a thousand dollars and then went for a thorough makeover at the local beauty salon. Suzana wanted to be in form that night and she arrived at Guaxuma bathed and changed, hair and nails freshly done. She drank a few whiskeys with PC and the others. At eleven PC's brothers made to leave, but Augusto and his girlfriend were persuaded to stay for a midnight supper of grilled king prawn kebabs and rice and left around one in the morning, Augusto later said. PC and Suzana were out on the verandah with the whiskey for another couple of hours, the domestic staff recalled, having what the manservant in the kitchen and the two armed security guards keeping watch on the beach side of the house later agreed was an animated conversation in raised voices. The guards and servants said it was after four on Sunday morning when PC asked to be woken at eleven, in time for a prelunch walk along the beach at low tide. He drank a bottle of Perrier water in the kitchen and took another to keep by the bed. By then it was nearly five.

The first version of what happened on Sunday, 23 June, as the sky lightened over the Atlantic at Guaxuma and the sun came up, had the merit of being clear, simple and strictly limited to the two persons later found dead in their bed. Which was that Suzana, distraught at the announced end of her life with PC, inflamed by whiskey and argument, had taken the Rossi thirty-eight out of her handbag and shot PC as he heavily slept. She had used her cell phone to leave several messages on the answering machine in São Paulo of the young dentist of the previous evening, whose name was Fernando. The first was recorded at ten or five to four in the morning. *I'm never going to forget you . . . I'm sure we'll meet again somewhere.* The second said the same thing a few minutes before five, and mentioned *eternity . . . I'm sure I'll meet you in the other world.* Four minutes later she left a last, fleeting message: *My love. Fernando. It's Suzana.* Then, it seemed, she had shot herself. The bodyguards patrolling outside, who had heard so clearly the voices raised in argument a short time before, said they heard neither of the shots fired in the bedroom. Neither did the waiter, the cook, the caretaker, or the couple who housekept and slept on the grounds. The wife was sweeping out the main room just after nine on Sunday morning when, she later said, she found a bullet on the floor. She called the bodyguards and the caretaker. All agreed that they then knocked on the bedroom door and received no answer. That they tried to open it but found it locked. That they went outside and broke open the bedroom window with an iron bar and saw the bodies. They said they saw what police later found, the scene the police forensic specialists photographed comprehensively that afternoon.

Two hundred and twenty police photographs show the scene around the house at Guaxuma from various distances and angles. Mostly they show PC and Suzana. PC is lying on his back in a pair of gray silk pajamas on the right side of the big bed. The pajamas in another account of the scene are blue, not gray, and polyester rather than silk. Gray silk was more PC's style than blue polyester and the specialist in forensic medicine who opted for polyester may have confused the costly shimmer of silk and the sticky nail-catching gloss of polyester. Suzana is lying on her back on the left, clad in a brassiere and a printed silk slip, two items of clothing that her family later insisted she had never worn together. The slip is hitched up over her widely splayed naked legs and the smears of blood on the sheets suggest movement over the sheets, movement that would have taken place when she thrashed around during the fifteen minutes she took to die. PC's body was already cold and stiffening and Suzana's body still partly warm when the people in the house said they called PC's brother on his cell phone. Augusto Farias arrived a little before midday. As a member of the federal Congress and prospective mayor of Maceió, he was politically well connected. He said that *after the shock* of finding PC and Suzana shot dead in their bed a few hours after he had eaten with them, he called not the police but the state minister for public security with the news. *I didn't notice anything strange,* Augusto said of his dinner with PC and Suzana. The state minister called the police and before midday an officer of the Alagoas police, chosen by the minister or the police chief, was at the house and in charge. The house was already full of people, PC's friends, relatives and employees, who had already been into the bedroom where PC's and Suzana's bodies still lay.

The scientific squad took their photographs and retrieved the revolver that was lying on the bed by Suzana's body and tested it for fingerprints. They found the holster in the glove box of Suzana's car. The bodies were taken to the city morgue in Maceió, where the postmortem examination, in the absence of more refined equipment, was conducted with a kitchen knife. Traces of powder were found on Suzana's hands, but not on PC's, and time of death for both of them was put at between five and seven in the morning. Before sundown police announced a crime of passion and the investigating officer said, *My conviction that Suzana killed Paulo César and then committed suicide is based on what the scientific tests and the autopsy have revealed.* PC's body lay in state in the showrooms of his tractor dealership and a lot of people came by to pay tribute. Suzana's went straight to the cemetery. The police went back to the beach house and stayed there until one o'clock on Monday morning, questioning the four bodyguards, the cook, the manservant, the housekeeper couple and the caretaker, but not Augusto Farias. In plumping for the crime of passion, the Alagoas police may have responded to the accumulated pressures of a lifetime of telenovela viewing or to other urgings of a more focused if no more clearly stated kind. They weren't, it soon became clear, working from the evidence. Were they surprised that on Monday nobody in Brazil believed their story?

XI

In Maceió

PC's funeral was a major event in Maceió. Augusto stood by the grave in a dark suit and wraparound shades as his brother's body was lowered into the ground. Not for long, however. Indignity pursued PC beyond the grave and he was dug up again a few days later for further tests. So was Suzana. Augusto's vigorous argument that Suzana alone caused PC's death left a lot of people unconvinced. People wondered about Fernando, who was relaxing in Tahiti with Rosane when his old intimate died and sent a brief message of regret. PC knew everything about Fernando. People wondered about the Maltas, who were apparently angry that PC had stopped sending them money. People wondered about Zelia, at whose corruption trial PC had been due to testify a few days after the murder. People wondered about the Brazilian industrialists who had paid so much for so little. People wondered about people they knew nothing of. Nobody seemed to wonder, in the very first days, about PC's own family.

But a neighbor, who soon fell silent, had spoken of seeing PC's body carried from the beach in the early hours of the morning. Suzana's body was mysteriously bruised, as though she had been knocked around before her death. The bodyguards and the servants started contradicting themselves about how and when they had discovered the bodies, and what had happened the night before. Suzana's stomach was empty. PC's was full of undigested prawns. There was no way the bodyguards outside could have failed to hear gunshots from the bedroom. The crime scene was contaminated before police arrived and a few days later the mattress and bedding were burnt. The police failed to test the staff's hands for firearm powder traces, and their account of the damage done to Suzana and PC turned out to be full of inaccuracies. Even when it was revised, forensic medical specialists showed the police version did not match the facts. The bullet's trajectory meant Suzana could have shot PC in bed only by floating in the air above him. Neither could she have shot herself the way the police had it, as the second bullet's trajectory showed. Both PC and Suzana had been standing when they were shot and the bedroom aftermath seen in photos by everyone in Brazil—PC lying on his back in silk pajamas under the covers as if asleep, Suzana beside him in her silk slip, her head flung back and bare legs splayed—had been carefully set up. Someone had even cleaned the blood from PC's bullet wound. The forensic specialist who pointed all this out quite soon found himself receiving death threats. PC's family clung to the theory of a murder-suicide by Suzana and Badan Palhares was brought up from São Paulo to investigate. He was Brazil's celebrity forensic pathologist, famous for having shown a few years before that a jawbone dug up from a Brazilian graveyard was a part of Josef Mengele. Palhares confirmed the thesis of a murder-suicide, but his report too turned out to be full of mistakes that invalidated its findings—crucially, it got Suzana's height wrong—and yet another inquiry was ordered.

From the day of the killings nobody urged that Suzana was the killer more stubbornly than PC's younger brother Augusto.

Cracks and contradictions were showing in Augusto's own account of his leaving PC and Suzana at one in the morning and returning to find them dead the following midday, but it was nearly two weeks before the police questioned him. He turned up for interrogation surrounded by twenty men armed with sub-machine guns and rifles. By that time PC's and Suzana's bodies had been dug up and reexamined. Augusto seemed tense and tried to attack a photographer outside police headquarters. He stuck to his story and his theory and made PC's four suspect bodyguards part of his own entourage. Later, his description of having had to climb through the bedroom window was undermined by proof that the bedroom door had already been opened from the inside. By whom, nobody knew.

It took less than six hours for the police to find that Suzana was the killer and over three years to undo the thesis. Other lines of inquiry stayed unexplored while the legal bickering dragged on until 1999. As clouds gathered over the bodyguards and the servants, Augusto Farias stood by them. The case was removed from the local police, and nearly two years after the killings the state prosecutor announced in 1998 that charges were pending against the bodyguards. Another year and a half of judicial silence followed. When the bodyguards were arrested in the middle of 1999, Augusto's lawyers defended them and Augusto's influence got them out of jail. Then in September that year a woman PC had known well started speaking about the furious arguments over money between PC and Augusto she had witnessed shortly before PC's death. Soon after that, the sister of PC's dead wife, Elma, claimed that Elma had been suffocated in her sleep while PC was in jail, the first victim of Augusto's determination to control PC's fortune. She said that during PC's time in jail Augusto had joined forces with some of PC's old associates and fought him savagely when PC tried to regain control of business. People said in Alagoas that Augusto had a domestic servant slip Elma a tranquilizer and suffocate her in the night.

PC had removed a billion dollars from Brazil during Fernando's short time in power—this was the estimate of Kroll Associates in the United States—and none of it was ever found. What PC had done with it was unknown. In Italy, however, police investigating payments associated with a shipment of five and a half tons of cocaine, which they had seized near Turin in early 1994, found themselves at the end of a long and complex paper trail looking at bank accounts held by PC. It seemed PC had used the proceeds of cocaine export to finance his flight from Brazil in late 1993. The Italians noted with some interest that a couple of million dollars ended up not where it would be accessible to PC but in accounts in New York and in Miami, where Fernando was spending his gilded exile. The trail associated with this particular shipment was not the only indication on the global money laundering circuit that PC was doing business with Cosa Nostra.

In Augusto's desire to keep what he had taken while PC was in jail, the police now had a motive. In November 1999 they indicted Augusto Farias and PC's four bodyguards and the four servants who were in the beach house that night for the murders of PC and Suzana. The bodyguards were charged with being the *material authors* of the crime, Augusto with being its *intellectual author* and the domestic staff with complicity. *There is no doubt the congressman led the whole operation.* The prosecutor studied the police case and forwarded it for action to the Brazilian chief prosecutor. As a federal congressman Augusto enjoyed parliamentary immunity and the whole Congress would have to vote on handing him over to the law. In February 2000, the chief prosecutor—causing some surprise, because Geraldo Brindeiro was *famous for closing the book on cases involving powerful people*—forwarded the indictment to Brazil's Supreme Court. The Supreme Court would ask Congress for permission to try Augusto.

Whether to release him for criminal trial for his brother's murder was not the only thing the Congress was going to have to decide about Augusto. In 1999, while the PC murder inquiry was dragging into its fourth year, the Brazilian Congress had coincidentally set up a parliamentary commission of inquiry to look into drug trafficking in Brazil. Members of Congress were put out to find that one of their own had lately cut off a man's arms and legs with a chain saw, and hammered nails into his head. Hildebrando Pascoal was a government member from the far western state of Acre, which bordered on Peru and Bolivia. It was the area where a hundred years earlier Roger Casement had documented the torture and murder of the índio workers by the rubber companies, and where Chico Mendes, the rubber workers' leader, was murdered by hired killers in 1988. Pascoal had nothing against the man into whose head he hammered nails other than the victim's friendship with another man who had shot Pascoal's brother. The victim's thirteen-year-old son was killed with acid. The witness to the chain saw killings had himself killed over fifty people for Pascoal, who was head of the military police in Acre at the time he wielded the chain saw. Pascoal was also the leader of a death squad in Acre, a leading importer of cocaine from Peru and Bolivia and heavily involved in the ancillary activities of arms dealing and money laundering. He worked in association with two state governors, three of Acre's seven judges, and most of the leading figures in the state's business milieux. Soldiers of the Acre military police did the organization's heavy work, using its ten aircraft, dozens of trucks and ten riverboats and working out of Pascoal's property on the border with Bolivia as a logistical base. When it heard this the

Brazilian Congress voted to revoke Hildebrando Pascoal's mandate for *lack of parliamentary decorum.* He tried to flee Brazil by air, but was arrested with several dozen others, mostly military and civilian police in Acre.

A week later, on the last day of September 1999, one of the organization's truck drivers told the commission that its main activities were drug trafficking, arms dealing, road cargo piracy and professional killing. Along with Pascoal, the truck driver said, one of its four bosses was Augusto Farias, and added in his evidence that *PC died to benefit his brother and other elements of the organization.* He said that after PC died, his interests were split between another leader of the organization—a São Paulo lawyer who had worked as a front for PC and now got the businesses registered in his name—and Augusto, who got the rest, including the money hidden overseas. The driver said the organization's leaders divided the territory among themselves and *met to decide drug purchases, arms distribution, truck dispatch to Bolivia, who was going to die, who would live and how to distribute income.* Very like the mafia. The organization was active in most of Brazil's states and in Bolivia. A week later still, the commission discovered that Augusto owned a two-thousand-hectare property near one of Brazil's transcontinental highways and very near another property belonging to the state congressman named as another of the organization's four leaders. The properties were in the epicenter of the transcontinental cargo piracy. When he was called to testify to the commission, Augusto waved his arms and banged the table and shouted that he was raising cattle on this notably poor land. The federal police found eight head of cattle on the two thousand hectares. They also found an aircraft landing strip, and another on the other ranch nearby.

The commission went to Maceió and found that the head of Augusto's bodyguards—one of those Alagoas military police now indicted for PC's murder—was active in the road cargo thefts. They discovered that the police officer who first headed the PC murder investigation (and found it was a crime of passion) had been arrested for arms trafficking and was now working for a security company that belonged to Augusto. They discovered that Augusto owned a whole string of other properties in the Brazilian interior. And the commission heard the celebrity pathologist Palhares accused by the same truck driver of selling his scientific services to organized crime. A former governor of Alagoas added that Palhares had received a quarter of a million dollars for his murder-suicide report on Suzana and PC.

Around the same time Augusto's name was floating to the surface of another episode of life in Alagoas. Late one afternoon in December 1998, a newly elected federal congresswoman from Alagoas, after speaking at a ceremony for the new representatives, went to see her newborn niece. The congresswoman was standing with family on the verandah of her sister's home in one of the better suburbs of Maceió at eight o'clock in the evening when four men arrived. *The congresswoman here?* one of them asked. *It's this one,* said another. The congresswoman Ceci Cunha was shot in the neck point-blank. The men then killed her husband, two others in the family, and left.

Eyes immediately turned on the congressman from Alagoas who owed his seat in Brasilia to Ceci Cunha's murder, being next on the slate. Suspicion deepened when Augusto Farias claimed a few days after the massacre that he had barely escaped assassination himself, ordered by the same congressman. The well-known professional gunman known as *Leather Hat* had been engaged to kill him, Augusto said, but had tipped him off instead. *I owe my life to a professional killer,* said Augusto. The Brazilian minister of justice, who was from Alagoas, met privately with Augusto and announced that he believed Augusto's story, condemning the congressman before the police investigation began. The accused himself accused the governor of Alagoas and Augusto of ordering the massacre and conspiring to incriminate him. *A psychopath,* said Augusto. *Who's he to say that of anyone?* snapped the congressman. Leather Hat himself, who was already sixty and nearing retirement after a long career as one of the premier hired killers of the Northeast, seemed to be equally good friends with both Augusto and the accused congressman. Police thought Leather Hat was Ceci Cunha's killer, so Augusto's testimonial was timely for him.

The congressional commission, hearing the allegations that Augusto was a leader of organized crime and that he had ordered the murder of PC and Suzana, was struck by the analogies between the killings of PC and Suzana and the recent massacre of Ceci Cunha and her family—in particular the rush to explain the crime. The governor of Alagoas had set the police onto the accused congressman within a few minutes of the massacre. A week later the governor, the Brazilian minister of justice and Augusto at a joint press conference all accused him of the murders. There was no proof at all, but like the crime of passion which explained PC's death, the new story removed Augusto from the affair, and in both cases Augusto himself was the architect of the theory police followed up. The commissioners took their time, but in November 2000, a year after his indictment for the murders of PC and Suzana, they decided to indict Augusto as a leader of the organization. Then nothing happened. Augusto remained a deputy in the Brazilian Congress. No new evidence emerged in either case. The chief prosecutor went on sitting on the murder charge for a second year, five years after the killings, as a year of inaction passed on the organized crime charge. In early 2002 it was still impossible to find news on what was happening to Augusto. On the face of it nothing was. He continued to fly between Brasilia and Maceió every week as a representative of the Brazilian people. I decided to have a look at Alagoas.

Maceió is on the coast, a city of beaches, one after another around the promontory on which the older part is built, then up and down the coast forever. I arrived late at night on a long-distance bus from the up-country drylands. It started raining as the bus neared the coast toward the end of the afternoon and soon the darkness and the driving lines of water and the condensation on the windows stopped you from seeing a thing. Every now and then the bus pulled over into a shallow lake and a passenger scurried off looking for shelter in the darkness. Or a bedraggled figure clambered aboard. Sometimes these were food sellers, irrepressibly cheerful in the rain and the dark and their failure to find a taker for a single homemade chicken pattie before they stepped out again into the night. There were no armed holdups and no accidents, though sometimes we slowed to a walking pace and there seemed to be no road under the bus at all, just open ground. The rain was heaviest as we entered Maceió. The night was black and the streets were torrents of rubbish. Spouts and gutters were overwhelmed. Hovels were falling to pieces under the force of the water and pieces of tin and wood and plastic and paper were being swept down the hill to the sea. The hotel in the old part of town was full. I ran through the rain to a cab and the cab got stranded in the flooded city. We went around and around looking for a road that was not underwater. Finally I found a place on the beach on the northern edge of town. I ate a pizza in a flooded pizzeria and fell asleep as the rain softened and petered out.

I woke to brilliant sun. I looked out on a building site and an orange and white relay tower for cellular phones. The air was luminous and the sea was just out of view, making its presence felt. Birds were swirling joyously in the sky and I watched them in delight. Looking more closely I realized the birds were much farther away than they seemed. They looked to be close because they were so big. These birds were big and black and they had an unmistakable identifying upward tilt of the feathers at the end of their long beating wings. They were *urubus*. They were carrion birds and they had just found something dead. The swirl tightened to a hovering black turbine of wings and sank out of sight toward something on the ground.

I went for a run along a string of beaches, running on the hard sand at the surf's edge, threading through the barefoot football players, dodging big surf fishing rods planted in the sand, and past a series of newish hotels and beachfront resorts, until the road above the sand petered out into a dirt track lined by scraggy palms and wasteland and punctuated by some decrepit housing and bar shacks on the beach with plastic chairs. The water was a little cleaner there. Farther back, by the big hotels and the smartest beaches, the water was turbid in big patches and from time to time your throat caught at a sweetish stench hanging in the air. Every so often the sand was cut by a torrent of black water rushing toward the sea from a little lagoon above the dunes, overflowing after the night's rain. These had been a lot of little streams feeding into the Atlantic, and must have been beautiful a few years earlier. Now they were open sewers draining effluent from the strip of apartment blocks and hotels that lined the road above the beach and spread inland. This was Fernando's work, the tourist development of Maceió's northern beaches he had promoted as mayor. He overlooked the sewers, and the lovely beaches the hotels were built to exploit were now permanently befouled. As you got closer to the city, around Green Point, where the biggest hotels and the most bars and restaurants were, and where Augusto lived in the flashiest block in town, the water stank.

As I was walking back from the beach that first morning, a

small silvery car pulled up and its driver leaned out inquiringly. She looked as though she wanted directions. I bent down into the car. The driver had a sleek pale brown body under cascading corkscrews of black ringlets with highlights. She seemed to be without any clothes at all, though there were a couple of fraying strands of what looked like raw string slung tensely between her exuberances or tightening into clefts. The pieces of string covered nothing at all, though they excited a sense of constraining tension about to give way under pressure. She leaned over farther, her hand on the inside door handle, and the string prepared to snap. Leaning across the passenger seat and looking up she spoke out of a mouth made richly emphatic by the wet look lipstick. *You look lost,* she said. The door opened a little. *Jump in.*

Something terrible happened that night. Stendhal and copious fluids made the amoebic dysentery bearable. I reread the *Chartreuse de Parme* almost without a break. Maceió's brightness faded in the softer glow of Parma and the search for Augusto evaporated before Gina Sanseverina's unconfessable love and her brilliant, futile one-woman war with the grim and contemptible absolutism of the Parma court. From time to time I tried to catch the news on the cheap TV. Lula juddered into view, looking as bad as he did all year. He was beginning his fourth and last run for the presidency and this was the start of his astronomically costly TV campaign. In the hands of a master publicist Lula had lost all trace of the taciturn northeasterner, the stubbornly pragmatic metalworker. He had been trained to smile frequently and weep with practiced fluency and talk about his feelings and his private life. His handsome, slightly irregular teeth had been filed down to harmless little inward turning stumps, or maybe capped, to make the smiles less threatening to the female voters who were still less keen on Lula than males.

It helped that for once the government candidate was a surly death's-head, with none of Fernando's evanescent flair or FHC's self-assurance.

Serious efforts had been made with Lula's hair, which stayed wiry, intractable, hostile and low on the brow. Every day that year they tried a different approach with the hair. None worked, and in the course of the campaign the hair took on a mean-minded identity of its own, and in their increasingly radical attempts to tame it you would see the stylists' panic rising as the vote drew near. The dense beard had been shaved down to a gray scurf, like the filed teeth, to make him more approachable. He was wearing a tightly buttoned dark suit that strained in the wrong places and a hideous tie. The tougher the raw material, the harder it was to make over was the lesson of the viewer-friendly Lula now being recycled by his handlers as *Lula peace and love.*

This was at once the slogan that he and the Workers' Party and the Workers' Party's media people hoped would make him leader of Brazil, and the phrase everyone used in a knowing, amused and embarrassed way to refer to the falsity of it all. *Lula peace and love* had never a bad word to say of anyone, least of all his opponents, and a welcome for anyone who wanted to leap aboard. People like the millionaire businessman who became his running mate. None of this was strictly necessary, since he was going to win anyway. But nothing was more Brazilian than a really cordial and seemingly inclusive social life. Lula had never seen the world as us and them. It was always Lula's quiddity, whose strength and weakness were conjoined, to be neither an ideologue nor an opportunist in a party which had plenty of both, and needed them too. His constancy was what made him so unpredictable and his charm was his own special blend of good sense and ignorance. Never, as he reached for the fruits this one last time, had he seemed more elusive. *Lula peace and love* was the icon of the dispossessed and the darling of the World Bank.

After twenty years the visible changes in the Workers' Party were sometimes deeply disconcerting. Its best known representative after Lula was the mayor of São Paulo, and Marta Suplicy was best known around Brazil for her own blond beauty, her French lover, her rock star son and her enormous wardrobe of designer clothes. Marta visiting a São Paulo slum evoked faint memories of Eva Perón—or might have done if she and the slum dwellers had not been so tough-minded. Marta was tough enough to expel from the party a councillor who required the Workers' Party in office to stick to its stated policy on education. The husband she had lately left, the party's first senator, looked like a Florentine aristocrat and rode a Harley-Davidson. The Workers' Party had never been a huddle of losers and now it looked less like that than ever. We could only hold our breath as 2002 passed its midpoint.

By now Clélia was dead. Fabrice was dead. Their child was dead. The duchess Sanseverina was dead. The prince of Parma was dead and succeeded by his neurotic bookish son. Mosca lived on, the consummate operator. I had finished the *Chartreuse* and it was time to get up.

———

On the narrow strip of coastal highway, just north of town, cars were zipping north and south every few minutes. Down in the red dust the only other person on foot was a shirtless black boy of about twelve, struggling to keep a cartload of green coconuts moving toward an uncertain destination. I asked him about PC's place and it turned out we were right outside. The boy just nodded his head at the big stone wall. My idea of a beach house was something in weatherboard at the edge of the sand, a place that needed painting, a place furnished with old bits and pieces, with a wooden verandah and screen doors. PC's beach place was not like that. There were hundreds of meters of landscaped garden between the house and the sand, and hundreds more between the house and the road. The front wall was three meters high, finished in a bluish polished slatelike stone with no trace of a crevice or toehold between one block and another. The wall looked as though it were about half as thick as it was high, but there was no way you could really tell from the road. It was visually and physically impenetrable. It ran for fifty or a hundred meters along the highway, and then started down the gentle declivity toward the beach and the tropical Atlantic. From the road you could see only the tops of some mango trees. The front wall blocked everything out. There was a point in the middle where the roadside wall turned obliquely inward to a massive double gate of wood as high as the wall, a gate that fitted into the wall without a chink. On the left side of the gate, set into the oblique wall, was the glass window of a gatekeeper's sentry box that had been built into the wall, but the sentry post was unmanned, its window a blank pane.

It was big and luxurious and the most modest of PC's homes. And despite its sheer stone perimeter walls the least secure. His town house in Maceió was surrounded by granite walls a meter thick and three meters high. The beach place had been empty since 1996 and now belonged to a local entrepreneur who planned to make it an expensive brothel. It was an ostentatiously simple affair, with a largely exposed white skeleton of reinforced concrete and a lot of glass and a big cantilevered sundeck. The floor space was all on a single level that jutted out over the sloping terrain and was supported on the ocean side by white concrete pillars. It was very early eighties, in the taste of PC's humbler beginnings. The grounds ran in an interminable landscaped declension right down to the fine white sand and the sea of what was effectively a private beach, since road access to the beach was miles away. After looking in vain for a way in, I walked back to Edimilson's car.

Edimilson was the taxi driver who helped me locate PC's house. An earlier driver had nearly killed me first and then abandoned me in the wrong place, miles from transport, miles from anywhere, certainly miles from Guaxuma, wandering by a fetid black swamp seething with unidentifiable creatures as darkness fell with its always startling rapidity. Edimilson was a daylight person and had seen Augusto at the airport a few days earlier. He knew people who knew things and would inquire for me. When we met again, however, he looked strained and anxious. His people had not been forthcoming. We talked about PC's murder and I wondered why everything had stalled for so long. *A person like that has a lot of influence in Alagoas,* Edimilson said. *He can arrange anything.* He meant Augusto. *But once it was in the hands of the Federal Police*— I began briskly. *The Federal Police are local people too,* said Edimilson urgently. *He can influence appointments, promotions. People owe their jobs to him. He can stop you ever working at all.* He looked unhappy. I changed the subject to the massacre of the congresswoman and her family. *Oh, God, yes, that too . . .* said Edimilson, trailing off and looking distraught. He promised to call me when he found things out. I held out the promise of long and rewarding drives in his taxi around Maceió, but I never heard from him again.

Days spent among Maceió's eccentrics and local historians, going through dusty fascicles of the local press in the state library, turned up nothing on Augusto. I did read, in the family paper, about Fernando's recent return to public life in Alagoas. The archbishop had celebrated a solemn mass in the church of Fernando's Virgin of the Poor, before most of the state's big landowners and sugar producers. *The law must be obeyed,* said the archbishop in his homily and quickly added, *even when the law is an unjust one.* There was a speech by Fernando, whose raven hair had gone gray in exile, and a photo of Rosane standing by his side as he spoke, legs apart, mouth open, eyes glazed.

The library in Maceió had its rackety charm but a very spotty collection of the state's principal daily. The files were more complete at the headquarters of Fernando's family organization. The *Gazeta de Alagoas* contained some gripping material. The history of the murder of the current governor's brother and its consequences waylaid me for an entire morning. The current governor, who no doubt had his reasons, never went anywhere without a posse of armed guards, and kept his own bulletproof vest on even when presiding over cabinet meetings in the Palace of the Martyrs. There was also a piece on male prostitution among the middle classes in Maceió, whose sons found it a pleasant and rewarding way of earning supplementary income. A young Bible student had so impressed a society lady after a fortuitous encounter that she had passed his name and number on to her friends. The friends were similarly impressed with the Bible student's performance and gave his name to other friends. The student himself had had to abandon his biblical studies in order to keep up with a busy and ever expanding round of commitments to Maceió's wives.

But about the federal member for Alagoas, and the charges pending against him for over two years for the murder of his brother and his brother's lover, or about the year-old charges in relation to organized crime in Brazil, or about any developments in the case of the massacre of another federal member for Alagoas and her family, I found nothing in the *Gazeta de Alagoas*. The *Tribuna de Alagoas,* which was the Farias family paper PC had longed for, contained very little of anything apart from the most sickening accounts of everyday violence against and among the poor that I have ever read. Working the phones, I reached the federal Congress in Brasilia and Augusto's congressional office. Augusto's secretary told me he would be in Maceió at the end of the week and she gave me the cell phone number of the adviser who was always with him, a man named Marcos. I had to speak to Marcos if I wanted to speak to Augusto. I rang Marcos and wondered if the congressman would have time for a chat when he came up at the weekend. A chat about what? Marcos's eyes narrowed audibly. *About his brother's death and one or two things that have come up since—* The voice that replied from Brasilia grew curter and thicker. Marcos said to call back the next day, when they were in Maceió. I did. I kept ringing Marcos and the ever sprightly secretary in Brasilia, but Augusto was always in a meeting, or a plane somewhere between Maceió and Brasilia and quite soon Marcos began switching off his phone the moment it started to ring.

———

Inland from Maceió, among the rolling, well watered and palm tree dotted green hills that make up the northeastern *agreste,* the middle zone between the coastal strip and the high drylands of the real interior, was my other reason for travelling to Maceió. So I went on a bumpy ride in a small bus, which muscled its way past mule drawn carts and kids on bikes. After the bus ride a dried out and white whiskered old man bailed me up, an old man with very few teeth and a much washed white shirt and braces, who even in his upright youth and even by the standards of the Brazilian Northeast must have always been on the short side. Now he was bent at ninety degrees above the waist and propped on a knotted stick about as long as my shin bone, talking with great vigor about things I imperfectly understood. As he spoke, a team of small boys bore down on us one by one, selling roasted sweet corn from baskets, rewrapped and proffered in its original green leaf. They looked like brothers, and were fanning out from a brazier and a senior relative around the corner and they were very determined. Corn was one of the few things you could eat with impunity in a town like this. The sweetish faintly fetid pall in the town's air whispered of a total absence of sewers. The tiny slow-hovering flies that landed at the corner of your mouth, the edge of your plate or the rim of your glass before you even noticed, the sense that you might have unknowingly swallowed one or two, the clammy stickiness of every surface you touched, especially the plastic chair and the plasticized tablecloth in the bar where I later stopped for a beer, a clean fresh airy place, relatively speaking, brought back the visceral memory of the dysentery that had so lately followed the last meal eaten in a small town of the interior.

The main square of this hilly town was less crowded than the streets, and had a little garden whose trees leaned over the spiked railing into the streets that surrounded it. The square was on a slope and I walked up and down, around the railed rectangle, trying to shake off the sick feeling and clear my mind. A motorbike taxi rider bluntly refused to take me out of town and this was a worry. Queasy and self-absorbed, I took no notice of a senior officer of the military police who was striding toward me. I watched him languidly, one more bustling figure in a very busy town, as I leaned on the railings. When he got close enough, I saw his close clipped mustache of graying bristles and the aviator shades with mirror lenses. Perhaps my own air of mild curiosity annoyed him. He was coming over very fast in a stiff bandy-legged stride and his face was dark with anger. He was not a tall man. He demanded to see my papers. I said I didn't have any and he gave a little whinny of triumph. My passport was in the hotel in Maceió but the officer didn't wait to hear. He was following another scenario. *You're coming with us,* he said. A vein pulsed on his temple, above one of the mirror lenses.

The thing seemed ridiculous and I didn't move. *Are you not*

wanting to understand what I'm telling you? he yelled. My periph-
eral vision picked up a sense of larger movement and when I
looked past the officer I saw a couple of cars had pulled up.
You're coming to the barracks, he said, leaning ever farther into my
personal space and giving an idea of what he would like to do
in the barracks. I backed away and saw that the commanding
officer was reinforced by soldiers, one of them a woman, who
were closing in with drawn guns. I had an impulse to run, but
when I looked down the slope I saw the soldiers were six or
eight and they were fanned out in a semicircle and had me
covered on three sides. Behind me was the spiked railing. The
soldier who scared me most was the woman. She was the closest
and I could see how tense she was. Her finger was on the trigger
and her lips were white and puckered, eyes tiny black dots. Some
wisps of blond hair had escaped from under her military cap.
She wasn't going to be less of a man than the men.

May I ask the reason for this intense interest? I asked, lounging
against the railing. A dozen nervous military police with their
weapons trained on you at close quarters surely qualified as
intense interest. Unfortunately my tongue cleaved to the top of
my mouth in midquestion and belied my air of easy command
of the situation, the attitude of being a mildly amused onlooker
rather than the person all the guns were pointed at. The insane
impulse to run seized me again. *Reason?* shrieked the commanding officer, who struck me as not entirely in control either.
*Unknown person acting suspiciously outside bank? Unable to furnish
proof of identity? Get him in the car.* As they grabbed my little
rucksack and shoved me into the back seat I noticed for the first
time that we were standing outside the Bank of the Northeast.
One soldier got in on each side of me and their commander by
the driver. It was a squash. Their thick thighs had meter-long
black truncheons strapped to them as well as the guns they had

put away for the car ride. The suspension was terrible and the air was rank with old sweat as we jolted over the stones toward the barracks on the edge of town.

The duty officer at the barracks was a fat little man in a squeaky swivel chair whose politely inquiring smile turned into a snarl when he saw the look on the commanding officer's face. The duty officer started shouting. Being without documents, which he'd picked up from the commanding officer's rant, meant you didn't exist. So they could do anything with you. He grabbed my rucksack and upended it over his battered metal desk. Out fell a plastic water bottle, spare hankie, sun hat, newspaper, a few aspirins and a collapsible umbrella. He seized on the umbrella, a neatly furled black cylinder, as hopefully containing prohibited substances or being some kind of offensive weapon. It turned out to be a collapsible umbrella.

Not so collapsible, however. Having got it up, the duty officer couldn't get it down. He swiveled in his seat and shook it angrily. Its overingenious mechanism defeated the duty officer. He panicked for a moment, waving the semi-erect English collapsible over his head like a man under threat from a fruit bat. The soldiers, if not their commander, relaxed a little. The commander and the duty officer were starting to look pretty foolish. The commander was striding up and down muttering about documents as the drama drained from the moment, the smell of violence floating off. The bank robber had turned out to be a tourist and the duty officer was still trying to fold up his umbrella. The commander wanted to have taken out a bank robber. *How many days have you been here?* he shouted. *Half an hour,* I told him. *Why did you leave your documents in Maceió?* That was clear enough. *I wasn't expecting to be held up at gunpoint here.* Traces of a smirk were showing on the faces of the foot soldiers. *Get in the car,* shouted the commanding officer. *The civilian police can check out your identity.* We piled back into one of the cars.

The tension had collapsed. Now everyone was trying to save face, including me. I was annoyed by the way they were pushing me around and so I said, as we bumped up the hill to the other police, *Now that I've had the pleasure of getting to know you gentlemen, I wonder if you can tell me something I'm curious about. A friend of mine in Pernambuco who knows someone in the force here told me the other day that the military police in Alagoas haven't been paid for months. Is that true?*

I tried to put an offhand conversational lilt into the question, but the words came out too fast and a dry catch in my throat turned my voice squeaky. The inquiry poisoned the atmosphere inside the police car. Normality vanished. The foot soldiers stiffened. The commanding officer went greenish and the thin lips under the bristle mustache disappeared altogether. He was probably thinking that if only I'd run he could have shot me outside the bank and no questions asked. That was what I was thinking. I looked around the car for some response to the question. The driver concentrated on the traffic. The soldier on my right stared out of the side window. *Or don't you know?* I said, too sharply, wanting to rub it in. Finally the soldier on my left, the blackest man in the car and the one whose physique least closely matched the coiled muscular tension cultivated in the force, murmured reassuringly, as if to quieten a fractious child, *It's okay. We've been paid. Everything's okay.*

The question was real. Things weren't great in Pernambuco, people had said there, but they were a lot better than over the border in Alagoas. Pedro's friend in the Alagoas military police hadn't been paid for months. It was happening all over Brazil. Some forces hadn't been paid for six or eight months and the troops were going on strike, to the indignation of the Brazilian president, who was getting his salary on time. Soldiers' pay, when it did arrive, was so low—maybe two hundred dollars a month—that a man's need to boost his income and feed a family obliged him to turn to private account the limited but formidable skills learned in the military police. What you learned in the military police was how to run a fugitive down and how to use techniques of cruel and unusual persuasion. In Recife I had been in crowds watching the military police beating people unconscious. Plus you learned how to shoot and kill. You could make enough money to live on by using these skills after hours as a private guard of property and person, as the four military police from the Alagoas force were doing for PC the night he and Suzana died.

We jolted along in the car, all sunk in silence after the conversation died. I was looking down at the high lace-up paratrooper boots into which the trousers of the men beside me were tucked and thinking of after hours work. These boots reminded me of a report I had read once in the *Diario de Pernambuco*. The item concerned a bunch of boys from the streets of Recife who had been found shot dead. As I remembered, they weren't street kids proper, in the sense of being utterly homeless and destitute, but poor boys who spent a lot of time on the streets and were getting on someone's nerves. Their bodies were found on the city rubbish dump and nothing would have been known about how they got there except that one of the boys had not quite died. He later recovered, apart from being paralyzed from the waist down by the bullet that severed his spinal cord, and he described how a group of men, whom he was unable to identify because their clothing was unmarked and he never saw their faces, had picked him and his friends up on the street one night, flung them onto the floor of a jeep and taken them to the city dump and shot them. The one thing he did remember vividly, from the time they were being driven to the dump, was the men's feet, all shod in the high lace-up boots of the military police.

There was a different mood at the civilian police station. No uniforms were on display, or anything else much, and when he appeared at last the affable detective I found myself dealing with had longish curly hair, a beard and a body hugging shirt in high gloss brown acetate, open to just above the navel to display several ropes of heavy gold chain nestling in the graying chest hair. I was glad to see the PC style lived on in the heartland of Alagoas. He seemed about to offer girls or money changing services, though he didn't. The gun thrust in his belt looked like a fashion accessory. The seventies had clearly been a special time for him. I shoved my heavy pasteboard visiting card under his nose. The cards were made up for moments such as this. Usually I forgot to use them. He sauntered off to ring the hotel. A person went past with a small battered aluminum pan and I noticed the lockup in the darkness behind the abandoned reception desk. A skeletal boy of about fifteen was clinging to the barred door. He was naked except for a pair of boxer shorts hanging slantwise from a cruelly delineated hip. When the plainclothes officer returned half an hour later to offer any assistance I might possibly require, someone discreetly swung the door shut on the street boy's cage, and as the officer graciously indicated the way back to the town center I almost forgot I was dealing with the Alagoan police.

Free at last, I found an old man in town with an old car who didn't care where he took me. We drove out of town and down to the Mundau River. Crossing the river, we drove along an unpaved road which, when it started rising into the hills on the other side, soon became little more than a sandy, stony track running between dense green pasture peopled by amazed cows. As we rose—at every jolt the axle seemed about to go—the grass gave way to trees and bushes which got thicker with altitude. Getting higher, the road from time to time gave views that stretched for miles, and I could see that we were in the middle of a vast convolution of green hills that went on as far as you could see in all directions. The hill we were climbing was the highest of all, though you only saw this intermittently through the vegetation. There were a great many palm trees in the area, rising above the general level of the trees, or soaring above grass. Every hill seemed to have a great palm tree on top of it, waving its ragged fronds like a flag in the slightly cooler air. After a while we reached the very top, and walking around the cleared space, and peering out on all sides, I saw how this hill commanded a vast extent of territory and had all approaches to it in its view. We were on the Serra da Barriga, in the heart of the heart of what had been that congeries of settlements where for nearly a century the Africans of Angola and the Congo, brought to Brazil as slaves, had made their redoubt and their free home in the New World.

XII

A Win

I didn't find Augusto in Maceió but I found something more valuable. Morosely surveying the contents of an outlet in Shopping Iguatemí, my eye fell on a new edition of Raymundo Faoro's *Os Donos do Poder*. I hauled it off—quite a weight—to the hotel, where it filled the gap lately left by the *Chartreuse,* filled the room again with the air of a masterpiece. The book had been mentioned by someone in Rio a year or so before, but stayed unopened as too daunting. Now I needed any help on offer and tried again. Neither my Portuguese nor my acquaintance with Brazil's long and anomalous history was really up to the challenge of it, but it lifted my spirit as it weighed down my hands. Faoro seemed to hold the key to what I was trying to understand in Brazil.

The Owners of Power was another epic synthesis of what was special and different about Brazil, but it had none of the racy glamour of Gilberto Freyre's. This one's origins were unpromising. The author was a jurist and his only other book was a study of Machado de Assis. He had dashed off *The Owners of Power* in the fifties—and soon rewrote it in its present much vaster form—to refute some Marxist talk about the feudalism of the early Brazilian settlement. Faoro went right back to the part played by the monarchy in the origins of Portugal's mercantile capitalism, to the relations of money and power in the beginnings of Brazil and so—moving with indescribable elegance of mind through all the intricacies of everything that happened after—to the nexus of money and power in Brazil today. Much eluded me, as I surfed Faoro's powerfully surging prose, but I began to understand why Brazilian society had never developed that sense of the common good, the res publica, which made other societies cohere—why power and money in Brazil were always personal and dynastic, why interests were personal, why wealth and political power clung so closely together. Faoro took the story only to the early twentieth century, but he let me see where Fernando and PC came from. Everywhere had its crooks and mountebanks on the make. The mystery had been how in Brazil they did it so easily. What kind of complicities had eased their way? Cloudily, I glimpsed how Brazil's uniquely monstrous concentration of wealth had come about and how it had made PC and Fernando possible, outsiders though they partly were.

Faoro didn't say, since his book was written before the military coup of 1964 and ended its tale with Getúlio Vargas seizing power in 1930, what might explain the forces that had ended Fernando's time in power so soon and so abruptly. There was nothing in *The Owners of Power* to explain why, in 1992, students and workers in the streets might have brought about the downfall of a crook who exemplified a Brazilian tradition. Many Brazilian leaders had been abruptly thrown out in the past, but always by another faction of the ruling group, never by the people. Nothing in Faoro's book foresaw the presence in Brazil's Congress of a party with a mass following, one able to express the desires of the young people in the streets through the institutions of government. Faoro explained a lot about Brazil's long and often terrible past, but nothing about the present, or about the future which seemed to be breaking over our heads. He explained the immobility, but not the change. He saw Brazil imprisoned in its past.

―――――

Getting out of Maceió was an idea which took hold fast. I would leave first thing on Monday on a bus for Penedo, and head on down to Bahia. The burden lifted, I arrived for a last meal at the Divine Throat less tense and impatient than on many earlier visits. The Divine Throat had been a late discovery, for the simple reason that many eating places in Brazil featured *Divine* in their name and many others *Throat,* meaning gourmandism, and they were universally dire. The hideousness of somewhere called Divine Throat was beyond imagining, and in Maceió I passed through many grim moments at table—except for the nice Bahian place around the corner where you ate under trees in the garden—before I gave it a go. The Divine Throat turned out to be an agglomeration of many rooms and alcoves and a little courtyard garden. It seemed to have grown very fast and tables were now spilling out onto the street at the front from lack of space inside. Grilled meats were served by an army of energetic youths and every evening the Divine Throat was full of local power people, good-time girls, young couples and families and sugar planters' widows. These last, rather grand ladies of considerable age, always drank a caipirinha whose cachaça the waiters were constantly required to top up, so the ladies could get through the evening on a single drink. My last visit was a Friday night, and soon after nightfall the Divine Throat was full.

One amber J&B after another tinkled over the ice cubes in the tall glass cylinder. I was at peace with the world, at a well positioned table in the covered open area at the front, a thick walled corner at my back and a 270-degree view of what was going on in several different areas. It was wonderful not to care anymore. The rare filet came on a black and smoking griddle. The macaxeira chips were perfect and J&B had never tasted so good. My eye fell more amiably and a little more languidly on the villains around me. People came and went. Ten o'clock came and went and newcomers kept on arriving, standing around on the outer edge of the light, hovering in darkness and poised to pounce on a table, but none of the rest of us made to leave. New tables were set up, nudging out toward the darkened road. I eyed the confusion with the benign complacency of the well-placed, eyed one little group edging in from the shadows directly in front of me, a couple of men in their forties, speaking to a passing big haired woman as the waiters cleared a table on the very edge of the light. There was a boy with them and the elder of the men had a bald head and a neatly trimmed beard.

Gut contracted. Back stiffened. Eyes narrowed. I knew this face. The waiter took the drinks over. They always took the bottle and poured the drink at table. Augusto was drinking Black Label and the other Red. I moved up to Chivas. Blue Label was also on the drinks list at fifty dollars a shot and on my first evening at the Divine Throat, I had wondered who in this place would ever order Blue Label. Now I knew. They also had grilled king prawn kebabs, PC's favorite. I did not have a billion-dollar crime empire to support my habit, but I came from a respectable whiskey drinking family and Chivas would do. I could not afford to meet Augusto with a tumbler of J&B in hand. Self-assurance surged as the squat bottle with the silver label and a bucket of fresh ice wound toward me over the heads of the crowd. A slug of Chivas—ice and water in a separate glass—steadied the nerves. *Bond felt the fire spread through his belly.* In the shadows it was clearly Marcos drinking the Red Label, the man who turned the cell phone off whenever I called to ask about PC's murder. The boy could only be PC's son, whose fortune Augusto now controlled.

I called for writing paper, which took a while to come. The Divine Throat was not a place where people wrote much. I had another Chivas while they unlocked the office, and when the sheets arrived whipped out my fountain pen and wrote a florid note to Augusto reminding him of my many calls and proposing we get together for a chat about his brother's death. *Anywhere, anytime.* I wrote the name of my hotel and said I'd call his home in the morning and that I was looking forward to hearing what he had to say. The waiter delivered the note on a tray. If I thought Augusto Farias might even like to clear up the matter of his part in his brother's and various other murders over a whiskey or two that very evening, and maybe add a little about what happened to the billion dollars his brother had moved out of Brazil and his own current interest in pancontinental road cargo hijacking and the intercontinental traffic in drugs and arms—and at that precise moment I really did think he might— I was wrong. Augusto did not share my eagerness for a full and frank criminal résumé over a drink. Augusto seemed not to respond at all.

A certain rigidity set in at Augusto's table when the note arrived, and here at least I had them. His problem was that he was in profile. I could survey a swath of people without moving and Augusto could not see who sent the note without turning through forty-five degrees and peering into the crowd. He tried to do this with great subtlety and patience, formidable control, yet just enough to give himself away and not enough to satisfy his curiosity. The others at his table seemed not to know what was in the note. Augusto decided to have a pee. The path to the gents ran plausibly past my table. He left no message as he passed, but I got a better look at him. In the photos he was always dressed for Brasilia in expensive pastel suits and ties, but for an end-of-week drink in his hometown Augusto wore black jeans with a western belt and

Cuban heeled boots and a red shirt. He was lean and mean and utterly unlike PC.

I had a final Chivas. A wave of weariness swept up from somewhere, a slight cloudiness of the head. Could I leave unseen? There was a great stretch of unlit road to walk, road without footpaths, road where anything might happen at night. I paid the waiter. The Farias table seemed deep in its own affairs. Whatever were they so intent on? Something pretty serious. I stood up silently. The hideous screech of the metal chair legs on the concrete made people jump and would have wakened PC from his slumbers, but his brother seemed not to notice. I steadied myself against the table and stood there for a moment. Then moved, as swiftly and silently as I could, yet relaxed and fearless in body language, toward the outer darkness. The tables were packed together, closer than they had been earlier. My thigh caught the corner of one and slopped half a dozen drinks. The chair legs were deceptively splayed. One tripped me and I nearly fell, but I recovered adroitly and continued with great dignity toward the cover of the night—not too fast, not too fast— concentrating very hard on following a straight line.

The morning was nearly over before I remembered to ring Augusto. The telephone rang and rang in the apartment without an answer. I asked at reception for messages but Augusto had not called. And never did. I made ready to leave and lightness came back into being. That weekend, posters went up on the big billboards all round Maceió warning people against Fernando's planned return to public life in Alagoas. During the night someone went out with a chain saw and cut the billboards down and then I was heading south. That afternoon I was in Penedo, on the bank of the still mighty São Francisco River, just before it reached the sea. Under a pergola that night, on the high cliff carved by the river, I chewed on alligator stew and gazed at the little clusters of lights beyond the vast tract of dark water, on the Sergipe side of the river. In the morning I would be out of Alagoas.

I crossed into Sergipe by riverboat. The boat was long and narrow like a long and high canoe that had been roofed in. It was not a greatly reassuring craft. Passengers had to sit below along each side but I seemed to be the only one. Two boatmen struggled to get my big suitcase onto the blue flat wooden roof. The case was now so full of books, newspaper clippings and photocopies, and *journeying mercies,* that a single person could not hold it off the ground for more than a few seconds. It looked exposed and insecure, lying on its smooth curved side with nothing to retain it. A sharp tip of the canoe, which looked all too ready to tip sharply, would send everything sliding into the waters of the São Francisco. Five minutes before we cast off, a crowd of people arrived from nowhere on the quay. They were country people carrying crates of watermelons, bananas and macaxeira and other fruit and vegetables and all these were heaped up on the roof with my suitcase. All of us were funneled down into the narrow space below, where we sat with knees touching.

More people kept arriving and were squeezed in long after the boat seemed full. Some of the passengers were aged about ninety, bent and toothless, and others were just starting school and loaded with exercise books, and others were infants still in arms. New cargo thudded over our heads. Apart from the single entrance each new passenger squeezed down through, the only openings were tiny windows closed by wooden slats. If the boat capsized, which the high piled cargo made it increasingly likely to do, we would drown like rats in seconds. Everyone sat silent and staring, paralyzed by the same terrible thought and doubtless fighting the same claustrophobic panic that was rising in me. Being a swimmer would be no use at all. An old man in his eighties, wearing a flat cloth cap on his sunburnt head and a collarless shirt under his braces, gave a cry of alarm and lunged for the opening. We were packed in so tight he had no chance against the several dozen folded legs packed between the seats, and by then we were swinging out onto the river. On the open water a stiff breeze whipped across the surface and the riverboat leaned over hard. The next half hour went on forever. It was my worst moment in a lifetime of public transport. But we lived. And so did the suitcase.

I found a bus to Aracajú and then another that went to Salvador. It was night and pouring rain when we got there. Next day, from a vast white room with a honey-colored parquet floor, its three sets of heavy green shutters flung open in the face of a sun blazing through the new washed air, I looked down on the Bay of All Saints. The island-dotted bay itself spread vastly into an area of white gold indeterminacy where water and air became indistinguishable. Closer in, the sea surface shimmered like the scales of a still wet fish through silver, copper, gunmetal blue. Hundreds of feet below the window was a small-craft harbor by a big nineteenth-century customhouse and just offshore a little sixteenth-century fort built on one tiny island, a perfectly circular gray stone fortress whose sides rose vertically from the water. Out of the beaten yellow sand of its enclosure rose, in the very center of the ring, the tuft of a tall and slightly listing palm tree. A cannon in the fort fired off a long salute, and a string of white smoke puffs rose straight up toward me through the golden air.

The Palace was a big cream art deco pile, once the smartest hotel in town, halfway up the formerly fashionable Rua Chile, which led up to the plaza with the great elevator that linked the old city with the waterfront below. The old city, jumbled along the high cliffs above the bay, was greatly changed. Seedy old Salvador had been made over and now it looked as extraordinary as the very notion of the European seventeenth century in the tropics—pastel-painted houses packed around cobbled squares and dominated by great baroque churches, thrown into relief by the steepness of the hills. It was all pitched at tourists— everywhere that wasn't a church was a bar or restaurant or craft shop—but the squares still worked as public spaces in the evenings, and drew the people of *the most African city in the Western Hemisphere* back to their own city's old center every night to make their music. It hadn't done this before. It was enough to make you think again about heritage.

The churches of Salvador were mostly empty. The only one that was buzzing with life was the slave church on the Largo do Pelhourinho. The Pelhourinho was the pillory, and the Largo was the steeply raked square where the slaves had been bought and sold, and where they were flogged. They could be flogged for anything. In a poem by Bahia's great satirist of the seventeenth century, Gregório de Matos, a luxurious lady made a slave scratch the white skin of her bare back, and had him whipped when she saw he was excited. Was this worse than having your eyes gouged out by scissors or a needle, which was what neglected wives might do to their husbands' slave girl lovers? On one side of the pillory square was the big church *of the blacks* which had been built over many years by freed slaves and which still had the feel, unlike the restored and more splendid monuments of the baroque not far away, of standing for something. It was lighter inside Nosso Senhor do Rosário dos Pretos, and a buzz of noise came from its side chambers and sacristry. People were cleaning, arranging flowers, and somewhere someone was cooking. Out the back was a sunny yard. The carved saints in the church were black, and one in particular had a finely done and vividly African head.

The insides of churches soon become too much, and when the gorgeous gilded riot of São Francisco's baroque cedar carvings began to oppress, I stepped out into a more austere space and wandered around the deserted sun-filled cloister. This turned out to be livelier than it seemed at first—studying the azulejos that lined the walls, and some of the saucy pictures the Portuguese artist had painted on the tiles to illustrate the moral precepts and spiritual exhortations written underneath, I found that words and pictures together made the messages equivocal. As I peered more closely, I heard a long drawn out moan that was unmistakably the sound of sexual pleasure. Startled, I looked around the empty cloister. Was it the sun beating down, a hallucination? I returned to the tiles. Another long orgasmic moan filled the space, lower now, more strangely drawn out, more abandoned, almost inhuman. My mind was clearly lost in the lubriciousness of seventeenth-century Bahia. I took a turn around the cloister, hoping to shake my head clear. At each corner by a pillar was a tall terracotta jar with a flowering plant spilling out of it. At the base of one of these jars I found the hidden lovers, two tortoises locked in an ecstatic and interminable copulation.

———

Pierre Fatumbi Verger was born in 1902, as simple Pierre Verger, into a family of that French bourgeoisie whose ways and tastes were being mimicked and adored by its aspiring counterparts in Brazil. The Paris of his early years was the city where Marcel Proust was still going out socially and tiny, immaculate Alberto Santos Dumont, whose father had been *the king of coffee* in Brazil, was spending his inheritance building and flying the most advanced and daring air machines in the world. The First World War came and went and Pierre Verger raced his sports car in Paris and spent his summers in Deauville. When the twenties were over and both his parents dead and the family business in receivership, Verger began to travel. First to Corsica, then to Tahiti. He also began to take photographs. In the new age of photomagazines he was able to earn a living as a photographer and for the next twenty years he traveled around Europe, the Pacific, Southeast Asia, Africa, North America, Central America, South America taking photographs with his Rolleiflex. Most of the photographs were of working people, people in the streets, which through remoteness of place and the passage of time would gain a powerful strangeness as images of the world at the end of the European empires. In 1946 he arrived in Brazil and gravitated to Bahia, which became his base and eventually his home.

From Bahia Verger went on traveling, and more and more often to Africa—African people and African cultures were what he photographed, between the poles of the African Brazil of Bahia and the West African countries across the Atlantic which had peopled Brazil. His photography became less and less the random images of the higher tourism or the commissioned images of photojournalism. The beholder's eye was no longer the metropolitan renegade's, seeking the exotic, and as it took on the participant's sympathy the pictures lost something of their visual edge. They became a record of the cultures and practices and beliefs of African people on both sides of the Atlantic. Verger himself was drawn into the African culture of Salvador de Bahia and became an adept interpreter of *candomblé,* the Bahian African rites that were practiced, in Salvador, in more locales than the Christian churches had.

As a *go-between* linking Brazil's African culture and its white, Brazil and Africa, Brazil and Europe, Verger—who now also had the candomblé name Fatumbi—became both more inward and more analytical. He gave up photography altogether in the end, and became a collector and narrator of the history of Africa in Brazil and Brazil in Africa. His first vast book—done as a thesis for the Sorbonne, in a late rapprochement to the Paris intellectual world he had always derided—was a history of the reciprocities the slave trade between Africa and Brazil had engendered. His second was a massive compilation of African herbal practices—the uses of different plants in all the varieties of medicine and magic. When I went to his house in Salvador, where after his death they kept the thousands and thousands of negatives in cabinets of little wooden drawers, where they kept his rather eclectic library and carried on his studies, they were still in the agitation of organizing the great exhibition of his photographs which had lately opened in Rio. Looking around, I was struck by a thought, and asked the archivist if Verger had known Gilberto Freyre. *Oh yes,* she said quickly. *They were friends.* She shot a needle-sharp glance at the assistant archivist. *They shared the same interests.*

Whatever interests she meant, Pierre Fatumbi Verger had done rather better posthumously than Gilberto. Pierre's house was humming with enthusiastic activity and full of the mostly young and mostly black. The master's monkish cot and his couple of wire coat hangers were not objects of particular reverence and Pierre's house was lost in a jumble of low rent dwellings halfway up a steep little hill. Gilberto's suburban mansion in Recife was a much grander place with a splendid double bed and a conference center had been built in the garden under the mango and cinnamon trees. The house itself was carefully kept as in life, down to the silver backed hairbrushes on the dressing table, and there was nothing in its appurtenances that wasn't European—nothing of Brazil's African or northeastern cultures. The library was quietly succumbing to what book dealers below the equator call *scattered insect damage,* and apart from the youth looking after the place there was nobody there at all. The mortal remains of Gilberto and his wife were surrounded by a slimy fishpond and in the conference center there was a lifesize mannikin of Gilberto himself, wearing one of his tropical suits and holding a Bahian cigar, seated before a bottle of his favorite homemade pitanga brandy. Gilberto's papier-mâché face was flushed, the bright red lips were smiling slightly and his head was tilted almost sideways.

The taxi driver who took me to Gilberto's spent half the trip arguing vehemently that Gilberto was a reactionary figure who hated black people. I was responding to his animadversions in a quiet kind of way as we hurtled along the broken roads when he switched in midsentence to insisting no less vehemently that black people were the source of all Brazil's troubles, perverse and beyond all help. It seemed that nothing about Brazil's past had been settled yet. We found common ground, just before arriving, in the failings of the present government.

———

Luis Inácio Lula da Silva was elected, by a very big margin and in an impeccably swift and democratic process that might have shamed the United States, president of the world's fifth largest country at the end of 2002. Nothing could have been less surprising, nothing harder to believe. It had taken thirteen years, four elections and a major makeover. Fidel Castro of Cuba was among the heads of state at the inauguration, and among the other invited guests were Gilberto's and Lula's other cousins from Long Plain in Pernambuco. The open Rolls-Royce limousine, an ancient gift of the British government, broke down as it carried the new president to his swearing in and had to be pushed. One of the mounted guards of honor fell off his horse, and the crowds drowned the inaugural ceremony by splashing in the ornamental lake outside the palace. The day after handing over to the new president, FHC, who maintained that *Lula is a myth,* flew off for a long holiday in France.

José Dirceu, the former political prisoner and clandestine

resistance fighter and the real architect of Lula's victory, began as chief of cabinet by recalling to those present the memory of comrades in the fight for democracy in Brazil who had not lived to see that day. Dirceu's place as president of the Workers' Party was taken by the former guerrilla fighter and torture victim José Genoino. The new government's minister of culture was the great black singer and composer from Bahia Gilberto Gil, who immediately made it clear that he saw his task as letting the vast and muffled people's culture of Brazil be heard and seen in the world. Another member of the new cabinet was Benedita da Silva, a black woman born in a Rio favela, who like Lula himself had grown up selling fruit and sweets and peanuts on the street. A little earlier Benedita had been governor of the state of Rio de Janeiro, and somewhere I had seen a picture of her in the governor's great and magnificent Orange Tree Palace in Rio. She was on her new home's splendid curved stairway in a short-sleeved pale lemon suit, a powerful woman with limbs like aubergines, striding up the stairs followed by a straggle of children and teenagers from the favela, showing her family around. A little later President Lula appointed Brazil's first black justice of the Supreme Court.

Not everyone did so well in the other elections of 2002. Fernando Collor was resoundingly defeated in his attempt to reenter Brazil's political life as governor of Alagoas. *If we don't deal with the thing, the thing will deal with us,* the past and now present governor of Alagoas had said earlier in the year, and the people of Alagoas understood. Something had changed. Another victim of the change was the federal deputy from Alagoas, Augusto Farias, who lost his seat in the Brazilian Congress, so losing too the various privileges and protections enjoyed by a federal congressman in Brazil. Suddenly there was, in theory at least, nothing to stop Augusto Farias from being tried like any other citizen in Brazil's criminal courts on the charges outstanding against him.

Perhaps coincidentally there was now a surprising little flurry of activity around Augusto Farias in the Brazilian judiciary. Days after the election and more than six years after the crime, PC's bodyguards, who still worked for Augusto, were formally indicted for the murders of PC and Suzana. Augusto was in the equivocal situation of still having a month to go of his cover as a congressman, and the judge was still—after nearly three years—waiting to hear from the chief prosecutor of Brazil on Augusto. In November the chief prosecutor, Geraldo Brindeiro, announced that in the three years he had been sitting on the case, although no new evidence of any kind had turned up, he had changed his mind and now thought PC Farias had been murdered in a crime of passion. All the scientific tests that had eliminated this story were thrown out. The case was closed. When Augusto Farias became an ordinary citizen at the end of the year he would have nothing to answer for, at least on that matter. The others, the organized crime charges from the con-gressional commission, and the Ceci Cunha family massacre, had fallen into a bottomless well of silence. Augusto was walking clear of everything.

Except that in early 2003 another thing happened. On yet another of Augusto's vast properties—the Fazenda Santa Ana in Pará, a place of twenty-one thousand hectares lying a thousand kilometers south of Belém—141 workers were found living in slavery. They had been lured there with the promise of work and held in a debt servitude which began with the cost of their long-distance bus fare. They were prevented from leaving, fed on rubbish, savagely beaten and lacked even clean drinking water. Many were suffering from untreated malaria, hepatitis, kidney disease or dengue fever. The investigating magistrate who visited the property said, *I have never seen free men treated with such cruelty.* Augusto, and his sister who shared the title to this property, had received about a million dollars in development aid from the government to raise cattle at Santa Ana. In February a judge ordered Augusto's arrest and his sister's, but Augusto disappeared. A small army of police was distributed to stake out the airports of Alagoas and each of the known homes and properties and business addresses of Augusto and his family and their closest friends. The search for Augusto presumably included the *Dom Farias,* the brothers' purpose-built twenty-meter yacht, dreamed of by PC and launched in 1999 with circular beds in its six mirror lined suites. Then Augusto went to the police and was immediately released pending developments. He is presumably still free, going about his business in Alagoas and on his many vast landholdings in remote Brazil.

I went back to Recife. Dona Lia came out from behind the bar. *Pedro,* she said. *You've heard?* Heard what? *Vavá is deceased. We lost him four months ago.* I expressed surprise but didn't feel it. The story was that Vavá, just before the end, had been in excellent form. The Bangüê had been done up with heritage money from the council and had a whole new kitchen and ugly new tiles on the floor and white plastic chairs out front. Vavá was said to have been thrilled. Alexandre's shop, the one Vavá had lost his refuge for, had failed and been written off but the new Bangüê had been going great guns. Then one night in bed with Lia, Vavá had felt a mortal chill come over him and started weeping unconsolably. A couple of hours later he suffered a heart attack and was dead by the time an ambulance arrived. There had been an event to remember him in the Pátio, and some pieces in the paper about his contribution to the cultural life of

Recife and the Northeast and this had gratified Dona Lia. The
crowd of young students, the ones who used to spend the afternoon of every New Year's Eve at the Bangüê, had chipped in to
have a local artist paint a portrait of the deceased, and his work
now hung in the Bangüê's place of honor. The artist had clearly
worked from a photo of a much younger Vavá than I had ever
known, which he seemed to have overlaid with blocks of simple
color—jet black hair with strongly pronounced sideburns, a puce
splotch representing a face with no identifiable features and a
screaming acid yellow shirt. Dona Lia's enlarged eyes glinted
out of her giant lenses as I admired the likeness.

One afternoon a great lady of Recife, a cousin of Gilberto
Freyre's now in her eighties, came into the Bangüê with the
help of a sturdy walking stick. She had worked with Vavá in
his busiest years, making northeastern artists known, organizing
exhibitions, festivals, meetings. They had traveled—had been to
São Paulo to take part in the opening of the great continental
art collection in Oscar Niemeyer's *Memorial da América Latina*.
Dona Lia brought out a sheaf of curling photos of those days.
When we were alone, the great lady grew conspiratorial. She
told me she had been Vavá's lover. I ventured the thought that
life—the circumstances of his own life, northeastern life,
Brazil's—and his own heedless generosity of feeling had undone
Vavá. We remembered the house in Porto de Galinhas, and she
talked about the good times there. Her voice dropped still further and she shot glances around the almost empty room and it
was harder and harder to pick up what she was saying. I caught
the phrase *the family* a few times and once, quite distinctly but
in reference to whom I never knew, *They killed him, you know.*

———

Somewhere in Recife I woke with arms around me. It was dark
now, so damp the air was palpable, and silent outside. The smell

of rank plaster filled the little room. It was peeling off the blue-washed walls in foamy patches. Extricated, I stood on the bed and stretched to reach the room's single window, a little square high in the wall, the vent of a former storeroom or a prison. In the world outside a fine and soundless rain was falling and a scarf of tiny droplets floated under the bulb of a yellow street-light. I could see the back wall of the old convent, solid, white and high, and its lichen spattered terracotta roof. Clouds parted and the moon glared white on the great baroque bell tower, and the ragged fronds of the palm trees that lined each side of the brick paved path to the door of the church. I lay down and embraced the sleeper, who did not wake, and drifted off to sleep again. The rain was heavier, drumming audibly now. Time stopped. A soft insistent tap on the door woke me later. *Number eleven, number eleven,* came a soft and singsong female voice beyond. *You've been in there for hours. It's time for you to go.* This was years and years ago now.

———

Sitting in Rio with a canny old Brazilian journalist, the editor of the *Jornal do Brasil.* We were drinking cold Antártica and looking out over the waterfront from the restaurant on the upper floor of what was left of a green art nouveau building that in Machado's day had housed Rio's fish market. Below us, shirtless fishermen were dropping desultory lines into the oily water below the wharf. It was Good Friday, hot and hazy and strangely still. The editor knew all the people involved in the rise and fall of PC and Fernando and had written an account of those years, an account that was in many ways authoritative, although for some reason he persisted in believing that Suzana had killed PC. *It's obvious,* he said now, lugubriously peeling another quail's egg. *I spoke to him a few days before she killed him. He was going to leave her.* It occurred to me that telenovela values were even more deeply implanted in Brazilians' minds than I had thought, and I remembered that the editor was a friend and admirer of Roberto Marinho, who was now lost to terminal dementia, and did not pursue the matter. He gave me Fernando's cell phone number, which I would never feel inclined to call, and we talked about Brazil and about Australia, about the parallels and divergences in the history of two great countries of the New World.

Things can change overnight here, he said suddenly. *Everything seems to go on the same forever, but things are happening out of sight, and then one day nothing is the same.* We were looking down on the Ilha Fiscal, a tiny island that lay a few meters offshore. The island was mostly taken up with a miniature turreted palace like a fairy-tale castle. It had been built in the time of the Brazilian Empire and had been the scene of a famous ball held in 1889 to mark the visit to Rio of the Chilean navy. It was a social event of great glamour and elegance—the menu of course was in French—a celebration of the Brazilian Empire's place in the world and of the prevailing order at home. A few days later the army surrounded the imperial palace, the emperor and his family were sent packing and Brazil was a republic. *You see,* said the old journalist triumphantly. Without saying so, I didn't see at all. It seemed to me that Brazil had been a long time waiting for Lula. Then our grilled fish arrived. I reached for a lime.

Sources and Readings

In English, Gilberto Freyre's trilogy *The Masters and the Slaves,* *The Mansions and the Shanties* and *Order and Progress* were last reprinted—from Alfred A. Knopf's originals—by the University of California Press in the 1980s. Euclides da Cunha's *The Drylands* is available in Samuel Putnam's translation as *Rebellion in the Backlands* in Picador Travel Classics. The major novels of Machado de Assis, *The Posthumous Memoirs of Bras Cubas, Quincas Borba, Dom Casmurro,* and *Esau and Jacob,* have been newly translated in a wonderfully exact and readable way at last for Oxford's Library of Latin America. All of the above translations are excellent and so are the various introductions. Montaigne's essay "On Cannibals," Shakespeare's *Tempest,* Conrad's *Heart of Darkness* and *Nostromo* are available in endless editions and Jorge Amado's novels are easy to find in English. Roger Casement's Brazilian diaries were recently published in *Roger Casement's Diaries, 1910: The Black and the White* (Pimlico), edited and with an introduction by Roger Sawyer.

The historical literature on Brazil in Portuguese is vast and formidable, sometimes splendid, yet a few of the best books were written in English. C. B. Boxer's *The Portuguese Seaborne Empire*

(Carcanet) and John Hemming's *Red Gold: The Conquest of the Brazilian Indians, 1500–1760* (Harvard) are superb. Robert Edgar Conrad's *Children of God's Fire: A Documentary History of Black Slavery in Brazil* (Princeton, then Pennsylvania State) is a complete and thoughtfully introduced compilation, and Stuart B. Schwartz's *Slaves, Peasants and Rebels: Reconsidering Brazilian Slavery* (Illinois) a very good academic study. Emilia Viotti da Costa's *The Brazilian Empire: Myths and Histories* (Chicago, then North Carolina) has great élan, and Robert M. Levine's *Vale of Tears: Revisiting the Canudos Massacre in Northeastern Brazil, 1893–1897* (California) is exhaustively detailed. Mike Davis's *Late Victorian Holocausts* (Verso) relates Canudos to other crimes and catastrophes of empire. On Machado de Assis, John Gledson's *The Deceptive Realism of Machado de Assis* (Francis Cairns) is a terse and useful historical reading between the lines of *Dom Casmurro,* and one of Roberto Schwartz's studies of Machado— see below—has just been translated into English as *A Master on the Periphery of Capitalism* (Duke). On Lula, *Without Fear of Being Happy: Lula, the Workers' Party and Brazil* by Emir Sader and Ken Silverstein (Verso) and *Brazil, Carnival of the Oppressed: Lula and the Brazilian Workers' Party* by Sue Branford and Bernardo Kucinski (Latin American Bureau) are useful on the earlier years but both a decade out of date.

Introductory books in English are Ben Box and Mick Day's splendid *Brazil Handbook* (Footprint), an immensely detailed travel guide that puts everything in its historical and cultural context; the very thoughtful and wide-ranging *Brazil Reader* edited by Robert M. Levine and John J. Crocitti (Latin American Bureau), and two recent short histories, Thomas E. Skidmore's *Brazil: Five Centuries of Change* (Oxford) and Boris Fausto's *Concise History of Brazil* (Cambridge), the former livelier and the latter more detailed. For a glimpse of Brazilian history in its continental and global economic context, the shock of Eduardo Galeano's forty-year-old *The Open Veins of Latin America* (Monthly Review Press) never seems to fade. Bradford Burns's little *Documentary History of Brazil* (Knopf, 1966) translates and links a number of documents, but doesn't include all of Pero Vaz de Caminha's letter to the king. For that in English you have to go back to William Brooks Greenlee's translation in the Hakluyt Society's volume of 1937, *The Voyages of Pedro Alvares Cabral to Brazil and India.* On Brazilian food in English, *Brazil: A Cook's Tour* by Christopher Idone (Clarkson Potter) is fine as far as it goes, which is not much farther than the Rio–São Paulo axis.

In Portuguese, Raymundo Faoro's magisterial and never translated *Os Donos do Poder* (Globo) received in 2001 the Brazilian edition it deserved, the third; and Euclides da Cunha's *Os Sertões* came out in a splendid centenary edition in 2002 (Ateliê Editorial and Imprensa Oficial do Estado). Da Cunha's war dispatches from Canudos are printed as *Diário de uma Expedição* (Companhia das Letras). The three books of Gilberto Freyre's trilogy, *Casa-grande & Senzala, Sobrados e Mucambos,* and *Ordem e Progresso,* are currently available in very good editions (Record) and most of his other books are also back in print. His 1939 book on sugar, with recipes, is *Açúcar: Uma Sociologia do Doce com Receitas de Bolos e Doces do Nordeste do Brasil* (Companhia das Letras). The (nearly) complete works of Machado de Assis are available on thin paper in three fat volumes as *Obra Completa* (Nova Aguilar). The thirty-one-volume edition of 1944 (Jackson) has more. There is also an excellent two-volume anthology of Machado's stories with an introduction by John Gledson, *Contos: Uma Antologia* (Companhia das Letras), and an interesting autobiographical assemblage put together by Josué Montello as *Memórias Póstumas de Machado de Assis* (Nova Frontera). Machado's novels are available in innumerable editions in Brazil and also, like *Os Sertões* and the letter of Pero Vaz de Caminha, on the Internet. Roberto Schwartz's studies of Machado, *Ao Vencedor as Batatas* and *Um Mestre na Periferia do Capitalismo* (Duas Cidades and Editora 34), are relentless but necessary. Paulo Lins's novel *Cidade de Deus* is published by Companhia das Letras. The poems of Carlos Drummond de Andrade, who is in some ways a later analogue in poetry of Machado de Assis, requiring great attention to what he doesn't say, have just been gathered in a magnificent centenary edition of sixteen hundred pages as *Poesia Completa* (Nova Aguilar). The seventeenth-century poems of Gregório de Matos are published in two volumes as *Crônica do Viver Baiano Seiscentista* (Record). Jorge Amado's *O Menino Grapiúna* (Record) is a short account of growing up poor in Bahia, first written for *Vogue,* with beautiful illustrations by Floriano Teixeira.

Of Brazilian history in Portuguese, apart from the Faoro and Freyre books mentioned above, the following minuscule sampling is pertinent here: Pierre Verger's *Fluxo e Refluxo do Tráfico de Escravos Entre o Golfo do Benin a Bahia de Todos os Santos dos Séculos XVII a XIX* (Corrupio), which came out first in French as *Flux et Reflux de la Traite des Négres Entre le Golfe de Bénin et Bahia de Todos os Santos du Dix-septième au Dix-neuvième Siècle* in an edition I have never been able to find—I believe an English translation exists too, but I have never seen this either; Sergio Buarque de Holanda's *Raízes do Brasil* (Companhia das Letras) and *Visão do Paraíso* (Editora Brasiliense) are fundamental; on Palmares and the quilombos *Liberdade por um Fio: Historia dos Quilombos no Brasil* (Companhia das Letras) edited by João José Reis and Flávio dos Santos Gomes was very helpful, along with the books in English by Schwartz and Conrad and the *Brazil Reader.* The four-volume *Historia da Vida Privada no Brasil: Cotidiano e Vida Privada na América Portuguesa* (Companhia das Letras), directed by Lilia Moritz Schwarcz and with contributions from a number of historians, contains fascinating material to complement Freyre on how Brazilians have lived over the centuries. Câmara Cascudo's *Dicionário do Folclore Brasiliero* (Globo) has information on practically everything. The records of the Inquisition's northeastern interrogations in the 1590s are in *Confissões da Bahia* (Companhia das Letras) and the letters to the Baron of Jeremoabo in the 1890s, collected in *Canudos: Cartas para o Barão* (Edusp), throw much light on those events, particularly their long and thoughtful introduction by Consuelo Novais Sampiao. In *Canudos Cinquenta Anos Depois* (1947, reprinted 1993 by Conselho Estadual de Cultura and Academia de Letras de Bahia), Odorico Tavares offers testimony from survivors who were still living fifty years after the destruction of Canudos. The early republican history of Alagoas is described in *Metamorfose das Oligarquias* (HD Livros) by Douglas Apratto Tenório.

On the most recent history, *Notícias do Planalto: A Imprensa e Fernando Collor* by Mario Sergio Conti (Companhia das Letras) is a very fluid and complete account of Fernando's fast rise and faster fall as seen by the journalists of Brazilian press and television, not least of whom the author. This book provided useful factual detail for the Collor-Farias strand in *A Death in Brazil*: endnotes on page 316 identify points for which *Notícias do Planalto* was a source and for which its author is thanked. The three volumes of *Histórias do Poder* edited by Alberto Dines, Florestan Fernandes Jr. and Nelma Salomão (Editora 34) contain long and fascinating interviews with nearly all the (still surviving) leading actors in Brazilian public life of the last thirty years. *Ousar Lutar: Memórias da Guerrilha Que Vivi* (Viramundo) by José Roberto Rezende with Mouzar Benedito is the autobiographical account of a young resister who was tortured and imprisoned for five years by the Brazilian military; Frei Betto's *Batismo de Sangue* (Casa Amarela) is a history of imprisonment, torture and killing by the military in the twenty years of their tyranny by a former political prisoner who is a close adviser of Luis Inácio Lula da Silva.

Lucas Figueiredo's *Morcegos Negros* (Record) is disorganized, overexcited and skimpy, but it includes some very interesting details on the later international operations of PC Farias. Other instant books on recent events are rather less useful, apart from *Todos os Sócios do Presidente* (Scritta) by Gustavo Krieger, Luis Antônio Novaes, and Tales Farias. The late Pedro Collor's *Passando a Limpo; A Trajetória de um Farsante* (Record) offers some remarkable glimpses of Brazilian family life. *Mil Dias de Solidão* (Geração) by Fernando's press secretary Claudio Humberto Rosas e Silva is sickening. The murders of PC and of Suzana Marcolino and the many other deaths that have punctuated the rise and rise of Augusto Farias have been meticulously reported over the last seven years in the weekly *Istoé* by Mino Pedrosa—who was the journalist who found Eriberto França in 1992 and persuaded him to testify against president Fernando Collor—and Mário Simas Filho (*Istoé*, passim, from June 1996). Many of their articles have been posted on the Internet.

Statistics on contemporary Brazil I found in *Síntese de Indicadores Sociais 2000* (IBGE, 2001) and in *Desigualdade e Pobreza no Brasil* (IPEA, 2000) edited by Ricardo Henriques. *Brasil em Números/Brazil in Figures* (IGBE, 1999) presents a compact bilingual summary of some basic data. Statistics concerning the landless I mostly found in *Le Monde Diplomatique*, and articles posted on the MST's Web site.

There are many Brazilian books on Brazilian food. I found the *Viagem Gastronômica Através do Brasil* by Caloca Fernandes (Senac) particularly attractive, useful and informative.

––––––

The look of the Northeast in the last century has been caught by some great photographers. The two best were French. Pierre

Verger's images of the Northeast are in *Le Messager/The Go-Between: Photographies, 1932–1962* (Revue Noire and DAP) and *O Olhar Viajante de Pierre Fatumbi Verger* (Fundação Pierre Verger). Marcel Gautherot's, which date from the same period and include more of inland life, are in *Bahia: Rio Saõ Francisco, Recôncavo e Salvado—Fotografias de Marcel Gautherot* (Nova Frontera). Verger's ethnographic photographs of religious ceremonies in Africa and northeastern Brazil are in *Orixás: Deuses Iorubás na Africa e no Novo Mundo* (Corrupio).

Another Frenchman, the anthropologist and structuralist Claude Lévi-Strauss, published a book of his Brazilian photographs as *Saudades do Brasil: A Photographic Memoir* (Washington), showing mainly the people of the Amazon rain forest but including some striking images of a still pastoral São Paulo on the eve of its industrial transformation in the 1930s. Sebastião Salgado has produced a very fine book of photographs of the landless in Brazil, which shows a great deal of the people of today's rural Northeast, in *Terra: Struggle of the Landless* (Phaidon). His unforgettable photographs of the gold miners of Serra Pelada are in *Workers: An Archaeology of the Industrial Age* (Phaidon). The Canudos war photographs of Flávio de Barros are collected in *Canudos: Imagens da Guerra* (Museu da República and Lacerda) and there are splendid photographs of the place today by Evandro Teixeira in his *Canudos: 100 Anos* (Textual). Mario Cravo Neto's large-format photos of the black people of contemporary Salvador in *Laróyè* (Aries) are more colorful in several different senses than any of the black and white austerities listed above.

Notes

Page

50   He set up new offshore . . . *v.* Mario Sergio Conti, *Notícias do Planalto. A imprensa e Fernando Collor* (São Paulo 1999) p. 296

51   *I'm staking everything* . . . *v.* Conti, *op., cit.* p. 284

      PC also spent $10.5 . . . *v.* Conti, *op., cit.* p. 295

      From then on PC received . . . *v.* Conti, *op., cit.* p. 300

68   On a visit to New York . . . *v.* Conti, *op., cit.* p. 405

70   She was deeply religious . . . *v.* Conti, *op., cit.* p. 285

      Whe he was nine, PC . . . *v.* Conti, *op., cit.* p. 285

71   As president of the students' . . . *v.* Conti, *op., cit.* p. 285

      Being known, as PC made . . . *v.* Conti, *op., cit.* p. 286

      This was when they started . . . *v.* Conti, *op., cit.* p. 286

72   Then he went into . . . *v.* Conti, *op., cit.* p. 286

73   PC was a special . . . Conti, *op., cit.* p. 288

      He put one of his . . . *v.* Conti, *op., cit.* p. 288

79   From his meeting . . . *v.* Conti, *op., cit.* p. 291

101   He was in the papers . . . *v.* Conti, *op., cit.* p. 22

      He bought votes . . . *v.* Conti, *op., cit.* p. 21

102   The man *who* . . . Conti, *op., cit.* p. 27

104   The sergeant's killing . . . *v.* Conti, *op., cit.* p. 466

145   He alone, in the stifling . . . *v.* Conti, *op., cit.* p. 14

235   Brazil was sinking . . . *v.* Conti, *op., cit.* p. 664

A Chronology

1000 B.C. (*circa*) Indigenous people of Amazon cultivate manioc as their principal food.

1415 The Portuguese take Ceuta on the Moroccan coast, their first outpost in Africa.

1433 Portuguese ships begin sailing down the West African coast.

1453 The fall of Constantinople to the Turks closes Europe's overland route to Asia.

1484 Portuguese ships reach the mouth of the Congo.

1488 Bartolomeu Dias rounds the Cape of Storms, renamed the Cape of Good Hope by the Portuguese king.

1492 Columbus makes landfall in the Caribbean.

1493   In the Treaty of Tordesilhas, the pope divides rights to the new Atlantic world between Spain and Portugal.

1494   Portugal renegotiates the Treaty of Tordesilhas with Spain to include the still undiscovered Brazil in Portugal's eastern share.

1499   Vasco da Gama returns to Lisbon after sailing around Africa to India.
       Amerigo Vespucci sails along the northern coast of South America and writes home about a *new world*.

1500   On the way to India, a Portuguese fleet under Pedro Álvares Cabral makes landfall in the Land of the True Cross, on the coast of what will be Bahia in northeastern Brazil.

1501   Amerigo Vespucci sails into the Bay of All Saints, Bahia.

1502   Gonçalo Coelho lands in Guanabara Bay on New Year's Day and imagines a river, O Rio de Janeiro.

1530   Portugal sends 400 men to colonize Brazil.

1532   Brazil's first sugar mills are built.

1534   Brazil is divided into fifteen horizontal territorial strips and given out among Portuguese nobles as captaincies.

1537   Olinda is founded in Pernambuco.

1538   The first slaves from Africa are landed in the Northeast.

1549   Salvador de Bahia is founded as capital of the Brazilian colony.

1555   France starts a colony in Guanabara Bay.

1556   Brazil's first bishop is shipwrecked off Alagoas and eaten on the beach.

1565   Rio de Janeiro is founded on Guanabara Bay.

1567   The French are driven out of Guanabara Bay by the Portuguese.

1591   The Inquisition begins its interrogations in Brazil, principally in Bahia and Pernambuco.
       The use of palm oil in cooking is described in an Italian writer's book on the Congo.

1595   The Inquisition returns to Rome.

1600   Twenty thousand African slaves are working on northeastern sugar plantations.

1605   Fugitive African slaves found a community at Palmares.

1612   The first military expedition is sent against Palmares.

1624   The Dutch briefly take Salvador de Bahia.

1630   The Dutch take Olinda.

1637   Recife is built by the Dutch.

1644 A hundred people are killed by the Dutch in a raid on Palmares.

1645 The Dutch attack Palmares again.

1650 The number of slaves in the Northeast nears 50,000.

1654 The Dutch withdraw from Brazil and the Portuguese attack Palmares again.
     Palmares, with 20,000 people, is one of Brazil's three biggest settlements.

1661 Antônio Vieira and the Jesuits are expelled by the settlers from Maranhão.

1670 The government of Pernambuco decrees the destruction of Palmares.

1676 The Portuguese raze a settlement of 2,000 houses in Palmares.

1678 Ganga Zumba's people sue for peace in Recife.

1679 Palmares drives back a military expedition against it.

1680 Palmares drives back a military expedition against it.

1682 Palmares drives back a military expedition against it.

1683 Palmares drives back a military expedition against it.

1684 Palmares drives back a military expedition against it.

1687   The governor of Pernambuco authorizes a bandeirante expedition against Palmares.

1693   Siege is laid to Palmares.

1694   Palmares falls; 400 die and 500 are sold back into slavery. Zumbi and others escape.

1695   Gold is found in Minas Gerais.
        Zumbi is captured and killed.

1727   Coffee is planted in Brazil.

1827   British economic dominance in Brazil is formalized in a commercial treaty.

1835   Islamic African slaves revolt in Salvador de Bahia and briefly capture the city.

1850   Importation of African slaves to Brazil formally ends. More than 4,000,000 Africans have been delivered to slavery in Brazil.
        The clandestine trade continues.

1858   Coffee is now Brazil's main export.

1873   Immigration from Italy overtakes immigration from Portugal to Brazil's Southeast.

1878   Great drought afflicts the northeastern interior. Half a million people die.
        Machado de Assis has a breakdown.

1880 *The Posthumous Memoirs of Bras Cubas* by Machado de Assis begins appearing in a Rio women's magazine.

1888 Slavery is formally abolished in Brazil.
A new and worse drought comes to the Northeast.

1889 The emperor of Brazil, Pedro II, is deposed by the military and a republic declared.
Northeastern labor is the world's cheapest outside Asia.

1891 The drought worsens in the Northeast.
The coffee boom ends.
Quincas Borba by Machado de Assis is published.

1893 Police try and fail to kill Antônio the Counselor.
The Counselor and followers start an agricultural settlement at Canudos in the Bahian drylands.
The population of Canudos reaches 15,000.

1894 The population of Canudos reaches 35,000.

1896 Bahian troops attack a group from Canudos and are driven off after killing 150.

1897 Five hundred government troops march on Canudos, are ambushed and routed.
A third army expedition of 1,300 troops is routed in battle at Canudos. A fourth expedition of 8,000 troops attacks Canudos.
The Counselor dies.

Canudos is destroyed and its people are massacred by the Brazilian army.

The war minister is killed in Rio in an assassination attempt on the president while welcoming troops from Canudos.

Dom Casmurro by Machado de Assis begins to appear in a ladies' magazine.

1900 *Dom Casmurro* by Machado de Assis is published.

1902 *The Drylands* (*Os Sertões*) by Euclides da Cunha is published.

Pierre Verger is born in Paris.

Heart of Darkness by Joseph Conrad is published.

1904 *Nostromo* by Joseph Conrad is published.

1908 Machado de Assis dies.

Roger Casement is appointed British consul general in Rio.

1909 Euclides da Cunha is shot dead by his wife's lover.

1910 Roger Casement travels through Brazil to Peru to report on the conditions of rubber workers.

1930 Getúlio Vargas seizes power and Lindolfo Collor draws up Brazil's first labor laws.

1933 Gilberto Freyre publishes *The Masters and the Slaves* (*Casa-grande & Senzala*).

1937   Getúlio Vargas proclaims the New State and governs Brazil by decree.

1938   The bandit Lampião is killed in the Northeast.

1939   Arnon de Mello marries Leda, daughter of Lindolfo Collor.

1945   Getúlio Vargas is deposed by the military.
       Luis Inácio Lula da Silva is born in Pernambuco.
       PC Farias is born in Alagoas.

1946   Pierre Verger arrives in Brazil.

1949   Fernando Collor de Mello is born in Rio de Janeiro.

1950   Getúlio Vargas returns to the presidency by election.
       Arnon de Mello is elected governor of Alagoas.

1952   Lula and his siblings are taken south by their mother.

1954   President Getúlio Vargas shoots himself.

1960   Brasilia is the new capital of Brazil.
       One adult Brazilian in four is allowed to vote in the presidential election.

1961   President Jânio Quadros resigns after seven months, blaming unidentified *hidden forces* for his fall.

1963   Fernando Collor's father shoots and kills another senator in the Brazilian senate.

1964 The military depose President Goulart and seize power in Brazil.

1966 Lula gets his first job as a metalworker in São Paulo.

1968 The Brazilian military begin repression, killing, imprisoning and torturing dissidents.

1969 The U.S. ambassador to Brazil is kidnapped and released in exchange for political prisoners, including José Dirceu, who is flown to Cuba and trains as a guerrilla fighter.
Lula's first wife and child die in childbirth.
Lula is elected to the local directorate of his union.

1973 The elected government of Chile is overthrown in a military coup. President Allende and thousands of workers, trade unionists, students and leftists are murdered.

1976 The military seizes power in Argentina.
Leftists and students begin to disappear.
In Brazil metalworkers win a small wage raise.

1978 Lula is reelected union leader with 98% of the vote.
Lula leads strikes by 150,000 metalworkers in São Paulo, the first in over 10 years.
Lula proposes forming a Workers' Party.

1979 Over 3,000,000 workers strike in Brazil.
Troops close down unions, invade churches and shoot activists.
A *process of slow and gradual opening* begins the long death of military dictatorship in Brazil and political exiles return under amnesty.

José Genoino, guerrilla fighter from the Amazon, is released from prison.

The film *Pixote* is released.

Fernando Collor is mayor of Maceió.

1980 The Workers' Party is formally founded.

Lula leads a new strike of 140,000 metalworkers. The strike is declared illegal and is violently suppressed. Lula is arrested and imprisoned by the security forces.

1982 The Workers' Party now has 400,000 members and eight seats in Congress after its first contested election.

1983 Lula and others found the CUT, Brazil's new national trade union body.

Fernando Collor enters the Brazilian Congress.

PC Farias's businesses go into receivership.

1984 PC runs election finances for sugar men in Alagoas.

1985 The Landless Rural Workers' Movement is founded.

There are 27 million TV sets in Brazil, up from half a million at the time of the military coup.

In Alagoas PC Farias is charged with fraud, forgery and tax evasion.

Tancredo Neves is elected president by the Brazilian Congress.

The Workers' Party boycotts the *indirect* election.

Neves dies and José Sarney becomes president.

1986 Lula is elected federal congressman with the most votes of any candidate in Brazil.

Fernando Collor is elected governor of Alagoas.

1987   Gilberto Freyre dies.

1988   In local elections the Workers' Party wins control of 38 major city administrations, including São Paulo.

Inflation in Brazil is 1,000% per annum.

Chico Mendes, the rubber workers' leader, is murdered in Acre.

1989   Fernando Collor's approval rating reaches 43% before the first vote.

Fernando Collor defeats Lula da Silva in the first democratic election of president of Brazil.

1990   Fernando Collor is sworn in as Brazilian president. Bank accounts are frozen. PC spends $23 million on electing the governor of Alagoas. Rosane spends $11 million of public money in her hometown.

The Workers' Party doubles its representation in Congress to 35.

PC buys his first jet plane.

1992   Fernando Collor resigns and is impeached.

The Workers' Party wins control of 55 municipal administrations.

Brazil's interim president is Itamar Franco.

1993   PC Farias vanishes.

Lula begins traveling to 400 cities and towns around Brazil.

PC appears in London and is arrested in Bangkok.

Inflation reaches 33% per month.

1994   The *real* is introduced in Brazil, pegged to the U.S. dollar.

      Fernando Collor is acquitted on charges of passive corruption and fraud.

      Pedro Collor dies in New York.

      Fernando Henrique Cardoso is elected president of Brazil with twice as many votes as Lula.

      The Workers' Party increases its congressional representation to 49 deputies.

1996   PC Farias leaves jail.

      Nineteen landless farmworkers are murdered by the military police in Pará.

      PC and Suzana Marcolino are murdered.

1997   The novel *City of God* by Paulo Lins is published.

1998   Fernando Henrique Cardoso defeats Lula again and is elected to a second term as president.

      Newly elected congresswoman Ceci Cunha is murdered with three of her family in Maceió.

1999   Congressman Hildebrando Pascoal is arrested on charges, among others, of cutting off a man's arms and legs with a chain saw.

      Augusto Farias and Pascoal are named as leaders of an organization of drug traffickers, arms dealers, road cargo pirates and professional killers.

      Augusto Farias and PC's bodyguards and servants are indicted for the murder of PC and Suzana.

2000   Rosane Collor is sentenced to eleven years for corruption, but the conviction is overturned.

The congressional commission on drug trafficking announces the indictment of Augusto Farias.

Fernando Collor returns to public life in Brazil.

2002　A colonel and a major of the military police are convicted, alone among 135 charged, of murdering 19 landless farmworkers in 1996; both are immediately released.

Lula is elected president of Brazil.

Fernando Collor loses the election for governor of Alagoas.

Augusto Farias loses his seat in the Brazilian Congress and his parliamentary immunity.

Brazil's chief prosecutor dismisses charges against Augusto Farias and others and closes case on murder of PC Farias.

2003　Luis Inácio "Lula" da Silva is sworn in as president of Brazil.

One hundred and forty slaves are found working on a property belonging to Augusto Farias.

The film *City of God* is released around the world.

An arrest warrant is issued for Augusto Farias.

Augusto Farias is detained and released.

A NOTE ON THE AUTHOR

Peter Robb was born in Australia and has lived for many years in Italy and Brazil. He is the author of *Midnight in Sicily* and a book about Caravaggio called *M*.